PERENNIALS

COMPLETE GARDENER'S LIBRARY™

NIALS

Maggie Oster

NATIONAL HOME
GARDENING CLUB

**National Home
Gardening Club**
Minnetonka, Minnesota

Perennials

Printed in 2006.

Tom Carpenter
Creative Director

Julie Cisler
Book Design & Production

Michele Stockham
Senior Book Development Coordinator

Gina Germ
Photo Editor

Nancy Wirsig McClure, Hand to Mouse Arts
Illustration

Justin Hancock
Copy Editor

7 8 9 10 11 / 10 09 08 07 06
ISBN 1-58159-185-3
© 2002 National Home Gardening Club

National Home Gardening Club
12301 Whitewater Drive
Minnetonka, Minnesota 55343
www.gardeningclub.com

Photo Credits

David Cavagnaro pp.: cover, 5, 10, 11, 23, 56, 68, 72, 74 both, 75, 77, 79 both, 83, 84, 85, 87, 88(2), 89, 90 both, 91(3), 92(2), 93, 95, 96, 99, 100(2), 101(2), 102 both, 103, 105, 109, 110(2), 111, 112, 114 both, 116, 117, 118, 119, 121, 124, 127, 133, 137 both, 138 both, 139, 140 all, 141 both, 142 all, 144 all, 145 all, 146, 147, 148, 149 both, 150, 151, 152, 155 both, 156(2), 158, 159, 160 both, 164, 166(2), 167, 168(2), 169, 170, 171, 172, 176, 178 both, 179, 180, 182, 183, 184, 187 both, 188, 189, 191, 194, 195, 196, 197, 199(3), 200, 201(4), 202(3); **R. Todd Davis Photography p.:** 1; **Michael Landis pp.:** 2-3, 14-15; **Bill Johnson pp.:** 4 both, 33, 78, 80, 81, 85(3), 94, 95, 97, 98, 101, 104(2), 107, 110, 111, 112, 113, 115 both, 118, 119, 121, 122, 127, 128, 129, 132, 133, 134, 135, 136, 139, 150, 151, 154, 162(2), 163, 165, 166, 168, 171, 173 both, 176, 179, 180, 181, 184, 185, 189, 190 both, 192, 193, 195, 196, 197(3), 198, 200(2), 202; **Walter Chandoha pp.:** 6, 11, 12, 13, 16 both, 18(2), 20, 24, 25, 26-27, 28 both, 29 both, 30(2), 31, 36, 37(2), 39, 45(2), 46, 47, 48, 51(2), 53 all, 57, 58 both, 66, 102, 109, 152, 153, 188, 200, 201; **Maggie Oster pp.:** 7, 12-13, 23, 24, 31, 33, 35, 38, 40, 45, 49, 59, 64 both, 65, 69, 70-71, 126; **Janet Loughrey pp.:** 8-9, 54-55; **Saxon Holt pp.:** 11, 25(2), 30, 42-43, 44, 48, 84, 97; **Jerry Pavia pp.:** 17, 18, 50(2), 51, 75, 89, 94, 98, 122, 123, 124, 125, 136, 154, 161 all, 162, 165, 166-167, 177, 197, 198(2), 200; **Derek Fell pp.:** 19, 20-21, 22, 38, 40, 41, 47, 49, 50, 51, 52(2), 67, 78, 81, 109, 121, 130, 148, 164, 169, 175, 192, 196, 198, 199; **Jim Block pp.:** 24, 34, 37(2), 39, 45, 48, 56, 57, 60-61, 62, 63, 73 both, 76 both, 77, 80, 82, 83, 86 both, 87, 88, 91(2), 92, 93, 94, 95, 96, 100(3), 103, 104, 105, 106 both, 108 all, 113, 117, 119, 120 all, 127, 128, 129, 130, 131, 132, 133(2), 134(2), 135, 143(2), 146, 150, 153(2), 156, 157 both, 159, 163(3), 170, 174 all, 175, 179, 185, 186 both, 193, 197, 201(2), 202; **Mark Turner pp.:** 32, 52, 129, 131(2); **Marge Garfield pp.:** 33, 34, 35, 36, 41; **Robert Perron p.:** 35; **Thomas E. Eltzroth pp.:** 66, 68, 123, 158; **Diane A. Pratt p.:** 67; **Rosalind Creasy p.:** 99; **Stephen R. Swinburne pp.:** 126(2), 127; **William D. Adams p.:** 143.

CONTENTS

PERENNIAL PLEASURE

I can remember it as clearly as if it were yesterday. There was this spectacular flower in our backyard, at just about eye level for a seven-year-old. The top was the purest white, the bottom was a deep purple color, and there was this wonderful fuzzy stuff on the lower petals. Mother called it an iris and said its name was 'Wabash', just like the name of the river in the Indiana state song, "On the Banks of the Wabash," that my father loved to sing.

Certainly this was not my introduction to flowers, as my parents had gardened since long before I was born. That there were flowers in their lives at that particular moment did speak volumes about the kind of people they were. A year-and-a-half earlier, their lovingly restored, century-old farmhouse had burned to the ground. There was scant insurance or income to rebuild, but somehow they managed, cutting lumber from the farm and doing the building themselves. During that time, my father continued to milk dairy cows, and my mother taught school. Yet there was also enough time and energy to plant a new flower border. No one will ever accuse my mother of being a spendthrift, so most of the plants were ones moved from around the old house or shared by friends, but for some reason, she splurged that year and ordered a 'Wabash' iris. There were other iris in the garden, but that was the one that stole my heart.

Perhaps it would make for a better story if I could say that at that specific moment I decided to study horticulture and write books about gardening when I got older.

Opposite page: Peonies are among the most popular of all perennials, offering countless forms and colors, splendid fragrance and longevity.

Maggie Oster.

That it was that particular flower or seeing my parents put so much importance on having flowers, even when other matters were so pressing, that immediately and profoundly touched me. The reality is that the process was much more subtle—but no less effective.

My mother's teaching mentor emphasized that children were taught, "Line upon line, precept upon precept." And so it was with me. There were untold numbers of ways that nature and flowers and gardening were a part of my family's everyday life. Sometimes it was being called out to see the first brave crocus in the spring, while at other times it might have been standing together on the front porch to watch a spectacular sunset and make a wish on the evening star, gathering a bouquet for the dinner table, or appreciating the smells and sounds of the different seasons. No matter what career path I might have chosen, my life would have been inextricably linked with the natural world.

What my parents had learned from their families and friends, and consequently passed on to me, was a love of the beautiful in nature, especially that of flowers. Without medical research or self-help books, they instinctively knew that when life was difficult and stressful, making time for flowers would raise their spirits. The same is true for any of us today.

But as important as it is to our health and well-being as individuals to have flowers in our lives, the benefits of our flowers and gardens on others can reach greater distances than we might ever imagine. You may never know how you've affected the people who walk by your garden each day. Maybe it will inspire that little child who can look eyeball to petal, or provide happiness for the elderly neighbor who can no longer garden. Or, since one of the overriding characteristics of gardeners is their propensity for sharing, be it divisions, seeds, advice, opinions, information or experiences, you may start a chain reaction with your deeds. The neighbor lady who inspired my mother to grow flowers when she was a little girl never directly knew the child who fell in love with an iris and grew up to write gardening books, but if not for her, you might be reading a very different book. So remember: You sow powerful seeds with your flowers, within your own heart as well as the hearts of others for generations to come.

Maggie Oster

◄ CHAPTER 1 ►
THE POSSIBILITIES OF PERENNIALS

Perennials, more than any other group of plants, turn a yard into a garden with their diversity of colors, bloom seasons, textures, shapes, sizes and forms. Add a few daylilies around the mailbox or lamp post, a cluster of ornamental grasses at the corner of the house, a groundcover of sweet woodruff under a tree or some rudbeckia among the foundation planting of shrubs, and your yard begins to take on a character of lushness and beauty. Expend a little more effort in creating beds and borders overflowing with the flowers and foliage of perennials, and you'll be on your way to having the kind of garden people fantasize about.

THE FLOWERS OF OUR DREAMS

Perennials certainly are nothing if not the stuff of fantasy. For some, it is the nostalgia for a grandmother's garden, overflowing with rainbow-colored iris, sweetly scented peonies and boldly rising spires of delphinium. For others, enticing magazine or book photos or maybe a visit to the gardens of England has beckoned us to perennials like a siren's song. Some people are drawn to perennials because of the many different types of plants available, while others were given transplants by friends explaining how easy they are to grow. Sometimes, people just tire of planting so many annuals every year. Whatever the reasoning or rationale, perennials have a remarkable ability to fulfill our daydreams.

Defining Perennials

By definition, perennials are herbaceous (fleshy) plants that grow, bloom and (usually) die back to the ground in the winter with the roots surviving cold temperatures; then they send up fresh growth and flowers each spring, repeating the cycle every year. Some perennials, such as peonies and bleeding hearts, often outlive us, while others, like delphiniums, may survive for only a few seasons. Other perennials develop woody stems that lose their leaves but do not die back, while others retain their leaves during winter.

To compare perennials with other flowers, annuals complete their life cycle in a single growing season; biennials produce leaves the first year, then bloom, set seed and die the second year; and bulbs grow and bloom year after year but are classified separately because of their root structure.

Through the centuries, gardeners have been drawn to perennials because of their ability to grow and bloom for years on end, theoretically saving labor, time and money; theoretically, because the tendency for many of us is not to be content with just a few perennials. In fact, the difficult aspect of perennials is not in growing them but in limiting ourselves to a reasonable number. For when the right perennials are chosen for a site, most are remarkably easy to grow, and they often have the good grace to generate new plants for transplanting and sharing.

Whether perennials are short or tall, upright or spreading, with fuzzy, grassy or fleshy leaves, they all have the ability to grow and bloom year after year without replanting.

Perennials adapt not only to many different garden styles but also to a wide variety of garden environments, including shade.

Since the majority of perennials are easily grown, the biggest difficulty encountered may be choosing from among the thousands of plant possibilities.

Choices, Choices and Choices

There are literally tens of thousands of plants from all over the world to choose among for your perennial pleasure. No matter what your given climate, soil, moisture, light conditions or type of design, be it hot and humid, cool and moist, dry soil or wet, acid or alkaline, formal or cottage garden, woodland or meadow landscape, there are perennials that will satisfy.

Utilize Chapter 2, The Garden Environment, to analyze your garden situation and get help selecting the plants most suited for your garden. You may want to try a few plants that seem questionable for your conditions, but by choosing the most adapted ones, you will make gardening much easier.

The choices are also many when considering how to use perennials in our gardens. There are any number of different ways of doing things; the most important person you have to please is yourself. Some people are content to get whatever perennials are available at their local discount department store. Others search out esoteric mail-order nurseries that carry the most obscure plant varieties. One gardener may like beds of flowers

There is no one right or wrong way to use perennials in the landscape. Some people relish the formality of traditional English-style perennial borders, with their mirror images reflecting each other across the lawn, while others find this style confining.

When adding perennials to your yard, step back and look at the many places they can be used. Why not start at the beginning, by emphasizing your driveway and mailbox with a colorful planting, such as these long-blooming gaillardia 'Goblin'?

while another prefers borders. You may want all one color and straight paths, while your neighbor combines colors with abandon along curving paths. No one method or technique promises either success or failure.

In this book you'll discover the various ways to use perennials, including in borders, beds, foundation and corner plantings as well as groundcovers, along with an assortment of garden themes. These ideas will inspire you to look at your yard with fresh eyes, opening you to the possibilities of perennials. If you desire artistic success, Chapter 4, Design Considerations, will help you integrate the many elements of perennials into a creative whole.

What may be the most intriguing aspect of perennials is their variety. Some perennials grow only inches tall, while others exceed 8 feet. They may creep, mound, sprawl or reach for the sky. Some have a light airy appearance,

with grasslike or feathery leaves, while others present a bold or exotic appearance. You never knew there were so many shades of green, gray, gold and white until you started studying perennial foliage.

Not only does flower shape and color run the gamut, but so does the blooming season. By careful selection, you can have flowers in all but the coldest months of the year. With the lists of suggested perennials throughout this book and the detailed descriptions of plants in the plant profile section, you'll have a starting point in choosing the best perennials for different garden sites with a multitude of uses and styles.

Perennials offer an amazing diversity of sizes, shapes, textures, colors and forms of both flowers and foliage, affording an unlimited palette.

Keep Them Healthy

Perennials do require some maintenance. I have heard countless beginning gardeners say that they want to grow perennials because they won't have to do anything. My first reaction is, "why bother?" One of the joys of gardening is the process itself—to get out there in the peace and quiet and putter around. Certainly there are some perennials that you can plant and pretty much forget about. But you should explore the pleasures and rewards when you put some effort into gardening with perennials.

Healthy, flourishing plants, however you use them in the garden, always bring satisfaction. To achieve that aspect of success, use the best and most efficient ways to care for your perennials. Just as we lead healthier, happier lives when we have a comfortable home, nutritious food, regular medical care and thoughtful attention from family and friends, your plants will respond with enthusiastic growth to well-prepared soil, consistent fertilization and watering, and reasonable care and maintenance.

Among my earliest childhood memories are those of the flowers that my mother, relatives and neighbors grew, shared and enjoyed. These gardeners' enthusiasm was contagious, and even many years later, I cannot imagine living anywhere, be it urban or rural, where I would not want to be surrounded by flowers. Vegetables, herbs, fruits and other plants bring their own particular satisfaction. But it is perennial flowers—with their versatility, adaptability, diversity and sheer beauty that return year after year—that hold a nostalgic place in my heart.

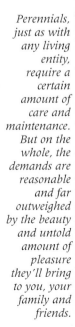

Perennials, just as with any living entity, require a certain amount of care and maintenance. But on the whole, the demands are reasonable and far outweighed by the beauty and untold amount of pleasure they'll bring to you, your family and friends.

❧ CHAPTER 2 ❧

THE GARDEN ENVIRONMENT

A well-grown garden has intrinsic beauty. But the first step in attaining that success is not in the work of growing the plants. Rather, it is in selecting those that are most closely adapted to your environment. Considerations include climate, soil, sunlight and the amount of moisture available. Certainly there are ways to modify the soil with amendments; to change the soil moisture with drainage tiles, raised beds or watering systems; to alter the light by trimming, removing or planting trees; or to find a protected microclimate within the yard for less-than-hardy plants. In fact, with only a few minor changes, a wider range of plants than normal can be grown. But to make large-scale, wholesale changes is usually very expensive, and, particularly in the case of irrigation, detrimental to our natural resources. How much more in tune with the natural world to choose wisely at the outset.

CLIMATE

When thinking of plants and climate, the first thing that occurs to most people is winter hardiness, or the ability of a plant to survive a minimum winter temperature.

The United States Department of Agriculture has processed data on the lowest temperatures that can be expected each year in the United States and created the USDA Plant Hardiness Zone Map (see page 203). This map includes ten different zones, with each zone representing a difference of 10°F. Almost all plant labels or catalog descriptions carry the hardiness zone for any perennial sold.

What makes gardening complicated and, for many people, an intriguing challenge, are the various other climatic factors that come into play. For example, there are microclimates that exist within these hardiness zones. Those who garden in urban areas often find that they may be an entire zone warmer than the surrounding region. Most likely you'll also find microclimates within your yard, such as a warmer area against a south-facing wall or cooler ones on the north side of the house or at the bottom of a hill.

Snow serves as natural protection for roots.

Climatic Factors Beyond Winter

Then again, even if a plant is considered hardy for an area, other climatic factors can affect its ability to survive winter. In areas with midwinter warm spells, perennials are particularly susceptible to what is known as "heaving," in which the roots are literally heaved out of the ground by the soil's alternate freezing and thawing. The remedy for this problem is mulching to keep the soil temperature consistent. Water drainage is another factor that affects hardiness, as many plants will not survive poorly drained soil during the winter. The amount and duration of snow cover during the winter are important, too. Gardeners in areas with a lot of snow are fortunate that snow acts as a natural insulator.

Be aware of microclimates within your yard. A south-facing stone wall absorbs winter sun, providing warmer winter temperatures at the base. But it's hotter here in the summer.

PERENNIALS FOR WARM CLIMATES

Not only will blistering summer days cause plants to deteriorate and weaken, but so will hot, humid nights. The following plants are ones that, with other growing conditions being correct, should actually flourish in such conditions, even through Zone 9. An even greater variety of perennials with thrive through Zone 8.

(spp. = species in the plural; cvs. = cultivars)

Acanthus spp.—bear's breeches
Achillea spp. and cvs.—yarrow
Amsonia spp.—blue stars
Aquilegia x *hybrida*—hybrid columbine
Aquilegia longissima—longspur columbine
Armeria plantaginea—plantain thrift
Artemisia absinthium—wormwood
Artemisia ludoviciana cvs.—'Silver King', 'Silver Queen' artemisia
Arum italicum 'Pictum'—variegated Italian arum
Asclepias tuberosa—butterfly weed
Astilbe x *arendsii* cvs.—astilbe
Baptisia spp.—wild indigo
Belamcanda chinensis—blackberry lily
Bletilla striata—bletilla
Boltonia asteroides—boltonia
Ceratostigma spp.—leadwort
Chrysanthemum x *morifolium* (*Dendranthema* x *grandiflorum*)—chrysanthemum
Chrysanthemum x *superbum* (*Leucanthemum* x *superbum*)—Shasta daisy
Chrysogonum virginianum—green-and-gold
Coreopsis spp. and cvs.—coreopsis, tickseed
Crocosmia x *crocosmiiflora*—crocosmia
Cyclamen hederifolium—hardy cyclamen
Dianthus spp. and cvs.—sweet William, pinks
Dicentra spp. and cvs.—bleeding heart
Digitalis purpurea—common foxglove
Eryngium planum—flat sea holly
Euphorbia myrsinites—myrtle euphorbia
Euphorbia wallichii—wallich spurge

Filipendula ulmaria—queen-of-the-meadow
Gaillardia x *grandiflora* cvs.—blanket flower
Gaura lindheimeri—gaura
Gypsophila paniculata—baby's breath
Helianthus angustifolius—swamp sunflower
Heliopsis helianthoides cvs.—sunflower, heliopsis
Helleborus foetidus—bear's foot hellebore
Helleborus orientalis—Lenten rose
Hemerocallis spp. and cvs.—daylily
Heterotheca villosa—golden aster
Hosta plantaginea—fragrant hosta
Hosta ventricosa—blue hosta
Hosta venusta—dwarf plantain lily
Hylotelephium (*Sedum*) x 'Autumn Joy'—Autumn Joy sedum
Hypericum calycinum—Aaron's beard
Iberis sempervirens and cvs.—evergreen candytuft
Iris spp. and cvs.—iris
Kniphofia uvaria and cvs.—red-hot-poker, torch lily
Lamiastrum galeobdolon and cvs.—yellow archangel
Lavandula spp. and cvs.—lavender
Liatris spp. and cvs.—gayfeather, blazingstar
Limonium spp. and cvs.—statice, sea lavender
Linum spp. and cvs.—flax
Liriope muscari cvs.—lily-turf
Lobelia cardinalis—cardinal flower
Lychnis x *haageana*—campion

Mertensia virginica—Virginia bluebells
Monarda spp. and cvs.—bee balm, bergamot
Omphalodes verna—blue-eyed Mary
Ophiopogon japonicus—dwarf mondo grass
Pachysandra spp. and cvs.—pachysandra, spurge
Paeonia cvs.—peony
Perovskia atriplicifolia—Russian sage
Phlox divaricata and cvs.—woodland phlox
Phlox maculata and cvs.—wild sweet William
Phlox nivalis—trailing phlox
Phlox subulata—moss phlox, creeping phlox
Physalis alkekengi—Chinese lantern
Physostegia virginiana and cvs.—obedient plant
Polygonatum spp. and cvs.—Solomon's seal
Rudbeckia spp. and cvs.—black-eyed Susan, coneflower
Ruta graveolens—rue
Salvia argentea—silver sage
Salvia azurea—azure sage
Salvia pratensis and cvs.—meadow sage
Sedum aizoon and cvs.—aizoon stonecrop
Solidago spp. and cvs.—goldenrod
Stokesia laevis and cvs.—Stokes' aster
Thermopsis caroliniana—southern lupine
Tradescantia x *andersoniana* cvs—spiderwort
Tricyrtis formosana—Formosa toad-lily
Verbena spp. and cvs.—verbena
Vinca spp. and cvs.—periwinkle
Viola spp. and cvs.—violet

Among the perennials that withstand the hot days and nights typical of warmer climates are 'Oxbow' sedums, hostas, shasta daisies and gaura.

Gardeners along a seacoast may have to contend with salt spray and sandy soil, but they have the advantage of temperatures being more moderate in both summer and winter compared to inland regions.

Latitude, elevation and the proximity of a large body of water also have an effect. For example, compare Atlanta, Georgia, to Seattle, Washington. Both are classified as Zone 8, but remember that the closer to the equator, the hotter the sun. Large bodies of water tend to cool the surrounding areas in summer and warm them in winter. Often, there is more fog or cloud cover in these areas, too, which also affects plant growth.

Strong prevailing winds are another climatic factor. They affect plant growth by causing the soil to dry out quickly, so plants transpire water faster than the roots can absorb and transport it to the leaves;

it also causes tall plants to blow over. For those who live with strong prevailing winds, shorter plants are a better choice, as are those adapted to dry conditions and sometimes even those that are at least a climate zone hardier. A windy site can be remedied by installing a windbreak of trees or shrubs. An open fence will also help, but not a solid one, as it just makes the effect of the wind even greater.

Another climatic factor is the first and last frost dates. Periods of warm weather before the last frost make it difficult to grow perennials that start growth early in the season. Conversely, in the autumn, plants that bloom then may be literally nipped in the bud by early frosts.

Many gardeners in the United States are particularly aware of the effects of summer temperatures and humidity on perennials. Because we tend to look so much to English gardens and gardening books, we are apt to want some of the plants that flourish in English gardens.

Unfortunately, many of these simply languish in midwestern and southern heat and humidity. Gardeners, of course, have learned tricks to offset these problems, such as providing light afternoon shade to successfully grow these cool-summer plants, but, even then, they never attain the splendid form they show when grown in their ideal climate.

It is impossible for any gardening book to address all the possible situations and specific adaptability of each plant for each situation. This is where talking with other gardeners in your area, visiting local private and public gardens, and utilizing local experts, such as your local county extension agent, is the best way to learn. The lists in this book will provide a starting point for choosing perennials for your garden. Keep in mind that some plants that will grow in your area may not be included in the lists, just as some plants listed may not grow well in your specific garden.

Loosely mulching plants with evergreen branches prevents the plant roots from being heaved out of the ground during alternate freezing and thawing winter temperatures.

An evergreen windbreak protects perennials from damaging winds, plus it provides a dramatic backdrop that accentuates the plants.

PERENNIALS FOR COLD CLIMATES

Gardening in Zones 3 and 4 offers the challenge of winter temperatures as low as -45°F, strong winds in both winter and summer and, frequently, dry summers. Fortunately, winter temperatures are consistent, and snow cover acts as an insulator. Plus, while summer temperatures may reach the 90s, humidity and night temperatures are usually moderate.

Achillea spp. and cvs.—yarrow
Aconitum spp. and cvs.—monkshood
Actea spp.—baneberry
Adenophora spp.—ladybells
Adiantum pedatum—northern maidenhair fern
Ajuga spp. and cvs.—bugleweed
Alchemilla mollis—lady's mantle
Anemone sylvestris—snowdrop anemone
Aquilegia spp. (not hybrids)—columbine
Aruncus dioicus—goat's beard
Asarum canadense—wild ginger
Asclepias tuberosa—butterfly weed
Asplenium spp.—spleenwort
Aster tartaricus— Tartarian aster
Aster umbellatus—flat-topped aster
Baptisia spp.—false indigo
Bergenia crassifolia—Siberian bergenia
Boltonia asteroides—boltonia
Bouteloua curtipendula—side oats grama
Brunnera macrophylla—Siberian bugloss
Caltha palustris—marsh marigold
Campanula carpatica—Carpathian bellflower
Campanula glomerata—clustered bellflower
Campanula persicifolia—peach-leaf bellflower

Centaurea hypoleuca 'John Coutts'—John Coutts knapweed
Cerastium tomentosum—snow-in-summer
Cimicifuga racemosa—bugbane
Cimicifuga simplex—bugbane
Clematis integrifolia—clematis
Clematis recta—clematis
Convallaria majalis—lily-of-the-valley
Coreopsis verticillata and cvs.—threadleaf coreopsis
Cornus canadensis—bunchberry
Cystopteris spp.—bladder fern
Delphinium elatum and cvs.—delphinium
Dennstaedtia punctiloba—hay-scented fern
Deschampsia flexuosa—crinkled hair grass
Dianthus arenarius—sand pink
Dianthus x *arvensis*—pink
Dianthus deltoides and cvs.—maiden pink
Dicentra spp. and cvs.—bleeding heart
Dictamnus albus—gas plant
Digitalis grandiflora (D. ambigua)—yellow foxglove
Digitalis lutea—yellow foxglove
Dracocephalum spp.—dragonhead
Dryopteris spp.—wood fern

Echinacea spp.—purple coneflower
Echinops spp. and cvs.—globe thistle
Erigeron speciosus cvs.—fleabane
Eryngium yuccifolium—rattlesnake master
Eupatorium maculatum—Joe-Pye weed
Eupatorium purpureum—bluestem Joe-Pye weed
Eupatorium rugosum—white snakeroot
Euphorbia polychroma—cushion spurge
Filipendula spp.—meadowsweet, dropwort, queen-of-the-prairie
Gaillardia spp. and cvs.—blanket flower
Galax urceolata (Galax aphylla)—wandflower
Galega spp.—goat's rue
Galium odoratum—sweet woodruff
Gentiana andrewsii—bottle gentian
Gentiana septemfida—crested gentian
Geum triflorum—prairie smoke
Gymnocarpium dryopteris—oak fern
Gypsophila spp.—baby's breath
Helenium autumnale and cvs.—sneezeweed
Helenium hoopesii—orange sneezeweed
Hemerocallis spp. and cvs.—daylily
Heracleum spp.—cow parsley
Heuchera spp. and cvs.—coralbells
Hosta spp. and cvs.—hosta, plantain lily
Hyssopus officinalis and cvs.—hyssop
Iberis sempervirens and cvs.—candytuft
Inula spp.—inula
Iris sibirica—Siberian iris
Liatris spp. and cvs.—gayfeather
Lobelia cardinalis—cardinal flower
Marrubium vulgare—horehound
Matteuccia struthiopteris—ostrich fern
Nepeta sibirica—Siberian catmint
Onoclea sensibilis—sensitive fern
Osmunda spp.—cinnamon fern, royal fern
Papaver orientale—Oriental poppy
Phlomis tuberosa—tuberous Jerusalem sage
Phlox spp. and cvs.—phlox
Physostegia virginiana— obedient plant
Phytolacca americana—pokeweed
Platycodon grandiflorus and cvs.—balloon flower
Podophyllum peltatum—mayapple
Polemonium spp. and cvs.—Jacob's ladder
Polygonum bistorta 'Superbum'—Superbum knotweed
Polystichum acrostichoides—Christmas fern
Primula auricula—primrose
Pteridium aquilinum—bracken fern
Pulmonaria saccharata and cvs.—lungwort
Ratibida spp.—Mexican coneflower
Rudbeckia spp. and cvs.—orange coneflower
Sanguisorba canadensis—Canadian burnet
Saponaria spp. and cvs.—soapwort
Sedum spp. and cvs.—stonecrop
Silphium spp.—rosinweed, compass plant, prairie dock, cup plant
Solidago spp. and cvs.—goldenrod
Sorghastrum nutans—Indian grass
Symphytum spp. and cvs.—comfrey
Thelypteris spp.—beech fern
Thermopsis spp.—false lupine
Trollius spp. and cvs.—globe flower
Veronicastrum virginicum—culver's root
Zizia spp.—golden alexander

Gardeners in cold climates have the advantage of low summer temperatures and humidity.

SOIL

Plant roots are dependent on the soil to anchor them, and supply water and nutrients for plant growth. Before planting, take time to analyze and improve your soil.

Soil Types

A soil that is predominantly **sand** has relatively large spaces between particles, which supplies plenty of air for plants and allows water to penetrate easily, but these spaces don't retain water for long and nutrients are quickly washed away. This necessitates frequent fertilizing and watering. Sandy soils warm up quickly in the spring, are easy to work, and roots can readily penetrate.

Clay soils have small spaces between the particles. This makes it difficult for water to penetrate and drain away. With fewer large spaces, there is also less oxygen in clay soil. All of this makes a clay soil stay cool much longer in the spring, and makes it more difficult for roots to penetrate. Clay is also more difficult to work; if clay soils are worked when wet, brick-like clumps will form. The advantage of a clay soil is that it is usually rich in nutrients.

The ideal soil, called **loam,** is composed of about two parts sand, two parts silt and one part clay

Seldom do we walk into someone's yard and exclaim, "Wow, those are great plant roots." Yet, that's how we need to think in order to have a beautiful garden. Plant roots don't just anchor the plant, they supply the water and nutrient building blocks essential for plant growth. How well they do this is dependent, in part, on the soil they are growing in. So before any plant is brought home, you need to consider the soil in your yard.

All soils are composed of inorganic mineral particles, originating from the rock that formed the soil. More importantly soil has organic matter, air and water. A good garden soil will be about 50 percent mineral particles and organic matter, 25 percent water and 25 percent air.

The mineral particles are a combination of, in descending order of size, sand, silt and clay. The highest proportion of mineral particles determines the soil type, or texture, which in turn is one factor in determining the amount of water and air available to plant roots.

PERENNIALS FOR HEAVY CLAY SOIL

As long as there is some drainage and no hardpan layer underneath, the following are some of the perennials that will tolerate soils high in clay content. Even with these plants, it pays to prepare the soil by incorporating organic matter before planting.

Acanthus spp. and cvs.—bear's breeches
Ajuga spp. and cvs.—bugleweed
Alchemilla spp.—lady's mantle
Anemone spp. and cvs.—windflower
Anthemis spp. and cvs.—chamomile, golden
   marguerite
Aruncus spp.—goatsbeard
Asarum spp.—wild ginger
Asclepias spp.—milkweed
Belamcanda chinensis—blackberry lily
Bergenia spp. and cvs.—bergenia

Boltonia asteroides—boltonia
Brunnera macrophylla—Siberian bugloss
Campanula carpatica—Carpathian bellflower
Centranthus ruber—red valerian
Chrysogonum virginianum—green-and-gold
Echinacea spp. and cvs.—purple coneflower
Epimedium spp. and cvs.—barrenwort
Geranium spp. and cvs.—cranesbill
Helleborus spp. and cvs.—Christmas rose,
   Lenten rose, hellebore
Hemerocallis spp. and cvs.—daylily

Hosta spp. and cvs.—hosta, plantain lily
Inula spp. and cvs.—inula
Lamium spp. and cvs.—dead nettle
Limonium spp.—sea lavender
Physostegia virginiana—obedient plant
Polygonatum spp. and cvs.—Solomon's seal
Prunella spp. and cvs.—self-heal
Rodgersia spp. and cvs.—rodgersia
Solidago spp. and cvs.—goldenrod
Symphytum spp. and cvs.—comfrey
Vinca spp. and cvs.—vinca

particles. Like Baby Bear's porridge, it is "just right," retaining some moisture but not too much, and enough oxygen, too. Loam is easily worked, roots penetrate without difficulty, and it has significant nutrients. Although there are plants that naturally grow in sandy or clay soil, the greatest number of plants thrive in loam.

An easy way to determine the texture of your soil is to take a handful of soil several days after a rain, form it into a ball in your hand, then poke the soil ball with your fingers. If it falls apart easily and feels gritty, you have a sandy soil. When the ball looks like a lump of clay, that's what it is. A loam will easily crumble apart into small, loose clumps.

Organic Matter

Don't panic if your soil is sandy or clay, nor exult if you have loam. Even though soil texture is very difficult to alter, there is another characteristic of soil, called structure. This refers to the arrangement of clumps, or aggregates, that the three soil particles form in the soil. These aggregates give soil its tilth, or friability, which increases its capacity to hold air and water, improves water absorption and drainage, and makes the soil easy to work and easy for roots to penetrate. The key to these clumps is organic matter.

In nature, organic matter is an amalgam created by animals above and below ground excreting and dying, plus leaves, stems and roots dying. Their organic matter is incorporated into the soil by the actions of earthworms and other below-ground creatures, plant roots and freezing and thawing. As it becomes a part of the soil, organic matter, whether produced in nature or provided by man, decomposes into humus, which contains sticky gums that bind the soil particles together into those all-important friable clusters, crumbs, clumps or aggregates.

Whatever the original soil texture, these clumps create a soil structure that enables your soil to behave as if it were the ideal. An added bonus is that as the soil microorganisms break organic matter down into its elemental components, nutrients become available to the plant roots, too.

A loam soil (left) is considered ideal, but even a sandy soil (center) or a clay soil (right) can have its structure improved with the addition of organic matter, which increases the soil's capacity to hold and release air and water, and makes the soil easier for roots to penetrate.

PERENNIALS FOR SANDY SOIL

Achillea spp. and cvs.—yarrow
Anthemis tinctoria—golden
  marguerite
Armeria maritima—sea pink
Artemisia ludoviciana cvs.—'Silver
  King', 'Silver Queen' artemisia
Asclepias tuberosa—butterfly weed
Baptisia australis—wild blue indigo
Belamcanda chinensis—blackberry
  lily
Chasmanthium latifolium—northern
  sea oats
Chrysanthemum pacificum
  (*Ajania pacifica*)—golden silver
Euphorbia spp. and cvs.—spurge
Gaillardia pulchella—blanket flower
Gaura lindheimeri—gaura
Heliopsis helianthoides cvs.—
  sunflower heliopsis
Hemerocallis spp. and cvs.—daylily
Kniphofia uvaria and cvs.—red-hot-
  poker torch lily
Oxalis spp.—oxalis
Panicum virgatum—switch grass
Yucca filamentosa—Adam's needle

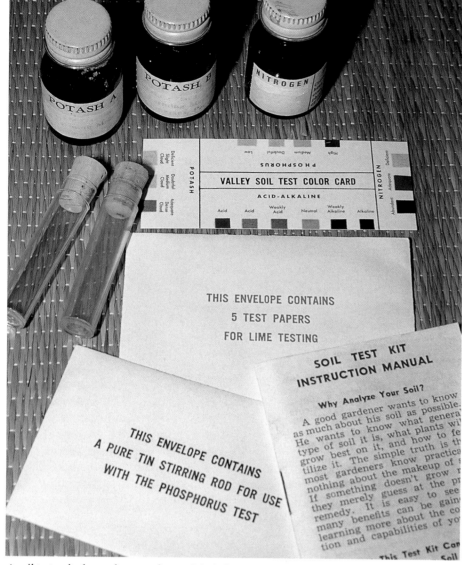

A soil test, whether at home or from a lab, helps you spend money wisely on fertilizer.

Acid vs. Alkaline

The acidity or alkalinity of the soil, or pH, is another factor to consider. A measurement of the concentration of hydrogen ions on a scale of 1.0 to 14.0, with 7.0 being neutral, the pH affects the availability of the essential elements to the plants. While some plants prefer a higher pH (or sweeter) soil and others need a lower pH (or more acid) soil, most plants grow best with a pH range of 6.0 to 7.0. Home soil-testing kits and professional laboratories can also determine the pH of your soil and offer recommendations for correcting it, if necessary or desired.

For more information on preparing and improving the soil in your garden, adding nutrients or adjusting the pH, see Chapters 6 and 7.

PERENNIALS FOR ALKALINE SOIL

These are some of the perennial flowers and ornamental grasses that either prefer or will tolerate alkaline soil (pH above 7.0).

Aquilegia canadensis—wild columbine
Begonia grandis—hardy begonia
Bergenia cordifolia—bergenia
Centaurea hypoleuca—knapweed
Centranthus ruber—red valerian
Chasmanthium latifolium—northern sea oats
Coreopsis lanceolata—lanceleaf coreopsis
Dianthus spp. and cvs.—pink
Dicentra spp. and cvs.—bleeding hearts
Dictamnus albus—gas plant
Echinacea purpurea—purple coneflower
Echinops ritro—globe thistle
Eriathus ravennae—ravenna grass
Geranium spp. and cvs.—hardy geranium
Gypsophila spp. and cvs.—baby's breath
Iberis sempervirens—candytuft
Leymus arenarius—lyme grass
Miscanthus spp. and cvs.—maiden grasses
Pennisetum spp. and cvs.—fountain grasses
Phlox subulata—creeping phlox
Plumbago ariculata—plumbago
Schizachyrium scoparium—little bluestem

Soil Fertility

Another important subject is plant nutrition and soil fertility. Even though plants manufacture their own food from carbon dioxide and water in the presence of light, they need certain minerals in order to carry out their life processes. These have been divided into three categories, depending on the amounts needed, but all are essential.

The three major nutrients necessary are nitrogen, phosphorus and potassium; the secondary nutrients are calcium, magnesium and sulfur; and the seven micronutrients, also called trace elements, are chlorine, iron, manganese, boron, zinc, copper and molybdenum. While some nutrients can be absorbed from the air into the leaves, most are taken up in water absorbed by the roots.

To determine the ability of your soil to provide the major nutrients, soil test kits are available from garden centers or mail-order garden supply companies. For the most accurate analysis, including determination of the minor or trace elements, there are professional soil-testing laboratories. To locate these, check the yellow pages or call your County Cooperative Extension Service for information. Both kits and professional testing will provide a recommendation for the addition of fertilizer.

WATER

Water, chlorophyll and carbon dioxide are the essential ingredients plants need to manufacture nutrients. Water also serves as the medium by which nutrients are then transported throughout the plant; it is also needed for the various physiological and chemical processes of plant growth. In addition, the mineral elements in the soil that plants need for growth must first be dissolved in water before they can be absorbed by the roots and transported upward.

While water is essential to plants, some plants need more or less than others, usually because of natural adaptation. Witness the cactus, which can survive drought because of fleshy, water-storing leaves, or the water lily, whose roots must be immersed in water to survive. Most plants have their roots concentrated 1 to 2 feet deep and grow best when there are roughly equal amounts of water and air around the roots.

Rainfall

When deciding what perennials to grow in your yard, first get a sense for the natural rainfall in your area.

For precise figures, the local weather service or the weather department of a local television station can supply figures for the average annual or monthly rainfall.

Drainage

Next, determine how well the soil drains in different parts of your yard. This can be done in a general way just by being observant— notice where water tends to stand, where the soil remains squishy long after other areas have dried, or where it is so dry that even weeds wilt soon after a rain. For more precision, dig a hole 24 inches deep and any width. Fill it with water and let it drain completely. Fill the hole with water again, and note the rate at which the water level drops. An area with adequate drainage will drop about 6 inches in 24 hours.

If the soil drains faster than that, you will need to improve water retention by incorporating organic

Water is essential to plant growth. The natural rainfall in your area will be another factor in determining which plants are ideally suited for your garden.

matter when preparing the soil. It would also be wise to choose plants that are more drought resistant. For poorly drained soils, solutions may include installing drainage tiles, building raised beds filled with well-draining topsoil and organic matter, or exploring the joys of bog gardening.

Micro Needs

Because of the variations in soil and slope and exposure to sun and wind, even an average-sized yard will likely have at least several different areas for plants with specific moisture needs. By selecting plants that are adapted to the natural moisture in your area and your specific site, the need for supplemental watering or major excavating can be kept to a minimum, saving time, money and resources. Rather, you'll be able to spend your time and money on the plants themselves. For suggestions of water-tolerant plants, see the chart at left. For a list of drought-tolerant plants, see page 41.

PERENNIALS FOR WET SOIL OR STREAMSIDE GARDENS

Acorus spp.
Aruncus spp.
Calamagrostis spp.
Chelone spp.
Filipendula spp.
Helianthus
    angustifolius
Iris fulva, I. hexagona,
    I. laevigata,
    I. pseudacorus,
    I. versicolor
Ligularia spp.
Lobelia spp.
Meconopsis spp.
Monarda spp.
Osmunda spp.
Ranunculus spp.

Rheum spp.
Rodgersia spp.
Sanguisorba spp.
Silphium spp.
Smilacina spp.
Thelypteris spp.

If you have a stream, pool or any area that is naturally boggy, why not turn the area into a garden by using perennials that thrive and flourish under such conditions?

LIGHT

By taking into account the climate, soil, rainfall and light in your garden, you can choose plants that are closely adapted to your environment, thereby increasing your chances for success.

Plants are unique in their ability to manufacture food from light. In the process called photosynthesis, light reacts in the leaves with the green pigment chlorophyll, water and carbon dioxide to create sugars. Some of these sugars are then converted into carbohydrates and proteins and transported throughout the plant. A by-product of photosynthesis of particular importance to us is the oxygen released into the air.

For many plants, the more light, the more food produced, the faster the growth and the more flowers produced. With a little less light, but still at least six hours of direct sun each day, sun-loving plants can still grow. Reduce the light much more and these plants can barely produce enough food to stay alive.

Fortunately for gardeners with shade, many other plants have adapted to lower light by having more chlorophyll in their leaves and by becoming more efficient at using the light they receive. Try to grow shade-adapted plants in full sun, and they wilt, burn or show other signs of stress.

Analyze Your Light

A little detective work yields information about the light patterns in your yard. Usually the south-facing areas receive the most direct sunlight throughout the day. The east side of your property probably gets mild morning sun and afternoon shade, while the west side has morning shade and hot afternoon sun. Areas on the north

A border can be designed for shade-to-sun.

The light under deciduous trees may be full shade in the summer, but in the spring it could be sunny enough for woodland wildflowers.

A garden with partial, or dappled, shade will receive some direct sun in the morning or afternoon or lightly dappled sunlight all day. A great range of plants can grow here.

side of walls get very little, if any, direct sunlight. Notice, too, that at the height of summer, the sun rises in the northeast and sets in the northwest. These various situations not only result in differing amounts of light available to plants, but they also have an effect on air and soil temperature, humidity and soil moisture.

Determining the areas receiving full sun is pretty easy. Determining shade conditions is a bit more difficult. Although shade is usually defined as any area receiving less than six hours of direct sun a day, there are nuances that must be taken into account. These have variously been divided into anywhere from three to five categories with a number of different names, including partial, or dappled, shade; light shade; open, or half, shade; full, or medium, shade; and heavy, deep or dense shade. For suggestions of plants to grow under shady conditions, see page 40.

Partial Shade

Partial, or dappled, shade areas may receive some direct sun in the morning or afternoon or lightly dappled sunlight all day. This type of shade occurs under open trees, under an arbor or lathhouse, or on

the east or west side of a building or fence. A great number of shade-loving plants, as well as a number of sun-loving plants, thrive in these conditions.

Light Shade

Light shade is the type of shade found at the south edge of a woodland, under young trees, or on the north side of a light-colored house. The area may receive as much as an hour or two of sun during the day. Most shade-loving and some sun-loving plants grow well with this type of light.

Many plants can grow in light shade.

Half Shade

Open, or half, shade gets no direct sun during the brightest daylight hours but lots of reflected or bright light. This includes areas with shade cast by north-facing walls, fences, or low buildings or the area under a fiberglass-roofed patio. Again, most shade-loving plants grow well in this type of shade, and so do some sun-loving plants.

Full Shade

Full, or medium, shade gets no direct sun. It may be on the north side of structures where there are also trees or other structures obscuring the light. It is also the area under large trees that have a dense, wide canopy. Many shade-loving plants can survive here, especially native woodland plants.

Heavy Shade

Heavy, or dense, shade is the deep, cool shade cast by tall buildings or mature evergreen trees. Very few plants can grow with this type of shade unless there is at least a small amount of reflected light.

Evergreens and mature deciduous trees can create an area of heavy, or dense, shade.

◆ CHAPTER 3 ◆

GARDEN STYLES

From the earliest waxen blooms of the Lenten rose battling late-winter winds and snow, to the exuberant willfulness of the last asters on a frosty fall morning, the perennial garden offers us the prospect of being surrounded by flowers for many months of the year. The inherent qualities of these flowers are such that even the most casually placed plants bring charm to the yard. By expending a little effort in considering where and how to place perennials in the landscape, we multiply our pleasures. Whether you have a minuscule urban property or extensive rural acreage, there are rewards in developing planted areas that suit your own particular needs, desires, tastes and life-style. Success lies not in rarity or numbers, but in how the plants are used and cared for. It is about passion and vision—and follow-through.

FORMAL OR INFORMAL

Whether on an estate or in a backyard, the elements of a classic formal garden are the same: a central axis with identical plantings on each side mirroring one another. Here the beds are edged in lamb's-ears and 'Brilliant' sedum, and accented by hollies.

The delineations between the design concepts of formal and informal are essentially a matter of balance, of symmetry versus asymmetry. At their most basic definitions, each side of a formal arrangement matches, or is a mirror image of the other, while an informal arrangement is defined by the two sides being different, but equal in value, or weight.

Formal

In translating these design concepts to gardening, formal gardens are generally those based on a central axis with identical plantings on either side. At their most extreme, these are large, elaborate affairs as part of an expansive estate and mansion, such as those built by European and English nobility beginning in the Renaissance.

Over time, this concept has been reduced and adapted to more modest plots and dwellings. Among the best examples of small-scale formal gardens are those of Colonial Williamsburg. As exemplified there, formal gardens are composed of beds with clearly delineated geometric shapes, be they rectangular, square, round or pie-shaped, usually outlined by low, clipped hedges and straight paths. Perennial plantings within the beds are also symmetrical, with plants chosen for their ability to stay in place and to maintain a uniform height.

Informal

At the opposite extreme is the most informal of gardens, that of the cottage. In its purest form, the true cottage garden is one of necessity,

An informal cottage-style border along the driveway reflects the building design.

with design elements being of little import. As such it is a higgledy-piggledy mixture of all kinds of plants, including perennials, annuals, herbs, shrubs, trees, roses, vegetables and fruits. A fence, wall or hedge encloses the garden and irregular steppingstones allow passage among the plants.

With the introduction of "design" into this garden, it evolves toward more clearly defined beds and borders, often with curving edges and paths, and plants of irregular shapes. In essence, the informal garden draws on nature.

On a large scale, this naturalistic approach to landscape design had its heyday in England with the garden at Stourhead, and in the United States with the gardens of Frederick Law Olmstead. No matter the scale, a well-designed informal garden has an asymmetrical balance at its core.

Combinations

Between the extremes of the formal and informal are infinite combinations. The predominant variation is to have the beds laid out in a formal pattern, but planted in a relaxed, informal way. Both large and small properties can have combinations of the different styles, often with a formal area near the house, while garden areas at the farthest edges of the property are more informally planted.

Perhaps it will be an existing landscape feature, such as a rock wall, that will be a determining factor in what type of planting style you choose.

BORDERS

Perennials and flower borders are thought of almost simultaneously by many people. Yet it has really only been in the last hundred years or so that this phenomenon has come about. In reaction to the beds planted with regimented rows of brashly colored flowers so favored by the mid-Victorians, two English gardeners, William Robinson and Gertrude Jekyll, turned the gardening world upside down. They designed long beds at least 9 feet wide, backed by a hedge or brick wall and filled them with masses of subtly colored perennials. Ideally, there were two borders, parallel and separated by a closely-clipped lawn.

The tallest plants were placed at the back and the lowest at the front. Colors were soft blues, pinks and white, with only the occasional gold or yellow, all to give the effect of an Impressionist painting. Colors were never to clash, but contrasting forms were put next to each other for interest, and bloom sequence was carefully planned. Significant examples of this type of perennial border still exist in England today, most notably at Wisley, Hampton Court and Great Dixter.

The Mixed Border

Just as the intervening years have wrought a multitude of changes in society, so too with the grand perennial border. Such borders require a great deal of space and labor. Most Americans do not have the advantage of the cool, moist English climate. Still, much has been gleaned from the era of Robinson and Jekyll, with the perennial border of today borrowing from them as well as from the informal cottage garden.

The result may best be labeled the mixed border, using as it does a wide range of plants in addition to perennials. These may include both evergreen and deciduous trees and shrubs, roses, bulbs, herbs and annuals. The woody plants provide a year-round framework as well as seasonal color, while the bulbs bring life to the garden in early spring and the annuals give summer-long color.

Certain rules still apply when creating a border, but only insofar as your desired effect. For instance, borders are now thought of in much smaller terms, usually no more than five feet across. A background still shows off the plants, but it now may be a simple fence or an assortment of shrubs planted in a curving line. Shorter, sturdier hybrid varieties are used to minimize the need for staking. The low-in-the-front, medium-in-the-middle and tall-in-the-back rule is

If straight lines aren't to your liking, try creating borders with softer, flowing edges.

Borders derived from the cottage style of gardening may utilize a wide variety of plants besides perennials, plus have curving edges and meandering paths that beckon one to go exploring. Here, a partially hidden sundial in the distance catches the eye.

Utilize disparate styles by combining an informal border of perennials and other flowers with a formally clipped boxwood or other low hedge.

much more freely interpreted, often with taller plants set more toward the front.

Taking the sequence of bloom into consideration when planning still makes sense, but the use of color is more broadly interpreted. As the section on color in Chapter 4 illustrates, there are many different types of color combinations. The shorter the border, the better to use monochromatic or analogous color schemes. With a longer border, it's possible to use more colors or color schemes, but the effect will be most pleasing if different areas are separated with shrubs or foliage plants.

One of the best ways to have a flower border looking good for much of the growing season is to incorporate roses, shrubs, annuals, herbs or other plants with the perennials.

ISLAND BEDS

The use of beds, open on all sides, is not a new concept in gardening, having been used in ancient times in the courtyard gardens of Persia, then again in the cloistered Medieval gardens and walled Elizabethan pleasaunce gardens. Formally arranged beds were the standard in ornate Renaissance gardens, and Victorians took the concept to exaggerated lengths with their stylized plantings of annuals in bedding schemes. Although Gertrude Jekyll is known for her perennial borders, the formally arranged beds she designed at Hestercombe show her willingness and ability to use beds of perennials. For gardens where a formal design is appropriate, beds are certainly still an excellent choice. Using the traditional geometric shapes, these beds are formed into a symmetrical arrangement composing a whole.

A completely different approach to gardening in beds are the island beds promoted by English perennial expert Alan Bloom. These are large and free-form in shape, and fit in with a naturalistic, informal landscape.

No matter their shape or size, the advantages of beds are not only that they can be appreciated from all sides, but also that they can be maintained from any perspective. In addition, light, air and moisture reach the plants more readily than when they are grown in borders backed by walls, fences or hedges. This means fewer disease problems and less need for staking.

In planting an island bed, the tallest-growing plants are placed near the center, with progressively shorter plants placed outward from the center to the edges. For the most balanced effect, the height of the tallest plants should be half the width of the bed. The overall look will also be more effective if plants of one kind are set out in groups.

Informal island bed plantings offer the aesthetic advantage of their beauty appreciated from all sides, while their free-form shapes fit in with naturalistic landscapes.

FOUNDATION AND ENTRYWAY PLANTINGS

No boring planting of yews or junipers at this house. Instead, colorful flowering shrubs like rose of Sharon and 'Wonderful' pomegranate are interplanted with long-blooming perennials such as rudbeckia and gloriosa daisies.

When landscaping a home, the first places most people consider are the foundation of the house, the driveway and the front walk and door. Traditionally, evergreen trees and shrubs form the basis of these plantings that are a first impression of the home and, potentially, the creativity of the owner. They are placed so that they hide the foundation from view, frame the house, outline windows and soften corners. Ideally, the trees and shrubs are not placed in a single row, but arranged in groups of different heights and forms.

But all those evergreens can get a little boring. And so can those rows of petunias put in every year. To shake up this part of the landscape, why not try adding perennials? Use the evergreens as the background for a new perennial border. In the winter, the evergreens provide form and structure to the front of the home, while in the summer, you'll have lots of colorful flowers welcoming people. In addition, a perennial planting will better tie the house to the surrounding landscape and emphasize the trees and shrubs.

LONG-BLOOMING PERENNIALS

The following perennials should bloom at least eight weeks, and even up to 12 weeks, depending mainly on climate and care. Most are summer blooming, but others will extend the season, either in late spring and early summer or in autumn. This list offers a variety of heights and colors as well as plants for both sun and shade, for borders as well as foundation and entryway plantings.

Achillea millefolium 'Fire King'
Armeria maritima
Aster x *frikartii* 'Monch'
Aster x *frikartii* 'Wonder of Staffa'
Aster novae-angliae 'September Ruby'
Chrysanthemum rubellum (*Dendranthema zawadskii*) 'Clara Curtis'
Chrysogonum virginianum 'Mark Viette'
Chrysopsis mariana
Coreopsis grandiflora 'Early Sunrise'
Coreopsis grandiflora 'Sunray'
Coreopsis verticillata 'Moonbeam'
Coreopsis verticillata 'Zagreb'
Corydalis lutea

Dicentra eximia 'Alba'
Dicentra x 'Luxuriant'
Gaillardia x *grandiflora* 'Baby Cole'
Gaura lindheimeri
Geranium sanguineum var. *striatum*
Hemerocallis 'Happy Returns'
Hemerocallis 'Stella de Oro'
Heterotheca villosa 'Golden Sunshine'
Hylotelephium (*Sedum*) x 'Autumn Joy'
Lychnis x *arkwrightii*
Malva alcea 'Fastigiata'
Nepeta x *faassenii* 'Dropmore'
Perovskia atriplicifolia
Phlox paniculata 'Eva Cullum'

Phlox paniculata 'Franz Schubert'
Phlox paniculata 'Sandra'
Platycodon grandiflorus
Rudbeckia nitida 'Autumn Glory'
Rudbeckia nitida 'Goldquelle'
Salvia x *superba* 'East Friesland'
Salvia x *superba* 'Lubeca'
Salvia x *superba* 'May Night'
Scabiosa caucasica 'Butterfly Blue'
Stokesia laevis 'Bluestone'
Verbena bonariensis
Veronica 'Sunny Border Blue'

Since these flowers are in front, you'll want them to look good for much of summer. That means choosing easily grown perennials with a long blooming season and few pest problems—and providing the best soil preparation, care and maintenance. This is not the site for single specimens or plants that have to be fussed over. You want to make a statement here, so, for the greatest effect, make groupings of perennials, preferably with triangular placement rather than rows. Depending on the space available and your preference, you may want to work up an area three to four feet wide in front of the shrubs. This allows you to have plantings of different heights progressing from back to front.

Don't forget about other areas in front of your home, such as the lamppost, where a large-specimen perennial is effective. Also consider using the space between the walk and the house for a planting of perennials. The strip between the drive and the property boundary is another possible area for perennials.

CORNER PLANTINGS

When planted with lilies, clematis, delphiniums and other flowers, the corner space between two stairs becomes a focal point near a deck. Look around your yard for areas such as this that can provide big rewards with little effort or money.

Corner plantings are not a widespread concept, but quite effective when you want a small, defined space for perennials. Working most effectively on small urban or suburban lots, it involves defining one or more of the outer limits of the property with a short length of fence or hedge. Purchased fencing usually comes in eight-foot lengths, so the basis for a corner planting would be a corner post with lengths of fencing at right angles. Low fencing, such as post-and-rail or picket works best. Of course, the concept can be enlarged, perhaps with an "anchor" plant, such as a spring-blooming or an evergreen tree. Within this triangular area, taller plants are placed near the corner, with progressively shorter plants toward the outside points and across the front.

Plantings of flowers make a stone wall and wrought-iron gate inviting.

Large hostas create a bold corner planting.

GROUNDCOVERS

Among the most versatile of perennials, hostas are staples of perennial groundcovers. Hosta foliage may be plain or variegated, in many shades of green.

A steep slope becomes an asset rather than an eyesore or problem area when stone terraces are installed and then planted with perennials. The creeping phlox is stunning in the spring with the redbud tree, while other perennials lend interest later in the summer.

Plants carpeting the ground are useful, as they prevent the soil washing away, and also bring beauty to the landscape.

The most important requirement of a groundcover is that it spreads quickly and efficiently. Plants chosen as groundcovers often have fibrous roots that bind the soil.

The second consideration is ease of maintenance. The area to be covered may be large or small, in sun or shade. Groundcover plants may grow close to the ground or with some height. Most often a single type of plant is used as a groundcover in a particular area, but sometimes several can be effectively combined.

The best known and most widely used groundcover for sunny areas is bluegrass. It withstands rugged use, but is, unfortunately, very high maintenance and can be particularly troublesome on slopes or under shrubs. It is also rather boring.

For shady conditions, bluegrass is superseded by fescue, with the same advantages and disadvantages. Woody evergreen plants, such as creeping junipers or English ivy, are chosen for groundcover use because they are green year-round.

For areas where there is little or no foot traffic, certain perennials are the plants of choice because of their various textures, forms and, in many cases, their flowers. Some are for sun, others for various degrees of shade.

Using perennial groundcovers not only can make garden chores easier, but also make your garden more interesting.

PERENNIALS AS GROUNDCOVERS

Ajuga genevensis, A. pyramidalis, A. reptans
Alchemilla mollis
Asarum europaeum, A. hartwegii
Bergenia cordifolia, B. crassifolia, B. stracheyi
Brunnera macrophylla
Cerastium tomentosum
Ceratostigma plumbaginoides
Chrysogonum virginianum
Convallaria majalis
Corydalis lutea
Dianthus gratianopolitanus 'Bath's Pink'
Epimedium alpinum, E. grandiflorum,
    E. pinnatum, E. x rubrum, E. x versicolor,
    E. x youngianum
Ferns

Festuca cinerea cvs.
Fragaria spp.
Galium odoratum
Geranium x cantabrigiense 'Biokovo'
Helleborus argutifolius, H. foetidus, H. niger,
    H. orientalis
Heuchera americana, H. x brizoides,
    H. micrantha, H. sanguinea, H. villosa
Hosta spp. and cvs.
Iberis sempervirens
Iris cristata
Lamium maculatum and cvs.
Liriope muscari, L. spicata
Lysimachia nummularia
Miscanthus spp. and cvs.

Myosotis palustris
Ophiopogon japonicus, O. planiscapus 'Nigrescens'
Pennisetum spp. and cvs.
Phlox divaricata
Phlox stolonifera
Polygonum affinis, P. bistorta 'Superba'
Pulmonaria angustifolia, P. longifolia, P. rubra,
    P. saccharata and cvs.
Sedum acre, S. spurium cvs.
Silphium spp.
Stachys byzantina, S. macrantha
Tiarella cordifolia and cvs.
Waldsteinia fragrarioides
X Heucherella alba 'Bridget Bloom',
    X H. tiarelloides

NATIVE PERENNIAL GARDENS

No plant from foreign shores can compete with the stunning appearance, come spring, of the various native woodland phlox.

A native garden is one that contains predominantly native wildflowers in a setting that is as close as possible to the one where they might be found growing in nature. The three most common native gardens are the spring-blooming deciduous woodland garden, the sunny prairie garden and the bog garden, which may be in sun or shade. When considering any of these gardens, the area of your yard to be used should already show a tendency for such a planting. For example, if an area of the yard has trees, then that would likely be an appropriate spot for a woodland garden. If a stream runs through your property, then planting along it with bog-type plants would be appropriate.

In designing native gardens, it's also logical to take your cues from nature. Study the types of areas you want to emulate. Any translation of a wild garden to a cultivated one should be preceded with a study of the trees, shrubs and flowers that naturally grow together. Observe the type of soil, light and moisture of the area where you will develop your wild garden.

When ready, clear the site, prepare the soil carefully and set the plants out just as you would for any new garden area. Do not dig plants from the wild and be sure purchased plants are nursery propagated. Weeding will also be necessary so that the plants you want to spread can do so. It is a fallacy that a native garden does not require planning or maintenance; a garden is a garden, no matter the style.

PERENNIALS FOR WOODLAND GARDENS

Actaea rubra	*Hepatica* spp.
Adiantum	*Iris cristata*
pedatum	*Jeffersonia diphylla*
Aquilegia	*Mertensia virginica*
canadensis	*Phlox divaricata, P.*
Arisaema	pilosa, P.
triphyllum	stolonifera
Asarum canadense	*Podophyllum*
Asplenium	peltatum
platyneuron	*Polemonium*
Chrysogonum	reptans
virginianum	*Polystichum*
Cimicifuga	acrostichoides
racemosa	*Sanguinaria*
Dentaria spp.	canadensis
Disporum spp.	*Trillium* spp.
Dryopteris spp.	*Uvularia* spp.

A deciduous woodland area provides an ideal setting for a planting of native spring-blooming perennials, such as these phlox and double trillium. When purchasing native plants, try to make sure that they have been nursery-propagated.

PERENNIALS FOR PRAIRIE GARDENS

Achillea spp.	*Panicum* spp.	*Solidago* spp.
Agastache spp.	*Penstemon* spp.	*Sorghastrum* spp.
Amsonia tabernaemontana	*Phlox* spp.	*Thalictrum* spp.
Andropogon spp.	*Ratibida* spp.	*Vernonia* spp.
Asclepias spp.	*Rudbeckia* spp.	
Aster spp.		
Baptisia spp.		
Boltonia asteroides		
Chrysopsis spp.		
Coreopsis spp.		
Echinacea spp.		
Eryngium yuccifolium		
Eupatorium spp.		
Filipendula spp.		
Gaillardia spp.		
Geranium pratense		
Helianthus spp.		
Heliopsis spp.		
Leucanthemum spp.		
Liatris spp.		
Miscanthus spp.		
Monarda spp.		
Oenothera spp.		

Wide borders of native prairie plants juxtaposed with finely clipped grass provides an intriguing contrast that is much more interesting than if either were used alone.

PERENNIAL FOLIAGE GARDENS

Foliage takes center stage in this planting of grasses with stachys and santolina.

A HOSTA PRIMER

Dwarf—eight inches or shorter. Best suited for rock gardens or containers.
Gold-leaved: 'Little Aurora', 'Blonde Elf'
Green-leaved: 'Baby Bunting','Gum Drop'
White-edged: 'Stiletto', 'Verna Lean'
Yellow-centered: 'Just So', 'Kabitan'

Edging—12 inches or shorter. Perfect for the outside edge of a border.
Green-leaved: 'Snow Flakes', 'Floradora'
White-edged: 'Aristocrat', 'Ginko Craig'
Variegated: 'Emerald Tiara', 'Geisha'
Yellow-edged: 'Scooter', 'Brim Cup'

Groundcover—20 inches or shorter. Vigorous; good choice for low-maintenance, mass plantings.
Blue-leaved: 'Blue Wedgwood', 'Halcyon'
Gold-leaved: 'Midas Touch', 'Day Break'
Green-leaved: 'Aoki', 'Invincible'
Variegated: 'Bright Lights', 'Janet'
White-edged: 'Francee', 'Fair Maiden'
Yellow-edged: 'Frances Williams', 'Yellow River'

Background—24 inches or more. Excellent for filling in at the backs of shade beds and borders.
Blue-leaved: 'Blue Vision', 'Wheaton Blue'
Gold-leaved: 'Gold Regal', 'Sun Power'
Green-leaved: 'Royal Standard', 'Honeybells'
White-edged: 'Antioch', 'Frosted Jade'
Yellow-edged: 'Wide Brim', 'Pizzaz'

Specimen—36 to 48 inches. Spectacular plants that make a strong focal point in the garden.
Blue-leaved: 'Blue Mammoth', 'Krossa Regal'
Gold-leaved: 'Sum and Substance', 'Golden Medallion'
Green-leaved: 'Edge of Night', 'Green Wedge'
White-edged: 'Regal Splendor', 'Crowned Imperial'
Yellow-edged: 'Sagae', 'Carnival'

Vinca becomes a fine-textured foil to the dramatic clumps of different hosta varieties that invite one to sit upon a bench and enjoy the splendors of the garden.

The leaves of perennials are usually thought of as an adjunct to the flowers, but in certain situations, focusing on foliage can have a dramatic effect in the garden. A garden where foliage predominates is more likely to produce a feeling of calmness in the viewer. Sometimes it can mean a garden that requires less maintenance. The stars of the perennial garden based on foliage are the hostas, the ferns and the ornamental grasses. Ferns are the only ones that truly do not produce flowers.

Hostas are the premier foliage plant for shaded situations in the landscape. They grow best in a soil that is rich in organic matter, and moist but well drained. Generally, variegated and golden-leaved varieties tolerate more sun than green- or blue-leaved varieties. The following are some suggested cultivars for various uses in the garden:

PERENNIAL GARDENS FOR BUTTERFLIES AND BIRDS

Birds and butterflies will make a home in your garden if it provides food, cover, nesting sites and a constant supply of fresh water.

Any garden is a veritable cosmopolitan ecosystem, complete with a full range of animals, insects and birds as well as assorted microorganisms and other critters large and small. Of these, birds and butterflies are among the most desired, particularly for the bright, flitting colors of both and the songs of the birds.

Some people may contend that the birds will feed on the caterpillars as well as bugs and berries, but unless you're trying to nurture a very rare species of butterfly, a balanced population of each can usually be reached. The one thing that you will have to give up, or at least minimize, in this type of garden is pesticides.

The most important aspect of encouraging birds and butterflies to your garden is providing adequate habitat. Birds need plants that will provide food, cover and nesting sites. Nectar plants for adult butterflies are necessary, along with larval food plants for caterpillars. Both birds and butterflies need a constant supply of fresh water.

PERENNIALS THAT ATTRACT HUMMINGBIRDS

Aquilegia
Asclepias
Heuchera
Iris

Lobelia
Monarda
Penstemon
Salvia

No bird is more welcome in the garden than the eastern ruby-throated hummingbird, with its glistening feathers and whirring wings. Besides the perennials and other flowers that attract these stunning creatures, you may also want to provide nectar feeders.

PERENNIALS THAT USE SEEDS TO ATTRACT BIRDS

Aster
Boltonia
Chrysanthemum
Coreopsis
Echinacea
Echinops
Gaillardia

Papaver
Penstemon
Rudbeckia
Salvia
Solidago
Spigelia
Vernonia

Lovely rudbeckia and goldenrod also produce seeds for birds.

PERENNIALS THAT ATTRACT BUTTERFLIES

For Nectar:
Achillea
Aster
Centranthus
Coreopsis
Echinacea
Eupatorium
Helianthus
Hemerocallis
Liatris
Lobelia
Monarda
Phlox
Rudbeckia
Salvia
Sedum
Solidago
Verbena

Host Plants for Larvae:
Artemisia
Asclepias
Foeniculum
Viola

Dame's rocket not only provides fragrance and excellent cut flowers, it also uses its nectar to attract butterflies, such as this eastern tiger swallowtail, to the garden. Remember that butterflies have larvae that eat plants, so grow enough for you and the caterpillars.

ROCK GARDENS WITH PERENNIALS

The challenge of creating a rock garden seems of little consequence to those who are drawn to its style and character.

People can spend years studying and constructing rock gardens. It requires a keen sense of imagination and practical skill to create an area that takes on the effect of a mountain setting. In planning a rock garden, you should choose a site in full sun with excellent drainage, never too close to trees where roots can take over. It's best to use rocks naturally found in your area so that the artificial outcropping you're going to create looks as appropriate as possible. At least some of these rocks should be of a large size, which means you may need the assistance of a contractor to place them with the bottom three-fourths buried. These rocks should be tilted toward the top of the grade to look natural and to channel water into the soil.

There should be deep pockets of soil between the rocks, with the soil mixture usually composed of one-half part garden loam, one-half part humus, one part half-inch crushed rock and one part coarse sand. Often somewhere in the rock garden is a scree, which is a heap of fine stones representing a rock slide or the tip of a glacial moraine. This should be about 12 inches thick, the bottom three inches

PERENNIALS FOR ROCK GARDENS

Achillea clavennae, A. tomentosa	Dicentra
Aquilegia	Filipendula vulgaris
Arabis	Gaillardia 'Goblin'
Armeria	Geum
Artemisia schmidtiana	Helianthemum
Aruncus aethusifolius	Heuchera
Asarum	Iberis
Aster dumosus	Linum
Aubrieta	Platycodon grandiflorus 'Apoyame'
Aurinia	Santolina
Bellis perennis	Saponaria
Bergenia spp.	Scabiosa
Campanula—selected spp.	Sedum—selected spp.
Cerastium	Sempervivum
Coreopsis auriculata 'Nana'	Teucrium
Coreopsis grandiflora 'Goldfink'	Veronica—selected spp.
Dianthus	

A rock garden in Colorado mimics the surrounding high mountain meadows with its rocks, gravelly soil, windblown tree, evergreens and perennials.

composed of two- to three-inch stone, and the rest a mixture of two parts half-inch crushed rock and one part garden loam. Because of the fast drainage, rock gardens must be watered regularly and deeply, but the soil should never be allowed to remain soggy.

The plants most often used in a rock garden are ones that may naturally grow in such a situation. Otherwise, in choosing plants for a rock garden, consider the size of the garden, the size of the plant, how much it spreads, its growing requirements and how it will look in the overall composition.

The art in developing a rock garden is in having it look as if the rocks "grew" there naturally. Large boulders should be "planted," with only a quarter of them showing.

PERENNIAL GARDENS FOR FRAGRANCE

Many of Grandmother's old-fashioned favorite perennials were chosen for their fragrance, such as these peonies and iris. Not all varieties will have a scent, or a good one, so check out plant descriptions to make sure before you buy.

One of the first things people do when confronted with a flower is smell it to determine if there is fragrance. Creating a perennial garden that focuses on fragrance most often means creating a mixed border or bed that utilizes traditional perennial flowers as well as perennial herbs, old-fashioned and shrub roses, annuals, bulbs, trees and shrubs. Fragrance will come from both flowers and foliage.

PERENNIALS FOR A FRAGRANT GARDEN

Agastache	Hesperis
Artemisia	Hosta plantaginea
Centaurea	Iris
Centranthus	Lavandula
Cimicifuga	Monarda
Convallaria	Nepeta
Dianthus	Oenothera
Filipendula	Paeonia
Galium	Perovskia
Hemerocallis	Phlox
(selected	Primula
cultivars)	Santolina

SHADE GARDENS

There are many different types of shade and a great variety of shady situations in a landscape. Shade should not be considered a problem in the landscape, but rather a wonderful opportunity for comfortable summer outdoor living surrounded by a wide assortment of beautiful plants. To successfully garden in the shade, it is necessary to analyze your site, matching the plant to the site as much as possible, and, when necessary or possible, adjusting the soil, moisture and degree of shade.

On a stifling hot summer's day, cooling breezes make a shady area of the yard seem the best place in the world. Don't neglect these areas when deciding where to have perennials.

No matter your climate or means, a garden should be your own unique expression, a place that is your joy and passion, a testament to your spirit and beliefs.

PERENNIALS FOR MOIST SOIL AND PARTIAL SHADE

A wide range of perennials will thrive in locations with partial (not deep) shade and moist but well-drained soil.

Acanthus	Hakonechloa
Aconitum	Helleborus
Ajuga	Heuchera
Alchemilla	Heucherella
Aquilegia	Hosta
Artemisia	Lamium
Aruncus	Ligularia
Asarum	Liriope
Astilbe	Lobelia
Bergenia	Monarda
Brunnera	Nepeta
Campanula	Oenothera
Carex	Phlox (some)
Chelone	Polemonium
Cimicifuga	Polygonatum
Convallaria	Pulmonaria
Corydalis	Ranunculus
Dicentra	Sanguinaria
Digitalis	Symphytum
Doronicum	Thalictrum
Epimedium	Tiarella
Filipendula	Tricyrtis
Galium	Vinca
Gaura	Viola
Geranium	Waldsteinia

PERENNIALS FOR DRY SOIL AND SHADE

The soil under large trees and shrubs is often especially dry and, because of the competition from roots, low in nutrients. Growing perennials in this situation is difficult, but several plants tolerate this situation. Even so, it's important to incorporate organic matter and fertilizer into the soil before planting, and to water regularly.

Alchemilla	Epimedium	Lamium	Stachys	Tricyrtis
Convallaria	Galium	Pulmonaria	Symphytum	Vinca

DROUGHT-TOLERANT PERENNIAL GARDENS

If you live in an area with little rainfall, have a garden with fast-draining soil or have other conditions that make the soil particularly dry, don't give up on creating a garden, or think that a massive amount of watering is the only solution. Consider creating a dry landscape, or xeriscape, composed of plants that are adapted to dry growing conditions. By utilizing plants from various arid regions of the world, you can have a garden that is beautiful and makes thoughtful use of limited natural resources.

Low rainfall or sandy soil needn't be a deterrent to gardening. With carefully chosen plants, this entrance garden is lush and welcoming without irrigation.

DROUGHT-TOLERANT PERENNIALS FOR SUN

Achillea
Andropogon
Anthemis
Artemisia
Asclepias
Baptisia
Belamcanda
Coreopsis
Cortaderia
Disporum
Echinops
Elymus

Euphorbia
Gaillardia
Gaura
Kniphofia
Liatris
Miscanthus
Rudbeckia
Salvia
Solidago
Stachys
Thermopsis

When natural rainfall is scarce, set plants farther apart from each other so that the roots of each have a wide area from which they can draw nutrients and water.

CHAPTER 4

DESIGN CONSIDERATIONS

Great garden designers are generally born, not made. But even the artistically challenged can learn to utilize the design principles of applied art to significant effect. Repetition, balance, sequence, contrast and rhythm—combined with the elements of form, texture and color—bring a visually satisfying appeal to any design, be it fabric, a centerpiece, a room or a garden. But designing a garden is still a challenge. Because the dynamic nature of plants combines with the complicating factors of climate, soil, moisture, light and different bloom seasons, it takes careful planning to create a breathtaking picture-book garden.

PLANNING PRINCIPLES

It is important to take the time to evaluate your garden environment, then decide how you want your garden to look, before you ever being creating a garden plan. Making lists of plants is also helpful, including lists of the best plants for your site and those you like, as well as lists of plants representing each of the elements of size, form, texture, color and bloom season. This way when you're looking for a bold-textured perennial with yellow autumn flowers for that moist, shady site, you'll see that Kirengeshoma is just the plant to use.

The planning stage can be some of gardening's most fun, because that's when we all have the perfect garden. So get lots of notepads, graph paper and tracing paper ready, with sharp pencils and those all-important erasers, get out the sketches and measurements of the areas you want to work on, surround yourself with plant catalogs and books and settle down for some serious doodling.

Planning Considerations

Make your goal a final plan drawn to scale on graph paper. Designing to scale helps you get a sense of space and proportion as well as the number of plants needed. First, determine the dimensions of the site and outline the shape of the bed or border on the graph paper. Next, lay a sheet of tracing paper over the graph paper. Using your plant lists, begin drawing in the clumps of plants on tracing paper.

As you design, it helps to include plant characteristics, such as height, form, color and bloom season. To save space, develop your own code for each of these. Using colored pencils or markers is a good way to indicate colors. Overlaying layers of tracing paper helps in experimenting with different combinations or seeing how the garden might look at different seasons. In spacing plants on the plan, consider that placing at least three of the same plants together gives the greatest impact.

As you go about this planning and design process, remember that no matter how good the plan, it is not foolproof. Acknowledging that fact in the beginning can make the whole process seem much less intimidating. Some plants will grow differently than you expected, or a color combination that seemed like such a good idea in your mind in January doesn't quite work in the light of June. A good spading fork can rectify any number of design errors.

Even those who don't consider themselves artistic can create a stunning garden if they take the time to consider the various principles of applied art when developing a garden plan.

DESIGN PRINCIPLES

There are five basic principles of garden design to consider: repetition, contrast, balance, sequence and rhythm.

Repetition

Repetition is the reappearance of the same plant, form, texture or color throughout an area. Whether naturalistic or stylized, this creation of a pattern provides visual pleasure plus a feeling of security and simplicity with its rhythm and movement. Think of it as the catchy chorus to a song. Repetition is used both within a single area and throughout the entire landscape.

By planting clumps of the white foxglove throughout the garden, the gardener has utilized the design principle of repetition, which gives a feeling of movement in the garden.

Contrast

Contrast accentuates the differences rather than the similarities. The juxtaposition of different sizes, textures, forms and colors of perennials creates interest in a garden. Or, to use the cliché, variety is the spice of life. Just remember that with too much spice you get heartburn. The use of a focal point in your garden is a prime example of good use of contrast. First your eyes are drawn to a particular plant or garden ornament, then gradually you examine adjacent elements.

Tall spiky irises provide visual contrast with rounded dianthus.

Balance

Balance may be symmetrical or asymmetrical, real or perceived, but there is always a sense of stability. To achieve balance, the size, form, texture and color must all be taken into consideration. With symmetrical balance, one side of a design will be a mirror image of the opposite side. In an asymmetrical arrangement, the two halves are different, but are of equal visual weight.

Straight lines, geometrical shapes and mirror images are the components of this symmetrically balanced garden designed by Gertrude Jekyll in England.

Sequence

Sequence, or scale and proportion, is the orderly relationship of sizes of plants and landscape materials to each other and to the landscape as a whole. In other words, a tall plant isn't used directly next to a short plant; rather a tall and a medium or a medium and a short are placed together. Or, for another example, a tiny planting area looks lost in a large yard. The ratio of size from one plant or planting to the next should be ½ to ⅓.

By repeating the use of yellow flowers in this garden, a rhythm is created that moves the eyes around this garden from the iris in the front, to the right, then to the back.

Rhythm

Rhythm is another method for moving the eyes around the garden, be it in a straight, circular or meandering line, or by a curve into a straight line (known as arc and tangent). It is achieved by the use of repetition of patterns punctuated by contrasts, causing the eye to hesitate, then be drawn onward. Such repetitions and contrasts should not be exact, or the effect will be as monotonous as a metronome. Think of how your favorite drummer might "play" a garden.

DESIGN ELEMENTS

Garden design elements include the size, form, texture, color and bloom season of the plants you use.

Size

Size is both the mature height and width of the plant. In considering the width of perennials, keep in mind how quickly the plant spreads, or multiplies. Some perennials spread rapidly from the center of the plant, while others remain relatively compact. The ultimate height of a plant will affect where in a garden the plant is placed, with taller plants usually going to the back of a border or the center of an island bed. The width has more effect on the spacing of the plants. A newly—and correctly—planted area can look sparse, so the temptation is to plant too closely. In what seems like no time at all, the plants are competing for light, water and nutrients, and you're out there digging up half the garden. Even in a perennial garden, where we're used to seeing plants close together, there should be a feeling that each plant has its own distinct space.

Just as in those group photos from class trips, perennial borders are usually planned with

Try incorporating the design elements of size, form, texture and color into your garden plan.

the tall plants in the back, medium-sized ones in the middle and the short ones in the front. Some plants confound the issue by being groundhugging except when in flower. In this case, plants are most often placed according to their foliage height. As described in the design principle of contrast, just to shake things up a little and make them interesting, taller plants are sometimes jutted out farther toward the front of a border. The following lists are meant as a general guideline; sometimes there are taller or shorter cultivars of certain plants available that push them into another category, and, some genera have plants of all sizes.

Utilizing the principles of scale and proportion between the plants, landscape and building has allowed this bold garden to delight the eye.

PERENNIALS BY SIZE

SHORT				MEDIUM	
Up to 18 inches tall	Campanula	Heuchera	Ornamental grasses	**18 to 36 inches tall**	Platycodon
Alchemilla	Cerastium	Heucherella	Phlox	Achillea	Salvia
Arabis	Chrysogonum	Hosta	Primula	Adenophora	Sedum
Armeria	Dianthus	Iberis	Pulmonaria	Amsonia	Solidago
Asarum	Dicentra	Iris	Scabiosa	Anaphalis	Stokesia
Aubrieta	Euphorbia	Linum	Sedum	Anthemis	Tradescantia
Aurinia	Ferns	Mertensia	Stachys	Aquilegia	Veronica
Bergenia	Galium	Nepeta	Veronica	Artemisia	
	Gypsophila	Oenothera	Viola	Asclepias	**TALL**
				Astilbe	**36 inches and above**
				Belamcanda	Aconitum
				Brunnera	Anchusa
				Campanula	Anemone
				Chrysanthemum	Aruncus
				Coreopsis	Aster
				Dicentra	Baptisia
				Dictamnus	Campanula
				Doronicum	Centranthus
				Erigeron	Cimicifuga
				Eupatorium	Clematis
				Euphorbia	Delphinium
				Ferns	Digitalis
				Filipendula	Echinacea
				Gypsophila	Echinops
				Helleborus	Eryngium
				Hemerocallis	Eupatorium
				Hesperis	Ferns
				Hosta	Filipendula
				Iris	Helenium
				Lavandula	Heliopsis
				Liatris	Hemerocallis
				Lupinus	Iris
				Lychnis	Kniphofia
				Lysimachia	Liatris
				Ornamental grasses	Lobelia
				Paeonia	Macleaya
				Papaver	Monarda
				Phlox	Ornamental grasses
					Phlox
					Physostegia
					Polygonatum
					Rudbeckia
					Thalictrum
					Thermopsis

Utilize plants of different sizes, to create a wave or flow in the garden.

Form

Form is the three-dimensional shape of a plant. These shapes can be broken down into any number of categories, but most perennial forms fall into five types:

- spiky, or vertical.
- mounding, or rounded.
- upright and spreading.
- low and creeping, or prostrate.
- open, or filler.

Keep in mind that plants may take on a different form when they're in bloom. Perennial gardens usually have a mix of these forms, but, once in awhile, it's interesting to use only one form. Since the majority of plants are upright and spreading, that is probably the shape that will predominate in your garden, with the other shapes providing contrast.

Most important to remember is that as living, growing entities, plants do not always fit rigid categorization, but the element of form is one that, with practice, can be used to make a garden more striking.

Plant form, or the three-dimensional shape of the plant, is one of the design elements to consider when developing a garden plan. These mums are an example of rounded form.

PERENNIALS BY FORM

Spiky or Vertical Perennials

Acanthus
Aconitum
Anchusa
Aruncus
Astilbe
Belamcanda
Campanula
Centranthus
Cimicifuga
Crocosmia
Delphinium
Dictamnus
Digitalis
Erianthus
Gaura
Hemerocallis
Iris
Kniphofia
Liatris
Lobelia
Lupinus
Macleaya
Penstemon
Polygonatum
Smilacina
Thermopsis
Verbascum
Yucca

Mounding, or Rounded, Perennials

Alchemilla
Armeria
Artemisia
Brunnera
Coreopsis
Dianthus
Euphorbia
Festuca
Geranium
Helleborus
Hosta
Lavandula
Nepeta
Santolina

Upright and Spreading Perennials

Achillea
Amsonia
Anemone
Aquilegia
Arisaema
Artemisia
Aster
Baptisia
Boltonia
Campanula
Centaurea
Chelone
Chrysanthemum
Dicentra
Doronicum
Echinacea
Echinops
Erigeron
Eryngium
Eupatorium
Gaillardia
Helenium
Helianthus
Heliopsis
Ligularia
Mertensia
Monarda
Oenothera
Paeonia
Papaver
Phlox
Physostegia
Platycodon
Polemonium
Rodgersia
Rudbeckia
Salvia
Sanguisorba
Scabiosa
Sedum
Solidago
Stokesia
Thalictrum
Tradescantia
Tricyrtis
Uvularia
Veronica

Low and Creeping or Prostrate Perennials

Ajuga
Arabis
Asarum
Aubrieta
Aurinia
Bergenia
Cerastium
Ceratostigma
Epimedium
Euphorbia
Iberis
Phlox
Pulmonaria
Saponaria
Stachys
Tiarella
Viola

Open or Filler Perennials

Alchemilla
Astrantia
Gypsophila
Heuchera
Heucherella
Limonium
Lychnis
Ornamental grasses
Perovskia
Patrinia
Verbena

Iris foliage provides a strongly spiky and vertical effect in the garden, while forget-me-nots have an open, or filling, effect.

Many plants are spreading or creeping.

Texture

Texture relates to how the plant looks in terms of fine, medium or coarse, not to how it actually feels to the touch. What determines texture is the size and density of the foliage and flowers. One of the complications is that the foliage may have one texture, while the plant in bloom has another. The element of texture has the ability to create spatial illusions in the garden. For instance, coarse-textured plants appear closer, while fine-textured ones seem farther away. Using coarse-textured plants at the back of a garden will make it seem smaller. Placing fine-textured plants in a narrow border gives it the illusion of appearing wider than it actually is.

Fine-textured plants provide the illusion of space in the garden. They will appear farther away than coarse-textured ones, plus give the appearance that an area is wider.

PERENNIALS BY TEXTURE

Fine-Textured Perennials

Achillea
Aquilegia
Armeria
Artemisia
Astilbe
Coreopsis
Dianthus
Dicentra
Foeniculum
Gypsophila
Hemerocallis
Lavandula
Liatris
Nepeta
Perovskia
Polemonium
Santolina
Thalictrum

Bold-Textured Perennials

Acanthus
Bergenia
Cynara
Digitalis
Echinops
Helleborus
Hosta
Ligularia
Macleaya
Mertensia
Polygonatum
Rodgersia
Sedum
Verbascum

Bold-textured plants appear closer than they actually are. And they will make an area seem smaller than it really is.

Warm colors, including reds, yellows and oranges, stand out in the garden and make a passionate statement.

A garden of golden yellow flowers imparts a sense of laughter and happiness as it reflects the sunshine and joyful days spent outdoors.

Color

Color is what the garden is all about, for it's the flowers, in their rainbow of colors, that continually inspire us. The best way to begin thinking about color in the garden is to first of all be aware of your favorite colors and what colors in the garden please you most. Remember, too, that what catalog and book writers describe as red or pink, you may call magenta, and what goes for blue in the plant world is usually purple everywhere else.

In planning a garden, it's helpful to understand some of the basic principles of color, with a standard color wheel providing assistance. The color wheel is based on the three primary colors of yellow, red and blue. All other colors are derived from these three colors. For instance, green is made from blue and yellow, purple from red and blue and orange from yellow and red. A pure color is called a hue. When white is added, the color becomes lighter, or a tint. With the addition of black, the color becomes darker, or a shade.

Plan Color's Effect

When considering colors for your garden, the first aspect to consider is their effect. Colors are considered either warm or cool, based on the feelings they impart. Warm colors, including red, yellow and orange, are the colors of passion. In the garden, they tend to stand out, seeming to advance toward the viewer. They make for dramatic displays, but also make an area appear smaller than it is. Cool colors, including green, blue and violet, are those of tranquility. They recede from the eye, making an area appear larger; they are best when viewed close up, and will make a hot location seem cooler.

If you're wondering where red-violet and yellow-green fit in, they have both warm and cool properties. Their effect in the garden depends on the other colors used with them.

Blues and violets are cool colors that are relaxing and give a feeling of tranquility. Used in the garden, they will make an area appear larger, but they are best viewed close up.

A garden with a monochromatic color scheme focuses on using flowers or foliage that is all of one color, such as this white garden of stachys, foxglove, Shasta daisy and pansies.

Using Color

In creating a garden, there are four basic ways to use color. These include monochromatic, analogous, complementary and polychromatic color schemes. Because there are so many perennials, with innumerable shades and tints, these four basic schemes multiply exponentially.

Monochromatic color schemes in the garden utilize flowers in various tints and shades of one color. Of course, no garden is truly monochromatic because there is always the green foliage. A monochromatic garden gives a feeling of harmony; it is relatively easy to carry out, perhaps with a color that complements the color of the house. The predominance of pink flowers in the plant world makes this a good choice, but the "white garden" at Vita Sackville-West's Sissinghurst Castle in England is the most famous monochromatic garden.

Analogous color schemes are meant to utilize the tints and shades of three adjoining colors on the color wheel, such as blue, blue-violet and violet. The reality in the garden is that the rule book doesn't always work. Taking those three colors as an example, what most often happens is that pink flowers are also included, and are actually what makes the combination come alive. Since pink is essentially a tint between red and red-violet, you're actually using four analogous colors. Call on your common sense.

Complementary color schemes combine colors that are opposite on the color wheel, such as yellow-orange and blue-violet. They are stunning and dramatic, with a definite vitality. Mismanage them, and the effect quickly becomes a nightmare. Again, don't be afraid to bend the rules a bit. In this case, the dogma is to stick to pure hues and use gray foliage or white flowers for softening. Maybe an artist would know a pure hue, but most of us just sort of scratch our heads. And flowers don't always bloom in the exact color we want. As an example, take a look at the color wheel, and think about analogous and complementary simultaneously. For

A color combination composed of colors opposite on the color wheel is a complementary color scheme. Here golden achilleas are combined with blue-violet delphinium.

instance, consider orange, yellow-orange and yellow opposite violet, blue-violet and blue. Now those are colors that can be thought of in terms of plants. The most important thing to keep in mind with an example like this is to plant the analogous colors in groups. Interplant all six colors randomly, and it won't be a pretty sight.

Finally, the color scheme for the rest of us: the **polychromatic garden.** In other words, any and every color. So who needs a book to tell you this? With either great skill or pure dumb luck, such combinations can give a rich and lively effect. A variation on this theme is when a garden progresses from one color scheme to another. Usually this is best attempted when both skill and a large property are present.

When combined in the garden, the analogous golds and oranges of lilies, rudbeckias and achilleas provide a dynamic effect.

A well-planned polychromatic garden softly blends an entire gamut of color.

PERENNIALS BY COLOR

Yellow Flowers

Achillea
Adonis
Alchemilla
Anthemis
Aquilegia
Aurinia
Baptisia
Centaurea
Chrysanthemum
Chrysogonum
Chrysopsis
Coreopsis
Corydalis
Doronicum
Epimedium
Helenium
Helianthus
Heliopsis
Hemerocallis
Iris
Ligularia
Lysimachia
Oenothera
Primula
Rudbeckia
Santolina
Sedum
Solidago
Thalictrum
Thermopsis
Trollius
Uvularia
Verbascum

Orange Flowers

Aquilegia
Asclepias
Belamcanda
Crocosmia
Gaillardia
Geum
Helenium
Hemerocallis
Kniphofia
Ligularia
Lychnis
Papaver
Primula
Trollius

Red Flowers

Achillea
Aquilegia
Aster
Astilbe
Bergenia
Chrysanthemum
Dianthus
Dicentra
Epimedium
Gaillardia
Helleborus
Hemerocallis
Heuchera
Lobelia
Monarda
Paeonia
Papaver
Penstemon
Primula

Pink and Magenta Flowers

Achillea
Ajuga
Anemone
Aquilegia
Armeria
Aster
Astilbe
Astrantia
Aubrieta
Bergenia
Campanula
Centaurea
Centranthus
Chelone
Chrysanthemum
Delphinium
Dianthus
Dicentra
Dictamnus
Digitalis
Echinacea
Erigeron
Filipendula
Geranium
Gypsophila
Helleborus
Heuchera
Iris
Liatris
Lychnis
Monarda
Oenothera
Paeonia
Papaver
Penstemon
Phlox
Platycodon
Primula
Pulmonaria
Rodgersia
Saponaria
Scabiosa
Sedum
Stachys
Stokesia
Thalictrum
Tricyrtis
Verbascum
Verbena
Veronica
Viola

Blue, Lavender and Purple Flowers

Aconitum
Adenophora
Ajuga
Amsonia
Anchusa
Aquilegia
Aster
Baptisia
Brunnera
Campanula
Centaurea
Ceratostigma
Corydalis
Delphinium
Echinops

Erigeron
Eryngium
Geranium
Hosta
Iris
Lavandula
Limonium
Lupinus
Mertensia
Perovskia
Phlox
Platycodon
Polemonium
Primula
Pulmonaria
Salvia
Scabiosa
Stokesia
Thalictrum
Tradescantia
Veronica
Viola

White Flowers

Acanthus
Achillea
Anemone
Aquilegia
Arabis
Aruncus
Aster
Astilbe
Baptisia
Boltonia
Campanula
Centranthus
Cerastium
Chelone
Chrysanthemum
Cimicifuga
Dianthus
Dicentra
Dictamnus
Echinacea
Erigeron
Galium
Gaura
Geranium
Gypsophila
Hosta
Iberis
Iris
Monarda
Phlox
Platycodon
Polemonium
Primula
Scabiosa
Verbascum
Veronica
Yucca

Delphinium and veronica are among the perennials grown for their blue flowers. Both of these perennials also have varieties in shades of purple, pink, rose and white.

Daylilies, lychnis and roses offer an assortment of orange, pink and red flowers.

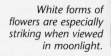

White forms of flowers are especially striking when viewed in moonlight.

Bloom Season

Now, for the real test. Can you coordinate all the other factors in this chapter with when the plants come into bloom? And for the length of time that they are in bloom? If you think about this for too long, you're apt to take up another pastime.

For those taking this chapter to heart, you may want to start with a perennial border that focuses the bloom time on just one of the three seasons of spring, summer or fall. Another way to alleviate the problems is to include annuals for their long bloom period, as well as some shrub roses. Another way is to use perennials with a longer blooming period than the average of two to four weeks.

As you gain experience and confidence, the three- or even four-season perennial planting can be planned and, ultimately, enjoyed.

Spring and early summer is the easiest time of the year to have a garden filled with glorious flowers. Many people plan parties around the height of the bloom in their gardens.

PERENNIALS BY BLOOM SEASON

Perennials Flowering in Spring

Alchemilla
Amsonia
Anchusa
Anemone
Aquilegia
Arabis
Arisaema
Armeria
Aubrieta
Aurinia
Bergenia
Brunnera
Chrysogonum
Dianthus
Dicentra
Euphorbia
Filipendula
Galium
Geranium
Helleborus
Hesperis
Iberis
Iris
Mertensia
Paeonia
Phlox
Primula
Pulmonaria
Sanguisorba
Smilacina
Trillium
Trollius
Viola

Perennials Flowering in Summer

Achillea
Adenophora
Anaphalis
Anthemis
Aruncus
Asclepias
Astilbe
Baptisia
Belamcanda
Campanula
Centaurea
Chrysanthemum
Cimicifuga
Clematis
Coreopsis
Delphinium
Dictamnus
Digitalis
Echinacea
Echinops
Erigeron
Eryngium
Filipendula
Gaillardia
Gaura
Geranium
Geum
Gypsophila
Helenium
Heliopsis
Hemerocallis

Heuchera
Hosta
Iris
Kniphofia
Lavandula
Liatris
Linum
Lobelia
Lychnis
Lysimachia
Macleaya
Monarda
Nepeta
Oenothera
Papaver
Phlox

Physostegia
Platycodon
Rudbeckia
Salvia
Scabiosa
Stokesia
Thalictrum
Thermopsis
Veronica

Perennials Flowering in Autumn

Aconitum
Anemone
Aster

Boltonia
Chrysanthemum
Coreopsis
Gaillardia
Helenium
Heliopsis
Ornamental grasses
Perovskia
Rudbeckia
Scabiosa
Sedum
Solidago
Stokesia
Tricyrtis
Vernonia
Viola

Here, bulbs take center stage in a mixed border in spring.

Later in the summer, perennials and summer-blooming bulbs are the focus.

In the fall, ornamental grasses, kale and mums bring the season to a close.

CHAPTER 5

ACQUIRING AND PLANTING PERENNIALS

What we've discussed up to now—understanding the garden environment, investigating garden styles, considering design principles and elements—is essential. But any gardening plan only becomes a success when healthy plants are selected or propagated, then planted correctly in properly prepared soil. You've heard the old phrase where the rubber meets the road? Well, these pages are about where the roots meet the dirt!

PROCURING PERENNIAL PLANTS

Each of these sources has advantages and disadvantages. Inveterate shoppers will revel in the possibilities, making the most of any and all possible sources for procuring perennials to use in every nook and cranny of the yard.

Merchants

For several months during the spring, hardware stores, home supply stores and discount department stores bring in plants for sale. Annuals are their bread-and-butter, and the perennials they offer are usually limited to the most common—and easily propagated—types growing in 4-inch or 1-gallon pots. If you need to buy in quantity for a mass planting, these places may prove a good source. The key is to get the plants soon after they arrive, before they've sat too long in the hot sun with infrequent watering. The real fun of shopping at these places is the adventure of finding something special. If you're the kind of person who likes to stop at yard sales, hoping to discover a genuine cameo for 50 cents, then this is your milieu.

One of the blessings (or banes, if your garden is already overflowing) of today's gardening is the ever-increasing selection of well-grown perennials available at local garden centers.

Depending on their focus, local nurseries and garden centers can range from offering little better than the mass merchandisers to having a wide range of perennials. Do your own personal research and talk with

Among the more provident aspects of early twenty-first-century life is the availability of goods, be they exotic cooking ingredients or the newest—or oldest—varieties of perennials. Gone are the days when only a handful of local nurseries offered perennials and the number of mail-order sources was limited. Today, perennials are widely offered for sale, from a basic selection at discount department stores in spring, to vastly stocked local garden centers and a staggering number of mail-order companies.

Local garden centers that specialize in perennials enable gardeners to select from among a wide range of varieties and sizes.

other gardeners in your area for suggestions of the best places. Again, plants are mainly available in 4-inch or 1-gallon pots.

Container-grown plants in this size pot are usually old enough to bloom the first season. Look for plants that are bushy and compact, with healthy green foliage and no signs of insects or disease. Plants that seem over-sized for the container are most likely root bound which can cause them to be slower in getting established in your garden.

Small Providers

Another local source that can be invaluable is gardeners who have gotten bitten by the gardening bug so badly that, as their gardens proliferate, they find it sensible to sell some of their extras. Often, these are people who collect and specialize, so it's a good chance to acquire hard-to-find varieties. To find these people, check the classified ads, roadside signs or local plant societies. The plants may be offered bare-root or growing in containers. A variation on this theme are the plant sales and swaps conducted by local plant societies.

Mail-Order

Mail-order sources provide the greatest selection of perennials. These range from mom-and-pop operations to large, long-established corporations. Some companies specialize in certain genera, while others offer the full range of perennials. The plants may be available as seed, dormant bare-root plants, young seedlings or older, larger plants in pots.

Make sure you understand what you're getting before ordering. Most of these companies, especially the smaller ones, are run by people who are dedicated plant enthusiasts, and are quite reliable. If you've never ordered plants by mail or have no first-hand information about the quality offered by a particular company, make your first order a small one.

Young plants, shipped in 4-inch pots, have been carefully packed to arrive in good condition. Open the box immediately and water well, place in indirect light, then plant or repot as soon as possible.

Those who have ever ordered anything by mail that is even vaguely garden related are probably already receiving catalogs from some of the major companies. For the smaller companies, you will have to call or mail a request for a catalog, usually including a nominal fee. The offerings may be a simple list or an elaborate catalog with color photos. The catalogs that contain detailed descriptions about the plants are among the most valuable sources of information about perennials.

Gardeners seldom suffer post-Christmas depression because their mailboxes are filled at this time with catalogs for poring over and planning the garden during the long winter nights. Companies ship dormant, bare-root plants in early spring, and container-grown plants are sent at the time of the last expected frost for your area unless requested otherwise.

Both bare-root and container-grown plants are ideally planted as soon as bought or received. Bare-root plants are the most difficult to handle if not planted immediately. They are usually wrapped in moistened packing material and plastic. Left too long in this, the roots will rot. Removed too soon, they will dry out. When planting right away is not possible, unwrap the plants, pot up in containers of potting soil, and put in a protected place outdoors. Small seedlings are also best potted up and cared for until they attain some size before planting into the garden.

PLANTING PERENNIALS

Carefully remove a plant from the container so as not to pull the top from the roots. If the plant is root bound, loosen the root ball with your fingers or cut the sides with a knife.

Preparing the soil before planting is crucial to successfully growing perennials as it's difficult, if not impossible, to improve the soil after perennials are planted. For details on this process, see the sidebar on Advance Soil Preparation.

Once both soil and plants are ready, try to plant on a cool, cloudy day when rain is predicted. Late afternoon is the best time to plant as the cool evening gives the plant time to adjust. Try to avoid hot or windy weather. When unavoidable, keep the plant watered and provide protection for several days, such as placing a cardboard box over the plant during the hottest part of the day.

Bare-Root

When planting bare-root perennials, don't let the roots dry out. It's best to soak them for several hours in a weak fertilizer solution. With a trowel or spade, dig a hole large enough for the roots to spread out. Set the plant in the hole so that the point where the roots meet the stem or crown is at ground level. Fill in with soil around the roots, tamping gently, then water thoroughly.

Container-Grown

The boons of container-grown plants are that they are already actively growing and, with a caveat, they can be planted any

ADVANCE SOIL PREPARATION—THE KEY TO SUCCESS

Nothing … *nothing* is more important to the successful growth of plants than proper advance soil preparation. Skip this all-important first step, and you're asking for trouble. Abide by it, and you've taken a huge step in ensuring a thriving, easy-to-care-for garden.

No matter what type of soil you have, from the lightest sand to the heaviest clay, a liberal addition of organic matter works miracles. Organic matter can be anything from compost to well-rotted leaf mold, fine fir bark, or peat moss. Almost every area of the country lays claims to indigenous, inexpensive organic material, readily available to gardeners.

A good rule-of-thumb is that the amount of organic matter you add should be equal to the depth to which you intend to turn the soil. If you're preparing the soil for raised beds, the minimum depth you should till is six inches; eight or 12 inches or more is that much better. This may contradict some traditional advice, but experience has proved it to be very successful.

If you intend to till the soil to a depth of 8 inches, then you should add 8 inches of organic material on top of the soil before you till to incorporate it to the full depth. This takes some doing, but it helps develop an extensive, healthy root system. This results in a hardy, vigorous, productive garden, able to withstand periods of drought and more resistant to disease and pests.

Depending on what you're planting and the characteristics of your soil, you may want to add fertilizer and lime as you incorporate the organic matter. Explain your situation to your local nursery staff or extension agent to find out if such additions are necessary.

After tilling the organic matter into the soil, rake the area smooth and plant your plants. Keep the area well watered for the first few weeks after planting. You'll be amazed at the growth the plants put on in such superior soil, even in the first year.

Container-grown plants can be set out anytime during the growing season, but be sure to prepare the soil well before planting, then properly care for the plants afterward.

time during the growing season. Planting in spring, near or after the last frost, depending on the hardiness of the plant, is still the best time because the cool spring weather gives the plant time to establish new roots before hot weather, and it probably has not become root bound yet.

When ready to plant a container-grown perennial, dig a hole, grasp the plant at the base near the soil, and gently tug it from the pot. If it doesn't easily come out, turn the pot on its side and tap it several times to jar the root ball loose. Use your fingers to loosen the roots slightly. If there is a mass of roots on the

outside of the soil ball, free them up even more or slash the sides of the root ball with a knife. This may seem cruel and unusual punishment, but it stimulates new root growth out into the soil. Place the plant in the hole, setting it at the same depth as it was in the pot. Water thoroughly.

STARTING PERENNIALS FROM SEED

An idiosyncrasy of people new to gardening is the desire to start plants from seed. Indeed, there are few processes as miraculous as watching a seed become leaves and flowers, but let's talk reality here. Starting a tomato is one thing; starting a perovskia is another—for a number of reasons.

First of all, perennials are a diverse group of plants, with many different conditions necessary for successful germination.

Second, we're talking delayed gratification. It's usually at least a year before the plants are big enough to set out into the garden, and then they may or may not bloom that year. In the meantime, they must be attended to in a nursery area, including watering them all summer and protecting them during the winter.

Third, perennials are often grown as a specific variety that will not come true from seed but only from vegetative propagation, such as division or cuttings.

Fourth, many perennials multiply quite handily on their own, readily providing new, blooming-size plants.

But ... there are times when starting perennials from seed does make sense. For one, maybe you just want to. This may be simple hardheadedness, a need for a great many plants at a reasonable cost or a desire to grow rare plants that do not readily multiply and/or do come true from seed. And some perennials do quickly germinate, grow and bloom the first year if

started early enough. These include certain varieties of English daisy, delphinium, shasta daisy and painted daisy.

How to Start from Seed

The procedure for starting perennial seed is much the same as for any other plant. There's a plethora of seed-starting paraphernalia available, but horticultural-grade vermiculite and a plastic seed-starting tray is simple and easy.

Read the instructions on the seed packet to determine whether there are special requirements, such as the need for heat, light, darkness, soaking, cold period or scratching the seed coat. Germination times vary greatly, so keep the growing media moist throughout the waiting period.

Once germinated, provide bright, indirect light, either by growing under fluorescent lights, or placing in a greenhouse or lathhouse.

Once several sets of leaves have developed, transplant the seedlings to larger pots or into a nursery bed, if all frost is past. Shelter them with shade cloth or lath or continue growing them in a cool greenhouse or indoors under lights until they start sending out new leaves again.

At this point, the seedlings can be kept growing in pots or set into a nursery bed outdoors. Water and fertilize regularly during the summer. Mulch the nursery bed in late fall after the ground has frozen or cover with a cold frame. The plants should be ready to set into the garden the following spring.

Well-tended seedlings yield many plants.

◦ CHAPTER 6 ◦

THE ART OF
GARDEN MAINTENANCE

For some, an hour or so a week is all the time that can be committed to the garden. Others will be out there every day for a couple of hours. Fortunately, both extremes, as well as all of us in the middle, are readily accommodated by perennials—when the garden style and size as well as the varieties of plants are chosen carefully in the beginning. If you're unsure, start out with a small area, using the plants that are the easiest to grow.

The following sections on garden care and maintenance provide the basics that have proved successful for most gardeners over the years. Reams more can and have been written, and certain plants or situations may be the exception to the rule. Nevertheless, these guidelines will stand most gardens and gardeners in good stead, requiring some effort but not so much that the garden becomes burdensome. In fact, the results should be so satisfactory that the biggest problem may be that you want to expand your beds or borders, growing ever more perennials.

MULCHING

Used correctly, organic mulches applied during the growing season are as close as it gets to a gardening panacea. The benefits include keeping weeds down, conserving soil moisture, keeping soil cooler in summer and warmer in winter, preventing soil erosion, improving soil structure, attracting earthworms, improving soil fertility and keeping plants clean and attractive.

Yes, there can be a downside to them, but not enough to not use them at all. For instance, in cool climates, the mulch should be pulled aside or applied later in the season to let the soil warm up. With plants that tend to rot with winter moisture, either draw the mulch away in the fall or place between the plants but not right up to the crown. Mulching creates hiding places for slugs and snails, so where these pests are a menace, more aggressive control will be necessary.

Non-decomposed mulches, such as shredded hardwood bark, tie up soil nitrogen as they decompose, so adding extra nitrogen (such as a fish emulsion solution) may be necessary. Another problem is likely to occur if you put the mulch on without loosening the soil surface just before applying. A mulch put on top of a crusted soil surface can result in an impervious layer developing between the two, defeating the goal of having the soil and mulch blend together into one rich layer.

Although any time is a good time to apply mulch, the ideal is in spring just as growth starts. Pull up any weeds, loosen the soil surface lightly, then apply 2 to 4 inches of an organic mulch over the surface of beds and borders, tapering it thinly near the base of the perennials. More can be applied during the growing season, if necessary. Some of the organic mulches to consider include half-rotted compost, buckwheat hulls, cocoa hulls, shredded hardwood bark, ground corncobs or leaves or composted manure.

Keeping several inches of organic mulch on the garden has many benefits. Before applying a mulch, be sure to pull up any weeds and loosen the soil surface slightly.

WATERING

Making sure plants get the right amount of moisture—neither too much nor too little—is one of the key areas where the observation powers of the gardener come into play. There is no one simple gauge, but rather a number of factors are involved.

Some plants are shallow-rooted, which means they're where the soil dries out quickly, while others have roots reaching down deep into the soil where it seldom dries out. Some plants need lots of moisture, while others are tolerant of drought.

New transplants need plenty of water until new roots get established.

When plants set their flowers is another time when moisture is crucial. Mulched gardens or areas where plants are closely spaced retain more soil moisture than raised beds.

You can't just go by the amount of rainfall received, since other environmental factors affect availability of moisture for plants. These include temperature, intensity of the sun and wind. The soil type affects moisture retention, too, with clay soil or soils rich in organic matter retaining more than sandy soils. So the adage of plants needing 1 inch of water a week is almost so general as to be worthless.

When and How to Water

The best way to determine if your plants' moisture needs are being met is to take all of these factors into consideration while keeping a watchful eye on both the plants and the soil. Particularly at the height of summer, walk through the garden at least once a day. The first hint of plants needing water is that the color of the leaves will be duller than normal. The next stage is wilting. While a slight amount of wilting is somewhat normal during the hottest part of the day, don't let plants wilt longer than a few hours, or they may not recover. The easiest way to determine soil moisture levels is by simply digging down a few inches to see if the soil is moist.

When natural rainfall is not adequate, the easiest, most efficient method of watering is to use a soaker hose, which puts water into the soil, not on the leaves where it can encourage diseases and their spread. Other methods include watering with a hose fitted with a soft-flow nozzle so that the water soaks into rather than splashes off the soil, or using a sprinkler. With either of these methods, water in the morning so the foliage has a chance to dry off before nightfall.

Whatever method you use, be sure to water deeply or not at all. Shallow watering makes for shallow roots that are more readily susceptible to drought. To conserve the valuable resource of water, don't waste it. Water slowly, allowing water to penetrate rather than run off, and apply just as much as necessary to soak the soil. To determine this, first keep in mind that perennial roots go about 1 to 1½ feet deep into the soil and that 1 inch of water penetrates sandy soils about 15 inches and clay soils about 5 inches. When you water, measure the length of time it takes to apply 1 to 3 inches, depending on your soil type. The next day after watering, dig into the soil to see how far the water has penetrated. This will give you the amount of time it takes to apply a certain amount of water, which you can then adjust accordingly.

Try to limit supplemental watering in order to conserve this natural resource. But when conditions do require watering the garden, soak the soil thoroughly to encourage deep rooting.

WEEDING

The gardener's joke about weeding goes, "The best way to make sure you are removing a weed and not a valuable plant is to pull on it. If it comes out of the ground easily, it is a valuable plant."

Hopefully, you have a better one-on-one relationship with your plants than that, but early spring weeding is particularly hazardous until you become familiar with the different perennials. The other keys to weeding are based on common sense.

- Make weeding a frequent and regular task, pulling the weeds while they are still small.
- When pulling, try to disturb the roots of the neighboring perennials as little as possible.

- If a large clump of soil is removed when weeding, bring in additional topsoil or compost to fill in the hole.
- To keep weeding chores to a minimum, work the soil lightly in spring and apply an organic mulch.

EDGING

Besides weeds popping up in a bed or border, there is the problem of the surrounding grass creeping into them. Of course, sometimes perennial areas have only paved or mulched paths between them, in which case this won't be a problem.

Since the vast majority of beds and borders are interspersed with lawns, keeping the two apart can be a real headache. One solution is to dig or pull out the grass several times a season. Another is to have a strong back or know someone who does who is willing to dig a space between the lawn and the perennials. The most efficient method is to install some type of barrier

Stones or other types of barrier edging retard the growth of grass into flower beds, while an organic mulch slows the growth of weeds and adds nutrients and humus as it decomposes.

edging, such as wood, plastic, brick, or stone. The edging can be installed at the same height as the lawn so that mowers can run over them, or it can be placed above, which necessitates some other method of cutting the grass next to it. While some people derive great pleasure from a crisp, defining line, others prefer to grow creeping, sprawling perennials next to it to soften the effect.

Use a hand- or machine-edger in the spring to retard the growth of grass into the flower beds. For the best plant growth, fertilize in the spring and again in midsummer.

FERTILIZING

To manufacture their food by photosynthesis and carry on other life processes, plants utilize a number of mineral elements, which are absorbed mainly in water from the soil.

Most soils have some nutrients naturally available, but the combination of nutrients being leached from the soil and used by the plants necessitates adding more in the form of fertilizers in order to get the kind of growth we expect in gardens.

Primary Nutrients

The primary nutrients required by plants are nitrogen, phosphorus and potassium. The three numbers on a bag or box of fertilizer, such as 5–5–5, represent the percentages by weight of these three nutrients, always in

Choose the right fertilizers to get the best growth from plants. Here, cannas, South American verbena, and wallflowers will bloom better if fed with a balanced fertilizer. Foliage plants, such as the bronze fennel and elephant's ears, produce more foliage if the fertilizer is slightly higher in nitrogen than the other nutrients.

the order of nitrogen, phosphorus, potassium. The remainder of the fertilizer is filler material, some of which may be other nutrients that can be utilized by plants.

Fertilizers that contain all three elements are called complete fertilizers. When one or two of the primary nutrients are missing, a zero appears in the three numbers, such as 21–0–0.

Gardeners use the ratio between these numbers as an indicator of the type of growth expected. In choosing a fertilizer ratio best for your various perennials, it helps to understand the roles of these nutrients.

Nitrogen is important in leaf and stem growth and health. It quickly washes away or is used up by plants.

Phosphorus is essential for healthy root growth, the production of fruit and seeds, and disease resistance. Much of the soil in the United States is deficient in phosphorus, and phosphorus is not easily dissolved in the soil, but once in the soil it remains there over a long period.

Potassium plays a number of roles in plant health and growth. It, too, is usually deficient in soil, except in the West. Although highly soluble in water, potassium clings tightly to soil particles, making an application last for a relatively long time.

Selecting a Fertilizer

When growing plants mainly for foliage, a fertilizer with a higher ratio of nitrogen is usually chosen, such as 6–3–3. For general growth, a balanced fertilizer, such as 5–5–5 is preferred. When

flowers or fruit are the goal, such as with most perennials, a ratio like 3–6–6 or 3–6–3 is a good choice.

The most accurate and efficient way to determine how much fertilizer to use is to look at results from a soil test. If the soil has been well prepared, including the addition of fertilizer, no further feeding is necessary the first year. A general rule of thumb for succeeding years is to feed once in the spring, using about 3 pounds of fertilizer with a ratio such as 3–6–6 or 3–6–3 per 100 square feet. Apply fertilizer again at the same rate in midsummer. A fertilizer with a different concentration but the same ratio is applied accordingly; for example, one and one-half pounds of 6–12–12 in place of the recommendation above. Always be sure to read the manufacturer's directions.

Fertilizer Forms

The choices among fertilizers are many. Some are applied in dry form, be it granules, crystals, powders or pellets. These are sprinkled on the soil and worked in lightly. Depending on the chemical makeup and form, the nutrients may be available for a short or long period.

Some fertilizers are made to be dissolved in water before applying to the soil or foliage (plants can also absorb nutrients through their leaves). These are taken up quickly by the plants, but they are also quickly depleted.

Another issue when buying fertilizer is whether it comes from an "organic" or "inorganic" source. Organic fertilizers may be from plant or animal sources, such as manure, fish by-products, seaweed, alfalfa meal, soybean meal, cottonseed meal or bloodmeal. Also included in this category are fertilizers from natural mineral sources, like rock phosphate or greensand, a mineral deposit found on the ocean floor.

Other Fertilizer Matters

There are environmental and ethical concerns with both inorganic as well as many organic sources. Proponents of inorganic fertilizers stress that the plant doesn't distinguish between organic or inorganic, the cost is less, and the effect faster. Advocates of organic fertilizers look to the larger picture of the negative long-term effects of inorganic fertilizers and the positive effects of organic fertilizers. Now that complete organic fertilizers are readily available (even vegan ones), the argument seems moot. Not only do organic fertilizers provide nutrients over a long period, but they also help to increase the all-important humus in the soil.

Over time, the use of organic mulches will lower the pH somewhat. It's a good idea to test the pH of the soil every spring. The best material to raise the pH is dolomitic limestone, available in powder or granules. Although it is best to follow soil-test recommendations, a basic guide to using it is that 5 to 10 pounds of dolomitic limestone to 100 square feet of garden will raise the pH one point. In lowering the pH, ground sulfur, calcium sulfate, iron sulfate or aluminum sulfate may be used, as may fertilizers designed for acid-loving plants. In lowering the pH, it is best to follow either the soil-test or product recommendations.

STAKING

Supporting perennials is not imperative, but for anyone who has had one (usually just coming into bloom) be blown over by wind, break off from its own weight or generally flop over and look untidy, the small amount of effort ahead of time is well worth it. Basically, there are two types of staking needs: one for tall, single-stemmed plants, such as delphinium, digitalis or monkshood, and another for plants with thin, floppy stems, like yarrow, aster, shasta daisy, echinacea or coreopsis. When properly used, supports become almost invisible as the plant grows during summer.

There are a number of different types of supports that can be purchased, including Y-stakes, linking stakes, and grids with legs or simply a ball of twine and bamboo or wooden stakes or poles. Supports can also be improvised from twiggy brush or saplings.

To support tall single stems, choose a sturdy stake or pole that is slightly shorter than the mature height of the plant in bloom, plus 12 inches. Insert the stake or pole 12 inches into the ground and 1 inch from the stalk in the spring or early summer. For purchased stakes with a "curl" on the top, "attach" the stem by slipping it into the circle. With a plain stake or pole, use a plant tie or piece of twine to loosely tie the plant

Plants with thin, floppy stems or heavy flowers benefit from having the stems supported. Whether homemade or purchased, put the support in place when the plants are about 8 to 12 inches tall, so that the stems can grow up through it.

stalk to the support. If the tie is too tight, the stem can be injured.

For floppy-stemmed plants, the support is put in place early in the season, or when plants are about 8 to 12 inches tall. Whichever of the following methods is used, be sure to insert the support stakes 6 to 10 inches into the ground. Grid supports are put directly over the plant. Another method is to put thin bamboo or wood stakes around the plant, then connect them with soft green twine. Or insert several twiggy tree or shrub branches, each about 18 to 24 inches long (depending on the mature height of the plant), into the soil around and among the plant stems.

To support tall, single-stemmed flowers, insert a bamboo, metal or wooden stake into the ground an inch from the stem. Use a plant tie or twine to loosely tie the plant to the stake.

PLANT CARE

Pinching, Thinning and Disbudding

Removing or pinching out the growing tip of a plant forces side branches to be more vigorous, making plants bushier and producing more flowers. With your fingertips, scissors or small pruning shears, remove a small amount of the top growth. This can be done once or several times in spring and early summer, as desired, but usually not after the end of June. Chrysanthemums and asters are the two perennials most often pinched.

Sometimes you may want to have fewer shoots, particularly if a plant tends to produce too many, causing spindly growth and disease problems because of poor air circulation in the middle of the plant. To prevent this, remove some of the stalks when growth is 4 to 6 inches tall.

In disbudding, some of the flower buds are removed, usually the side buds around a central one. This enables the plant to put all its energy into the remaining bud on each stem. Remove the buds early in their development.

Deadheading

Rather than a reference to a rock band's groupies, the term deadheading is a self-explanatory gardening term referring to the removal of the dead or faded flowers. This is not just compulsive behavior to keep everything neat and tidy, although it certainly does serve that purpose. But deadheading also prevents seed development, which can weaken a plant, cause it to stop blooming, or allow it to become a nuisance with a plethora of seedlings. Of course, sometimes the seedlings are desired; the choice is yours.

Insect and Disease Control

Most perennial gardeners are seldom bothered by pests. The main exceptions are those people who live in a Japanese beetle zone or those who grow a great number of plants from a single genus. Instituting preventive measures increases your advantage over pests even more. These include:

- selecting plants best adapted to your climate or site;
- keeping plants regularly watered and fertilized so that growth is vigorous and not stressed;
- growing disease-resistant varieties;
- checking plants regularly and treating for any pest at the first sign;
- regularly removing and destroying dead or distressed leaves or flowers;
- cleaning up plant material thoroughly in the fall so pests and winter hiding places are minimized;
- hand-picking injurious insects and destroying them;

Encourage ladybugs, as well as other natural predators, to inhabit your garden.

- making your garden a haven for natural predators, such as birds, bats, toads, ladybugs, praying mantis and others;
- laying boards in the garden at night to attract slugs and earwigs, then destroying the pests in the morning.

If a serious insect or disease problem develops, use an organic pest control according to the manufacturer's directions. Some of the safest yet effective organic insect controls include insecticidal soaps, pyrethrum and rotenone.

Removing the faded flowers from perennials not only keeps the garden looking tidy, but can also strengthen the plant, encourage repeat blooming and prevent self-sowing.

For caterpillar-type pests, use Bacillus thuringiensis, or Bt. You will probably have to read the fine print on the container to determine exactly what the active ingredient in the product is. The natural controls for fungal diseases are dusting with sulfur, thinning out growth to improve air circulation, keeping the soil evenly moist and avoiding wetting the foliage when watering. There are no controls for viral diseases; plants must be destroyed. To prevent further occurrences, choose naturally resistant plants and control the aphids or leafhoppers that spread viral diseases.

Pests in a perennial garden can be kept to a minimum by choosing the right plants for the site, feeding and watering adequately, and encouraging natural predators such as toads.

DIVIDING PERENNIALS

With each passing year, most perennials send out an ever-widening circle of new plants from the roots. As these spread and grow, each perennial not only is competing with others for water, nutrients and space but also with itself. The process of digging up the entire plant, composed of many plantlets, and breaking or cutting these apart is known as division.

Dividing perennials is an important part of their upkeep as it serves to rejuvenate an aging plant and control its size, as well as provide additional plants.

How and When to Divide

Those perennials that bloom in the spring and summer are usually dug up and divided in late summer or fall, except in areas where winter temperatures are -20°F or colder. In these colder climates, spring division allows plants to have a full growing season to become established. For plants that bloom very early in the spring, wait to divide them until after they finish flowering. Fall-blooming plants are also divided in early spring.

To have the greatest success when dividing, water the plants well several days ahead of time, then try to divide on a cool, cloudy day. When the center of the clump has not died, it is often possible to use a trowel or spade to dig up portions at the outer edges of the plant.

Otherwise, dig up the entire clump. Use your hands to divide the clump into smaller sections with two to four buds, sprouts or stems in each portion. For roots that are tightly bound or thick and carrot-like, use a knife or sharp-edged, heart-shaped Dutch perennial spade to cut the roots apart. When dividing plants in active growth, cut the tops back by half.

Fill in the hole from which the clump was removed with a mixture of topsoil, organic matter, and a handful of a fertilizer higher in phosphorous and potassium than nitrogen. If desired, replant one or more of the divisions in this spot, using the others in another part of the garden or sharing them with friends. Keep newly divided plants well watered until established and sending up new growth.

Digging up and dividing plants in the spring or fall, usually every 3 to 5 years, can rejuvenate them as well as control the amount of space they take up in the garden.

PROPAGATING FROM STEM AND ROOT CUTTINGS

Although far fewer perennials can be propagated from stem cuttings than can trees and shrubs, for the ones that can be done by this method (see the Perennials A to Z Chapter), it is an efficient way to get additional plants without digging up the parent plant. Spring is usually the best time to take stems cuttings of summer-blooming plants, and early summer is best for plants blooming in the spring and fall.

Stem Cuttings

To take a stem cutting, cut a piece 4 to 8 inches long from the top of the stalk, cutting just below the point where leaves join the stem. Remove the leaves on the lower half of the cutting, moisten this portion, dip in rooting hormone powder, and insert in a pot of moistened soilless seed-starting mix or vermiculite. Insert a label with the name of the plant and date written on it. Cover the pot with a clear plastic bag. Place in a warm spot with bright, indirect light.

Mist the cuttings several times a day with water, and keep the potting mix moist. Most cuttings will root in about a month. A good clue that cuttings are rooted is that new growth will start. At that time, transplant to a larger pot or a nursery bed. When plants are large enough, transfer to the garden.

Root Cuttings

Root cutting is a method to use when a large number of new plants are wanted from among the perennials that are able to be propagated this way. Best done in early spring, either the entire plant is dug up and all or part of the roots are cut up or a few of the outer roots are cut off without disturbing the rest of the plant.

For plants with fine roots, such as phlox, yarrow, sea holly, spurge, blanketflower, sage and stokesia, cut the roots into pieces 2 inches long. Spread them horizontally over the surface of a tray of moistened potting mix. Cover them with ½ inch more of potting mix. Keep the soil moist until sprouts develop, then transfer the plants to individual pots, caring for them until the plants are large enough to be set into the garden.

For plants with large, fleshy roots, such as bee balm, bleeding heart, baby's breath, poppies and peonies, cut the roots into pieces 2 to 3 inches long, making sure you keep the top ends facing the same direction. Plant these pieces vertically, top ends up, in moistened potting mix with ¼ inch sticking above the soil. Keep the soil moist until sprouts develop, then transfer to individual pots, caring for them until the plants are large enough to be set into the garden.

FALL CLEANUP AND WINTER PROTECTION

Cleaning up plant debris in the autumn not only makes the garden more pleasant to look at during the winter, it also reduces the places where pests can overwinter. After several frosts have killed plants back to the ground, cut off the dead stems to 2 to 4 inches tall and compost. Woody or evergreen plants are not cut back until the following spring, when winter damage is assessed.

Even when plants are fully hardy in your area, applying a winter mulch is a good insurance policy. This protection is particularly important in keeping shallow-rooted plants from being heaved out of the ground from alternate freezing and thawing of the soil during the winter. For the risk-takers among us, a winter mulch is the main method of keeping marginally hardy plants alive.

Wait to apply the winter mulch until the ground has frozen to a depth of 2 inches and plants are completely dormant. Using a loose, open organic material, such as oak leaves, salt hay, pine boughs, or straw, spread a 3- to 6-inch layer around plants. Use a thicker layer for the more tender perennials. Remove the winter mulch in the spring, gauging both the weather and plant growth carefully, with the mulch around some plants removed earlier than others.

Although some perennial foliage or seedheads can add interest to the garden in winter, the rest of the plant debris should be cleaned up in the fall before adding a loose mulch.

❦ CHAPTER 7 ❧

PERENNIALS A TO Z

The goal in choosing the perennials profiled in this book was to offer a wide range of plant types. Some have been grown by gardeners for centuries, while others have become favored only recently. One criterion was that a perennial plant should make an aesthetic contribution to the garden for as much of the growing season as possible: either from a long or repeat blooming period, or with foliage that remains attractive. In cases where this criterion is not met but the plant is still included, the rationale was the popularity of the plant or that it has the good grace to disappear, allowing other plants to fill in.

Maintenance was another important criterion. Life is complicated enough these days. However much relaxation and pleasure gardening gives us, there is a point of diminishing returns. Of course, we grow certain plants in spite of their fussiness. But overall, flower gardening pleasure is best enhanced with perennials that are seldom bothered by pests, sturdy enough to stand on their own without staking, and adaptable to a wide range of soils, moisture conditions, heat and humidity. That's what you'll find here.

A

ACANTHUS
(ah-*kan*-thus)
Bear's breeches
Acanthaceae—acanthus family

The large mounds of stiffly arching leaves give the various species of acanthus an architectural quality, fitting as the leaves inspired the decoration on Corinthian columns. Evergreen and invasive in milder climates, acanthus make a striking statement in the garden. The spikes of hooded, mauve flowers can be used fresh or dried.

Growing Guide
Full sun to partial shade, especially in hot, humid climates. Fertile, humus-rich, moist but well-drained soil. Winter mulching is necessary to prevent cold damage until plants become well established. Cut off flower stems when finished blooming.

Propagation
Division, root cuttings or fresh seed.

Uses
As an accent or focal point, singly or *en masse*. Give plenty of space.

Species, Varieties, Cultivars, Hybrids
A. mollis (*mol*-lis). Bear's breeches. Mediterranean. Grows 4 feet tall and 3 feet wide. Long, deeply cut leaves with spikes of white and mauve flowers in summer. The variety most often seen is 'Latifolius'. Can become invasive. Although it can tolerate colder temperatures, it grows best in those areas of Zones 8 and 9 that are not hot and humid.

A. spinosus (spin-*oh*-sus). Spiny bear's breeches. Southeastern Europe. Grows 4 feet tall and 3 feet wide. Dark green, glossy, deeply divided leaves to 3 feet long and 1 foot wide. Abundantly produced spikes of spiny white and mauve flowers in summer. More tolerant of both heat and cold and more free-flowering than *A. mollis*. The variety *spinosissimus* has leaves more deeply divided with silvery points, making it more beautiful but decidedly more vicious. Zones 6 to 10.

Acanthus mollis.

BOTANIZING

The plant descriptions here include both the botanical name, or Latin binomial, as well as the most widely used of the common names. While common names vary among locales, the Latin names are the same throughout the world. To ease the pain of learning these, a pronunciation guide is included with each one.

Scientists have devised a system of classifying all creatures, both plant and animal, into a hierarchical system. The system of botanical names is based on varying degrees of taxonomic differences—and similarities—between plants, mainly focused on flower structure. Plants with certain characteristics in common are grouped into a genus. This generic name is the first word in a Latin binomial. To differentiate between the members of a genus, a species name is given as the second part of the binomial. Sometimes this is broken down further, either into a subspecies (spp.) or variety (var.) name. The major frustration with this system occurs when, with research, taxonomists regroup or rename plants. To help alleviate the resulting confusion, both old and new names are included in the descriptions. Finally, either in nature or with the help of plant breeders amateur or professional, further differences are created among plants. A garden form, sport, clone or result of a hybrid cross is called a cultivar, with the cultivar name enclosed in single quotation marks.

ACHILLEA
(ah-*kil*-lee-ah or ah-kil-*lee*-ah)
Yarrow
Compositae—daisy family

A staple of perennial gardens for their beauty, ease of growth and long life, achilleas are prized for their feathery foliage and long-blooming, flat-topped flower clusters of white, yellows, pastels or reds. Cut when the pollen is visible, the flowers are excellent for arrangements. For dried use, pick them just as they become fully open.

Growing Guide
Full sun. Well-drained average to poor soil. Deadhead for repeat bloom.

Propagation
Division, stem cuttings.

Uses
Beds, borders, foundation, corner and meadow plantings. Use dwarf species and cultivars at the front of the border or in rock gardens. Fresh or dried flowers.

Species, Varieties, Cultivars, Hybrids
A. **x 'Coronation Gold'.** Grows 2 to 3 feet tall and wide. Well-branched, aromatic, gray-green leaves and golden flower heads 3 to 4 inches across. Does not need staking. Will bloom for 8 to 12 weeks. Zones 3 to 9.
A. **x 'Moonshine'.** Grows 2 feet tall and 18 inches wide. Gray-green leaves and pale yellow flower head to 3 inches across. Susceptible to leaf diseases in hot, humid climates. Will bloom for 8 to 12 weeks. Zones 3 to 8.

Achillea rilipendulina.

A. **grandifolia** (grand-i-*foh*-lee-uh). White yarrow. Southeast Europe. Grows 2 to 3 feet tall and wide. Gray-green foliage and white flowers on strong stems 3 to 4 feet tall. Seldom available but a much better white-flowered form than *A. millefolium.*
A. **millefolium** (mil-luh-*foh*-lee-um). Common yarrow. Europe. Grows 2 to 3 feet tall and wide. A spreading plant with white or pink flowers and aromatic, dark green foliage, it has a long-standing medicinal herb tradition. A number of cultivars and hybrids are available, including 'Cerise Queen', intense pink-red; 'Fire King', red fading to pink; 'Red Beauty', dark red; 'White Beauty', white; 'Summer Pastels'; and the 'Galaxy' hybrids, including 'Appleblossom', medium pink; 'The Beacon', crimson; 'Great Expectations', amber; 'Paprika', red with a white eye; 'Salmon Beauty', salmon pink.

In summer heat, many of these grow thin, flowers fade and plants need staking. Zones 3 to 8.

For the rock garden, consider *A. chrysocoma, A. clavennae* and *A. tomentosa.*

Pale Achillea *x* 'millefolium'.

ACONITUM
(ak-oh-*nye*-tum)
Monkshood, wolfsbane
Ranunculaceae—buttercup family

Lovely, underused plants, aconitums have delphinium-like leaves and spires of hooded, 1-inch flowers, mainly in shades of purple or blue, which contrast particularly well with yellow-flowered perennials. A few species have yellow or rose-colored flowers. Depending on the species, bloom may be in summer or early fall. Roots, leaves and stems are poisonous, and, as one common name attests, this quality has caused it to be used as a poison for wolves. The heart sedative aconite is derived from one species.

Growing Guide
Full sun to light afternoon shade in hotter climates. Humus-rich, moist but well-drained soil. Mulching and regular fertilization are especially beneficial.

Leave in place as they do not transplant well. Staking may be required.

Propagation
Division; seed, if sown as soon as ripe, but it is slow to germinate and will not flower for 2 to 3 years.

Uses
Middle or back of beds or borders; bog edges; wild gardens; planted in masses. Cut flowers.

Species, Varieties, Cultivars, Hybrids
A. x bicolor (*bye*-kul-or) (*A.* x *cammarum*). Bicolor monkshood. Grows 3 to 4 feet tall and 18 to 24 inches wide. Hybrids of *A. napellus* and *A. variegatum*. Dark green, glossy, deeply cut leaves and branching stems. Blooms in summer. Varieties include 'Bicolor', white with blue edges; 'Bressingham Spire', violet-blue; 'Ivorine', ivory-white; 'Newry Blue', navy blue; 'Spark's Variety', dark blue and 'Night Sky', deep-violet. Zones 3 to 7.

A. carmichaelii (kar-mye-*keel*-ee-eye). Azure monkshood. Eastern Asia. Grows 4 feet tall and 18 inches wide. Thick, leathery, dark green leaves. Blooms in early fall with short spikes of flowers in various shades of blue. *A. c. wilsonii* grows to 6 feet tall with violet-blue flowers. 'Kelmscott' has lavender-blue flowers. 'Barker's' has deep blue flowers and comes true from seed. The best variety is 'Arendsii', with intense amethyst-blue flowers. Zones 3 to 7.

A. napellus (nap-*pell*-us). Common monkshood. Europe. Grows 4 feet tall and 12 inches wide. Glossy, dark green leaves and branched spikes of indigo-blue flowers in mid- to late summer. There are cultivars with white or flesh-pink flowers. Zones 3 to 8.

Aconitum napellus.

ACORUS
(ah-*koh*-rus)
Sweet flag
Araceae—arum family

With semi-evergreen, grasslike leaves, this is a popular plant for boggy areas, especially in its variegated form. Because the leaves emit a spicy odor when crushed, they were used in earlier times for strewing on the floors of castles and manor homes.

Growing Guide
Full sun to partial shade. Constantly moist to wet soil.

Propagation
Division.

Uses
As specimen plants or mass plantings in bog and water gardens.

Species, Varieties, Cultivars, Hybrids
A. calamus (*kah*-lah-mus). Sweet flag. Asia, North America. Grows 3 feet tall and 12 inches wide. Aromatic, sword-shaped leaves. Insignificant flowers. The form 'Variegatus' has green and white striped leaves, sometimes flushed pale pink in spring. Grows in up to 10 inches of water. Zones 4 to 9.

A. gramineus (grah-*min*-ee-us). Japanese sweet flag. Asia. Grows 12 inches tall and 5 inches wide. Dark green, grasslike leaves. 'Pusillus' grows to 10 inches tall; 'Variegatus' has leaves striped with white. Zones 6 to 9.

Acorus calamus *'Variegatus'*.

ADENOPHORA
(ad-e-*noff*-o-ruh)
Ladybells
Campanulaceae—bellflower family

Perennials with an old-fashioned charm, ladybells are appreciated for their spikes of nodding, light blue flowers, which give them an appearance similar to campanulas.

Growing Guide
Full sun to partial shade. Fertile, well-drained soil.

Propagation
Seed; stem cuttings. Avoid division as the deeply growing, fleshy roots are easily damaged.

Uses
Front or middle of borders. Use *A. tashiroi* in rock gardens or as an edging, as it grows 4 to 12 inches tall. Cut flowers. Fragrant.

Species, Varieties, Cultivars, Hybrids
A. liliifolia (lil-ee-eye-*fol*-lee-uh). Lilyleaf ladybells. Europe. Grows 2 feet tall and spreads to 12 inches. Stout spikes of nodding, pale blue, bell-shaped flowers bloom in mid- to late summer above egg-shaped foliage. Spreads rapidly in proper conditions. White-flowered form available. *A. confusa* has deeper blue flowers, but it is less heat tolerant. Zones 3 to 8.

Agastache *'Licorice Blue'*.

AGASTACHE
(ah-*gah*-sta-kee)
Giant hyssop
Labiatae—mint family

A genus of about 30 species, all native to North America and Mexico except for one from Japan, agastache is appreciated by herb gardeners for its aromatic foliage and spikes of small, edible flowers. Recommending it for the perennial garden is its ease of growth, adaptability and mid- to late summer flowers. The name comes from the Greek *aga*, "very much," and *stachys*, "spikes," referring to the many flower spikes.

Growing Guide
Full sun to light shade. Just about any soil with good drainage. Plants do not live long, but readily reseed, which can be good or bad.

Propagation
Seed, stem cuttings.

Uses
Bed and borders, cottage, meadow or native plant gardens.

Species, Varieties, Cultivars, Hybrids
A. foeniculum (fee-*nik*-yew-lum). Giant blue hyssop. Eastern North America. Grows to 3 feet tall and 18 inches wide. Coarse, triangular leaves are toothed. Many cylindrical 4-inch spikes of small, dusky indigo-violet flowers are produced in summer. There is a white form, as well as hybrids in pastels. Zones 4 to 9.

Adenophora liliifolia.

AJUGA
(ah-*joo*-guh)
Bugleweed
Labiatae—mint family

The common bugleweed (*A. reptans*) is a widely adaptable, vigorous perennial groundcover grown mainly for its foliage, with a number of highly colorful cultivars available. The slightly taller-growing species are less vigorous, which can be considered an advantage in this case, with somewhat more prominent flowers. In the right place, the ajugas are wonderful plants.

Growing Guide
Partial to half shade. Just about any moist but well-drained soil.

Propagation
Division is easy at any time during the growing season.

Uses
Groundcover, but not where it will overtake a lawn or less robust plants.

Species, Varieties, Cultivars, Hybrids
A. genevensis (gen-e-*ven*-sis). Geneva bugleweed. Europe. Grows to 12 inches tall and at least as

Ajuga reptans *'Burgundy Glow'*.

wide. Rounded, toothed leaves to 4 inches long and 2 inches wide with whorled spikes of blue, pink or white flowers in summer. Although robust, it is not invasive. With constant soil moisture, it will tolerate more shade than other ajuga. 'Brockbankii' is a hybrid with bright blue flowers. Zones 4 to 9.

A. pyramidalis (peer-ruh-mid-*ah*-lis). Upright bugleweed. Europe. Grows to 9 inches tall and as wide. A handsome plant with dark semi-evergreen leaves and blue flowers. The cultivar 'Crispa', sometimes listed as 'Metallica Crispa', has deep blue flowers and red-brown, crinkled leaves with a metallic sheen; it is outstanding. Zones 3 to 9.

A. reptans (*rep*-tanz). Common bugleweed. Europe. Grows to 8 inches tall and spreads as far as it wants to go. Plant where its invasive qualities will not be a problem, such as under trees or on banks. Used as an edging, it can potentially take over a lawn. There are a number of cultivars selected for unusual foliage, which can revert to plain green; remove these to maintain the unique coloring. Selections, all with blue to violet flowers, include 'Atropurpurea', dark bronze-purple leaves with best color in full sun; 'Bronze Beauty', dark bronze-purple leaves with metallic sheen; 'Burgundy Glow', 'Multicolor' and 'Rainbow' are all similar, with white, pink, rose and green variegation on leaves; 'Gaiety', bronze-purple leaves; 'Silver Beauty' and 'Variegata', leaves variegated silver and green, with best coloring in shade. Zones 3 to 9.

Ajuga reptans.

Alchemilla mollis.

ALCHEMILLA
(al-kuh-*mill*-uh)
Lady's mantle
Rosaceae—rose family

Mounds of velvety, pale green, scalloped leaves make alchemilla endearing, especially to those of us who work to grow it in hot, humid climates. With cooler summers and more abundant growth, it may be taken for granted. The froth of yellow-green flowers rising in an airy cloud above the leaves in summer is like icing on the cake; these are also very good for bouquets. The genus name is derived from the use of the plant by alchemists, while the common name is a Latinized version of an Arabic name.

Growing Guide
Full sun in cooler climates to partial shade in hotter ones. Humus-rich, moist but well-drained soil. In hot climates, cut back in midsummer to stimulate fresh growth as days begin to cool.

Propagation
Division. Readily grows from fresh seeds. Deadhead unless you want it to self-sow.

Uses
Informal edging plant or groundcover. Looks particularly good as a foil for other flowers. Cut flowers.

Species, Varieties, Cultivars, Hybrids
A. mollis (*mol*-lis). Lady's mantle. Asia Minor. Grows 12 to 18 inches tall and 24 inches wide. Sprays of tiny, chartreuse-colored flowers are held six inches or more above the rounded, 4-inch-wide leaves during summer. Plants sold as *A. vulgaris* are usually *A. mollis*. There are more than 200 other species, the smaller ones being useful for the rock garden. Zones 4 to 7.

AMSONIA
(am-*sohn*-ee-uh)
Blue stars
Apocynaceae—dogbane family

Although they'll never be traffic stoppers, amsonias are easily grown North American natives that deserve greater use in perennial gardens. They emerge early in the spring with fine-textured, dark green leaves and are unusual in that they have significant fall color, in this case a bright gold. Loose, rounded clusters of star-shaped, pale blue flowers cover the upright clumps for about a month in spring and early summer. The genus is named after Charles Amson, an 18th-century physician.

Growing Guide
Full sun if soil is constantly moist, or partial to light shade. Widely adaptable but does best in deep, humus-rich moist soils that are mulched.

Propagation
Division, seed or stem cuttings.

Uses
Beds and borders, along the edges of woodlands or streams, native plant gardens.

Species, Varieties, Cultivars, Hybrids
A. tabernaemontana (ta-bur-nee-mon-*tay*-nuh). Willow blue star. North America. Grows to 3 feet tall and 2 feet wide. Thin, willow-like leaves to 6 inches long on upright stems. Open clusters of numerous, star-shaped, pale blue flowers to 1 inch across in early summer followed by soft, hairy seed pods. Golden fall color. Zones 3 to 9.

Gardeners in the South should also consider downy amsonia, *A. angustifolia* (*A. ciliata*). Zones 7 to 10.

Amsonia tabernaemontana.

ANAPHALIS
(ah-*nah*-fa-lis)
Pearly everlasting
Compositae—daisy family

A tough plant long prized for its woolly, silvery-gray foliage and large heads of small white flowers that are easily dried, anaphalis is particularly suited to gardens with moist soil where other gray-leaved plants might perish. To dry the flowers, cut when the blooms just begin to show their centers; put in a vase of water for several hours, then hang upside down in a dark, dry place.

Growing Guide
Full sun to partial shade in moist but well-drained soil. Can benefit from midsummer pruning if growth becomes leggy. May host fungal diseases in hot, humid summers or suffer caterpillar damage in early summer.

Propagation
Division, seed or stem cuttings.

Uses
Near the front of beds or borders; naturalized areas. Use in white gardens or to tone down warm colors.

Species, Varieties, Cultivars, Hybrids
A. triplinervis (tri-plee-*ner*-vis). Himalayan pearly everlasting. Himalayas. Grows to 18 inches tall and 12 inches wide. Growing in a zigzag, the stems form bushy, compact plants with woolly leaves and tight masses of small, creamy white, yellow-centered flowers from mid- to late summer. 'Summer Snow' is shorter-growing and flowers are a brighter white. Zones 3 to 8.

Also consider Indian pearly everlasting, *A. cinnamomea* (*A. yedoensis*), a taller-growing plant that takes several years to become established, and American pearly everlasting (*A. margaritacea*), growing to 4 feet tall and more tolerant of drought.

Anaphalis triplinervis.

ANCHUSA
(an-*kew*-suh)
Italian bugloss
Boraginaceae—borage family

Its life in the garden may be short, but anyone who has been smitten by the intense blue flowers of anchusa doesn't mind; better a brief, stunning affair than a long, boring one. The airy clusters of flowers, resembling forget-me-nots, bloom in early summer. The genus name is from a Greek word meaning "to paint," a reference to the use of the root as a dye. The common name is also from a Greek word, this one translating as "ox tongue," referring to the shape and roughness of the leaves.

Growing Guide
Full sun to very light shade. Deep, humus-rich, moist but well-drained soil. Cut back and fertilize after flowering to encourage a second blooming. May need staking.

Propagation
Division, seed or root cuttings.

Uses
At the back of beds or borders.

Species, Varieties, Cultivars, Hybrids
A. azurea (a-*zoo*-ree-uh). Italian bugloss, Italian alkanet. Caucasus. Grows to 5 feet tall and 2 feet wide. Coarsely textured, the oblong leaves grow to 8 inches long. The bristly stems bear spiraling clusters of ½-inch, deep blue flowers in early summer for about 4 weeks. A number of selections have been developed, including 'Dropmore', to 4 feet tall with deep blue flowers; 'Little John', to 18 inches tall with dark blue flowers; 'Loddon Royalist', to 3 feet tall with azure blue flowers; and 'Royal Blue', to 3 feet tall with dark blue flowers. Zones 3 to 8.

Anchusa officianalis.

ANEMONE
(ah-*nem*-oh-nee)
Windflower
Ranunculaceae—buttercup family

The many and varied anemones found around the world provide us with flowers from early spring through autumn on plants of different shapes and sizes. While the early blooming ones are charmers (and highlighted as a group later), it is the fall-blooming anemones that are the stars of this clan, with their tall, elegant foliage and a profusion of pastel flowers at a time of year when we cherish every single blossom.

Growing Guide
Full sun to partial shade. Fertile, moist but well-drained soil. Requires several seasons to get established enough to bloom their best.

Propagation
Division.

Uses
Specimens, mass plantings or back of beds and borders.

Species, Varieties, Cultivars, Hybrids
A. x hybrida (*hib*-ri-duh). Japanese anemone. May also be listed as *A. japonica*. Grows to 4 feet tall and 2 feet wide. Each leaf composed of 3 leaflets. Open, branching clusters of single or double flowers to 3 inches across in white or shades of pink to rose. There are a number of excellent named hybrids from which to choose. Zones 4 to 8.

A. tomentosa (toe-ment-*toe*-suh). Grape-leaved anemone. May also be listed as *A. vitifolia*. Asia. Grows to 3 feet tall and 18 inches wide. Very similar to *A.* x *hybrida* but with lobed leaves, more rapid spreading, and bloom beginning earlier. White flowers. 'Robustissima' grows to 4 feet with pale pink flowers. Zones 5 to 8.

There are a number of low-growing, spring-blooming perennial species particularly suited either for planting in masses, especially with spring bulbs, or for naturalized plantings. All have white flowers; they include *A. canadensis* (Zones 3 to 7), *A. magellanica* (Zones 2 to 7), *A. nemerosa* (Zones 4 to 8) and *A. sylvestris* (Zones 4 to 8). For the front of the border, *A.* x *lesseri* (Zones 5 to 8) blooms in early summer with white, yellow, rose or red flowers.

Anthemis tinctoria *'Golden Marguerite'*.

ANTHEMIS
(*an*-them-is)
Chamomile
Compositae—daisy family

The anthemis of choice for the perennial garden has sunshine yellow daisy-like flowers along with fine-textured foliage and an ability to thrive in dry soil.

Growing Guide
Full sun. Well-drained average to poor soil. May need staking.

Propagation
Division, stem cuttings.

Uses
Middle to back of beds and borders.

Species, Varieties, Cultivars, Hybrids
A. tinctoria (tink-*toe*-ree-uh). Golden marguerite. Europe. Grows 2 to 3 feet tall and 2 feet wide. Leaves resemble parsley. Abundant yellow flowers to 1½ inches across. Does best in areas with cool summers. A number of hybrids between this species and *A. sanctijohannis* are available, with plants ranging in height from 1 to 3 feet and flowers in shades varying from cream through yellows to golds and oranges. Zones 3 to 7.

Other species to consider include *A. cupaniana*, dwarf chamomile, forming dense, gray-green mats with white flowers (Zones 5 to 8) and *A. marschalliana* (*A. bierbersteinii*), with fernlike, silvery foliage and golden flowers (Zones 5 to 7).

Anemone tomentosa.

AQUILEGIA
(a-kwil-*lee*-gee-uh)
Columbine
Ranunculaceae—buttercup family

Their springtime bloom period and life span may be short but the gaily colored, unusually shaped flowers of easily-grown columbine have endeared it to generations of gardeners. Besides the many hybrids, there are a number of species that make excellent garden plants. The resemblance of the flowers to birds is illustrated in the names: *columba* for dove and *aquila* for eagle.

Growing Guide
Partial to half shade in most climates, but can tolerate full sun in cooler ones. Humus-rich, moist but well-drained soil. Destroy foliage riddled by leaf miner insects.

Propagation
Seed as soon as ripe or in spring. Division in spring of young plants only. Plants readily hybridize among themselves and self-sow, with the resulting colors a surprise.

Uses
Massed in shaded wild gardens. Beds and borders. Use shorter types in rock gardens.

Species, Varieties, Cultivars, Hybrids
A. x hybrida (*hib*-ri-duh). Hybrid columbine. Grows 1½ to 3 feet tall and 1 foot wide. Gray-green, finely divided leaves and spurred flowers in shades of white, yellow, pink, purple, red and orange. Many excellent named hybrids are available. Zones 3 to 9.

Among the species, consider *A. alpina*, to 3 feet with blue or white flowers (Zones 3 to 8); *A. caerulea*, to 2 feet with blue and white flowers; *A. canadensis*, to 2 feet with red and yellow flowers (Zones 3 to 8); *A. chrysantha*, to 3 feet with yellow flowers (Zones 3 to 9); *A. flabellata*, to 18 inches with light blue flowers (Zones 3 to 9); and *A. longissima*, to 3 feet with yellow flowers and very long spurs (Zones 4 to 9).

Aquilegia.

ARABIS
(*air*-uh-bis)
Rock cress
Cruciferae—mustard family

A large genus with many plants for the rock garden collector, one species is more widely adapted for garden use. It celebrates spring with a cascade of tiny, fragrant white flowers. The name is derived from Arabia, referring to its preference for dry soils.

Growing Guide
Full sun. Average to poor, neutral to alkaline soil. Cut back the flowers after blooming.

Propagation
Division, stem cuttings.

Uses
Edging or accent along walls, banks or the front of beds and borders.

Species, Varieties, Cultivars, Hybrids
A. caucasica (kaw-*kas*-ee-kuh). Rock cress. Mediterranean. Also known as *A. albida*. Grows 10 inches tall and 18 inches wide. Small, oval, toothed, gray-green leaves form a loose mat that is particularly effective climbing over rocks or cascading down walls. Fragrant white flowers are held above the leaves in loose sprays. There are variegated and pink-flowered varieties as well as one with double flowers that is especially long blooming. Zones 4 to 7.

Arabis caucasica.

ARISAEMA
(air-ris-*ee*-muh)
Jack-in-the-pulpit
Aracae—arum family

Jack expounding from his sylvan pulpit is one of the treasures of the woodlands of eastern North America, but the perennial cognoscenti are all aflap over the Asian varieties with their striking forms and colorations.

Growing Guide
Partial to half shade. Humus-rich, moist but well-drained soil.

Propagation
Division; fresh seed in fall.

Uses
Woodland shade gardens. Mass plantings are most effective.

Species, Varieties, Cultivars, Hybrids
A. candidissimum (kan-duh-*dees*-si-mum). China. Grows 12 inches tall and 18 inches wide. The white-striped, pink-hooded spathe appears in early summer, followed by broad, lobed leaves. Zones 7 to 9.

A. sikokianum (sik-koke-ee-*ah*-num). Japan. Grows 18 inches tall and as wide. Silvery-green leaves and a dark purple hooded spathe striped white. Zones 5 to 9.

Besides the beloved Jack (*A. triphyllum*), another North American native is *A. dracontium*, dragonroot, with a rather bizarre form. There are about 75 Asian species, more of which are being offered by specialty mail-order nurseries.

Arisaema sikokianum.

ARMERIA
(ar-*mee*-ree-uh)
Thrift
Plumbaginaceae—plumbago family

Armeria maritima *'Splendens'*.

Would thrift be such a widely seen plant if it was not so easy for garden centers to propagate the plants? Probably not. Still, ready availability should not preclude it from the garden. Though diminutive, thrift is a sturdy, neat plant that does its job well.

Growing Guide
Full sun to partial shade in hotter climates. Sandy to average, well-drained soil. Deadhead regularly.

Propagation
Division, seed.

Uses
Rock gardens, between flagstones, along walls or at the front of beds and borders.

Species, Varieties, Cultivars, Hybrids
A. maritima (mah-*ri*-tah-mah). Common thrift, sea pink. Europe. Grows 6 to 12 inches tall and 12 inches wide. Dense tufts of grasslike, evergreen leaves. Rounded, 1-inch clusters of tiny flowers on leafless stems. Depending on selections, flowers may be pink, lilac, red or white. Found growing naturally along coastlines. Zones 4 to 8.

Other species to consider include *A. juniperifolia* (*A. caespitosa*), Pyrenees thrift, 6 inches tall with lilac flowers (Zones 4 to 8); and *A. plantaginea*, 18 inches tall with wider leaves, pink flowers, and the cultivar 'Bee's Ruby' usually chosen (Zones 4 to 9).

ARTEMISIA
(ar-tem-*meez*-ee-uh)
Wormwood
Compositae—daisy family

With a cast of hundreds, the artemisias run the gamut from sagebrush to tarragon, with aromatic foliage a common thread in their use for thousands of years. For the ornamental garden, the focus is placed on those with fine-textured foliage that mainly runs to silver. An added bonus is that many of these are staples for making dried arrangements and crafts. The genus name is from the goddess Artemis, while the common name of wormwood refers to early herbalists' use of the plant to kill parasitic worms.

Artemisia schmidtiana.

Growing Guide

Full sun. Dry, well-drained soils. Cut back in midsummer to get fresh growth, particularly in hot, humid climates where rot can occur.

Propagation

Division, stem cuttings.

Uses

One of the best foliage plants for sunny beds and borders, providing a foil to flowering plants with its texture and color. Fresh and dried arrangements.

Species, Varieties, Cultivars, Hybrids

A. abrotanum (ab-*roh*-tan-um). Southernwood. Southern Europe. Grows 3 feet tall and 18 inches wide. A woody plant with threadlike leaves having a fruity scent. Insignificant yellow flowers. Zones 5 to 8.

A. absinthium (ab-*sin*-thee-um). Wormwood. Europe. Grows 3 feet tall and 2 feet wide. Woody plant with finely divided, silvery-gray leaves to 5 inches long. Insignificant, tiny gray flowers. Was used in the French liqueur absinthe, which turned out to have deleterious effects beyond the alcohol, as evidenced by Degas. Selections to be sought out include, 'Lambrook Silver' and 'Huntington Gardens', plus *A.* x 'Powis Castle'. Zones 3 to 9 for species, variably less for cultivars.

A. lactiflora (lak-ti-*flor*-uh). White mugwort. Asia. Grows to 6 feet tall and 4 feet wide. This is the oddball ornamental artemisia, what with dark green leaves and spectacular sprays of creamy flowers in late summer and fall. Good for background plantings and fresh-cut flowers. Needs moist soil. Zones 5 to 8.

A. ludoviciana **var.** *albula* (lew-doe-vik-ee-*ah*-nah *al*-buh-luh). White sagebrush. Western North America. Grows 3 feet tall and 2 feet wide, but watch out; it can spread fast and far. Both stems and leaves are silvery white. Long and pointed, the jagged-edged leaves are up to 4 inches long. Insignificant gray flowers in late summer. Prime candidate for summer pruning to freshen growth. Selections include 'Silver Frost', 'Silver King', 'Silver Queen', and var. *latiloba*.

A. schmidtiana (shmit-ee-*ah*-nah). Silvermound artemisia. Japan. The form almost universally offered is 'Nana', or 'Silver Mound'. Grows 12 inches tall and 18 inches wide. Forms a silken mound of finely cut silver foliage. Tiny yellow flowers in summer. Superb in cool-summer climates, less so with heat and humidity. Zones 3 to 7.

Aruncus dioicus.

ARUNCUS
(ah-*run*-kus)
Goatsbeard
Rosaceae—rose family

Large and stately, the North American goatsbeard is a long-lived, must-have plant for shaded areas. Magnificent clusters of creamy-white flowers in early summer create a striking effect.

Growing Guide
Partial shade. Tolerant of a wide range of soils, but best with humus-rich, moist but well-drained soil.

Propagation
Division, seed.

Uses
Back of the shade border, among shrubs, woodland wildflower garden, near a stream or pool.

Species, Varieties, Cultivars, Hybrids
A. dioicus (dee-oh-*ee*-kus). Goatsbeard. Eastern North America. Also listed as *A. sylvester*. Grows 5 feet tall and and as wide. Compound, serrated leaves resemble those of astilbe. Plume-like clusters of tiny ivory flowers in early summer. The variety *astilbioides* grows to 2 feet, 'Kneiffii' grows to 3 feet with finely divided foliage and 'Child of Two Worlds' has dropping flower clusters. Zones 3 to 8.
Another aruncus to search out is *A. aethusifolius* from Korea. It is a diminutive plant growing to 12 inches tall.

ASARUM
(ah-*sah*-rum)
Wild ginger
Aristolochiacae—wild ginger family

These are not the culinary gingers, which are *Zingiber*, but the leaves and roots do emit a similar fragrance. The value of the asarums lies in their low-growing, heart-shaped leaves; they make a good groundcover for moist, shady conditions. Taxonomists have now classified the evergreen types as *Hexastylis*, so you may find plants under that listing.

Growing Guide
Partial to full shade. Humus-rich, moist but well-drained soil.

Propagation
Division.

Uses
Edgings, front of shade borders, groundcover.

Species, Varieties, Cultivars, Hybrids
A. europaeum (oh-roh-*pye*-um). European wild ginger. Europe. Grows 8 inches tall and as wide. Glossy, dark green, evergreen leaves to 3 inches across. Purple-brown, urn-shaped flowers at ground level under foliage in early spring. Zones 4 to 7.
A. shuttleworthii, native to the Southeastern United States, is more tolerant of heat; it has lovely silvery-white markings on the evergreen leaves (Zones 6 to 8). *A. caudatum* (Zones 4 to 8) and *A. hartwegii* (Zones 6 to 8), both evergreen species, are native to western North America. More hardy (Zones 3 to 8) is the deciduous native wild ginger, *A. canadense*. There are also species native to Asia just coming into commerce.

Asarum europaeum.

ASCLEPIAS
(uh-*sklay*-pee-us)
Milkweed, silkweed, butterfly weed
Asclepiadaceae—milkweed family

Long-lived and easy to grow, butterfly weed is true to the name, attracting scores of butterflies to the clusters of waxy orange, yellow or scarlet flowers in summer. All plants of the milkweed family have a sticky white sap, hence the name. The canoe-shaped seed pods are distinctive, too, with the silken threads attached to the seed giving the group another common name. The flowers can be used for cutting if the cut end is seared in a flame to seal off sap flow.

Growing Guide
Full sun. Sandy to average well-drained soil. Plants are slow to emerge in the spring, so mark their site well. Deadhead to extend the bloom season beyond 6 weeks.

Propagation
Division, but with caution as the fleshy roots go deep. Fresh seed in fall. Root cuttings.

Uses
Sunny borders, meadows.

Species, Varieties, Cultivars, Hybrids
A. tuberosa (tew-bah-*roh*-suh). Butterfly weed. Eastern North America. Grows 3 feet tall and 2 feet wide. Stocky stems with narrow, pointed, bristly leaves to 4 inches long. Somewhat flat, tightly packed clusters of waxy flowers, mainly orange but with yellows and reds sometimes occurring. Zones 4 to 9.

Asclepias tuberosa.

Asphodeline lutea.

ASPHODELINE
(as-fod-eh-*lee*-nee)
Jacob's rod
Liliaceae—lily family

The grassy leaves of asphodeline provide fine texture to the garden, while the spikes of yellow flowers in early summer offer vertical form. They are sturdy and easy to grow in warmer climates.

Growing Guide
Full sun to partial shade in average to humus-rich, well-drained soil.

Propagation
Division, seed.

Uses
Groups in middle to back of beds and borders. Mass plantings. Cut flowers. Fragrant.

Species, Varieties, Cultivars, Hybrids
A. lutea (*lew*-tee-uh). Jacob's rod. Mediterranean. To 3 feet tall in bloom and 1 foot wide. Gray-green, grassy leaves to 10 inches long. Slim stalks of star-shaped, fragrant yellow flowers in early to midsummer. 'Flore Pleno' has double flowers. Zones 6 to 8.

Aster amellus.

ASTER

(*ass*-ter)

Aster, michaelmas daisy
Compositae—daisy family

Asters are indispensable in the sunny landscape in the summer and fall. With over 600 species and thousands of selections, choosing is a process of elimination by intimidation. Ranging in size from 6 inches to 8 feet tall, all have small, daisylike flowers, usually with yellow centers, in shades of blue, lavender, purple, pink, red or white. Foliage is relatively small, oval, pointed with smooth or jagged edges. The name is from the Latin for "star."

Growing Guide

Full sun to light shade. Humus-rich, well-drained soil. They grow best in cool-summer climates and need a winter mulch. Stake taller varieties. Pinch back in early summer to encourage branching, shorter growth and more flowers. Choose disease-resistant varieties.

Propagation

Division in spring, at least every 2 years, to keep plants vigorous. Terminal stem cuttings in spring or early summer.

Uses

Short ones near the front or middle of beds and borders; taller ones to the back. Meadow gardens. Cut flowers.

Species, Varieties, Cultivars, Hybrids

A. alpinus (ahl-*pine*-us). Alpine aster. Europe, Asia. Grows 10 inches tall and 18 inches wide. Tufts of gray-green, spoon-shaped leaves. Blue to purple, to 1-inch flowers in early summer. Best for cool-summer climates.

A. amellus (ah-*mel*-us). Italian aster. Southern Europe. Grows 2 feet tall and as wide. Rough-textured stems and leaves. A number of selections available in various colors, with 2-inch flowers in fall. Drought tolerant. Does best in Zones 5 to 6, but hardy in Zones 4 to 8. *A.* x *alpellus* is a cross between *A. alpinus* and *A. amellus*; it grows 15 inches tall and as wide. Sometimes listed as 'Triumph'. Blue flowers with orange centers.

A. divaricatus (duh-var-ah-*cah*-tus). White wood aster. North America. Grows to 3 feet tall and as wide. Great quantities of 1-inch white flowers from summer through fall. Good for dry soil and light shade. Zones 4 to 8.

A. x *frikartii* (fri-*kart*-ee-eye). Grows 3 feet tall and as wide. One

Aster novae-angliae.

of the best asters for the garden. Long-blooming, with 2- to 3-inch lavender-blue flowers. Selections include 'Monch' and 'Wonder of Staffa'. Zones 5 to 8.

A. novae-angliae (*noh*-vee-*ang*-lee-ee). New England aster. North America. Grows to 6 feet tall and 4 feet wide. Many selections available, but especially look for 'Alma Potschke' and 'Harrington's Pink', both shorter cultivars with pink flowers. May need staking. Do not overfertilize. Zones 4 to 8.

A. novi-belgi (*noh*-vee-*bell*-gee-ee). New York aster. Eastern North America. Size varies greatly, depending on the selection, of which there are many. Full aster color range, with some beginning to bloom in summer, but most with late-summer and autumn flowers. Zones 4 to 8.

A. tartaricus (tar-*tar*-eh-cus). Tartarian daisy. Asia. Grows 6 feet tall and 3 feet wide. Blue to purple flowers are particularly late blooming. Stout stems seldom need staking. Zones 4 to 8.

Aster *x* frikartii *'Monch'*.

Aster novi-belgi *'Professor Kippenburg'*.

ASTILBE
(ah-*stil*-bee)
Astilbe
Saxifragaceae—saxifrage family

Among the best plants for shaded areas, astilbes are long-lived and easily grown. Although each individual flower is tiny, the overall effect is of a fluffy plume in shades of pink, red or white. The foliage composed of divided leaves may be deep green to bronze. The name comes from the Greek *a*, without, and *stilbe*, brightness, referring to the dull color of the leaves of some species.

Growing Guide
Can be grown in all but the deepest shade. Needs a humus-rich, moist soil. Boggy soils can be tolerated, but dry soils cannot.

Propagation
Division.

Astilbe *x* arendsii *(pink).*

Uses
Shade beds and borders, along streams and pools. At their best planted in masses. Cut flowers.

Species, Varieties, Cultivars, Hybrids
A. x *arendsii* (ah-*rendz*-ee-eye). Astilbe. Hybrid origin. Hybrids under this classification were originally developed by German plantsman Georg Arends (1862–1952), with others following. Selections range in height from 2 to 4 feet tall and to 2 feet wide, with various colors and bloom times from early to late summer. Zones 4 to 9.

Although the vast majority of astilbes sold each year come under *A. x arendsii*, there are others with merit. These include *A. simplicifolia*, growing to 18 inches tall with starry, white flowers (Zones 4 to 8), and two that are more tolerant of dry soil: the creeping *A. chinensis* 'Pumila', growing to 18 inches tall with magenta-pink flowers (Zones 3 to 8), and the late-blooming *A. taquetii* 'Superba', growing to 4 feet with magenta-pink flowers (Zones 4 to 8).

Astilbe *x* arendsii *(red).*

ASTRANTIA
(ah-*stran*-tee-uh)
Masterwort
Umbelliferae—carrot family

Much-touted perennials by aficionados, masterworts are not showy plants and can be a bit difficult to grow. Their charm lies in their subtleties, including airy branches of small but unusual flowers over a long period in summer and the long life of these flowers when cut. With a domed center surrounded by pointed bracts, the whitish, pink or red flowers are the source of the name, an allusion to their star shape.

Growing Guide
Does best in partial to light shade but tolerates full sun in cooler climates. Must have humus-rich, moist but well-drained soil. Grows best with cool night temperatures, partial shade and consistently moist soil.

Propagation
Division. Self-sows.

Uses
Toward the front of beds and borders so the flowers can be seen closely. Near streams and pools. Massed under open trees.

Species, Varieties, Cultivars, Hybrids
A. *major* (*may*-jor). Great masterwort. Europe. Grows to 3 feet tall and 18 inches wide. Deeply lobed and toothed leaves. Wiry stems topped by open clusters of flowers. Starts blooming in early summer, stops during heat, then resumes in the fall. 'Involucrata' has a particularly large "ruff." Other selections differ mainly in the color of the flowers. Zones 5 to 7.

AURINIA
(aw-*rin*-ee-uh)
Basket-of-gold
Cruciferae—mustard family

Formerly classified as an *Alyssum*, the form remains the same—mounds of creeping or cascading plants are covered with bright yellow flowers in early spring.

Growing Guide
Full sun. Average to poor, well-drained soil. Cut back after flowering. Does best in cool-summer climates.

Propagation
Division, seed, stem cuttings.

Uses
Edging for paths, steps, or front of beds and borders. Rock gardens. Cascading over stone walls.

Aurinia saxatilis.

Species, Varieties, Cultivars, Hybrids
A. saxatilis (saks-ah-*til*-us). Basket of gold. Europe. Grows 12 inches tall and 18 inches wide. Mounds of fine-textured, gray-green leaves. Tiny, four-petaled flowers of bright golden or lemon yellow in early spring, depending on the cultivar. Zones 3 to 7.

B

BAPTISIA
(bap-*tis*-ee-uh)
False indigo
Leguminosae—pea family

North American natives, the baptisias hold their own in perennial plantings. Long-lived and easy to grow, they are shrubby plants with leaves divided into pointed, oval segments. The pealike flowers are blue, yellow or white, depending on the species. The flowers were used at one time as a dye, substituting for true indigo. Baptisias are attractive even after flowering, as they develop black seed pods that last through fall.

Growing Guide
Full sun to partial shade. Humus-rich, moist but well-drained soil. Because of the deep taproot, they are somewhat tolerant of dry soil.

Propagation
Seed, sown outdoors as soon as ripe. Division is possible, but difficult because of the taproot.

Uses
Back of beds or borders. Cut flowers; seed pods for dried arrangements.

Species, Varieties, Cultivars, Hybrids
D. australis (ah-*strah*-lis). False indigo. Eastern United States. Grows to 4 feet tall and as wide. Branching, upright stems with bright blue-green leaves. Blooms for a month in early spring with spikes of indigo-blue, 1-inch flowers, followed by the black seed pods. Zones 3 to 9.

White-flowered species for the garden include *B. alba*, from the southeastern United States (Zones 5 to 8), and *B. leucantha*, from the Midwestern prairies (Zones 4 to 8).

The most widely grown yellow-flowered form is *B. tinctoria*, from the Southeast (Zones 5 to 9).

Baptisia australis.

BEGONIA
(buh-*gon*-ee-uh)
Hardy begonia
Begoniaceae—begonia family

Among the thousand-plus species of begonias, only one has any significant hardiness. To make it feel at home, grow in shade among ferns, hostas, and Japanese anemones.

Growing Guide
Partial to light shade. Humus-rich, moist but well-drained soil. Needs a protective winter mulch in Zone 6.

Propagation
Small bulbs form in the leaf axils. These can be allowed to "self-sow," or can be gathered and stored over winter in dry peat moss, potted up the following spring, then transplanted several months later. Stem cuttings.

Uses
Front to middle of shade borders, woodland gardens.

Species, Varieties, Cultivars, Hybrids
B. grandis (*gran*-dis). Hardy begonia. Asia. May also be listed as *B. evansiana* or *B. discolor*. Grows to 2 feet tall and 1 foot wide. Waxen, glistening heart-shaped leaves are red-tinted beneath. Succulent, angular stems. Sprays of drooping red buds open to 1-inch pink flowers from late summer into fall. There is a also a variety with white flowers. Zones 6 to 9.

Begonia grandis.

Belamcanda chinensis.

BELAMCANDA
(bell-am-*kan*-duh)
Blackberry lily
Iridaceae—iris family

Not a flashy plant, but delightful for small charms. Leaves resemble those of iris, and, in midsummer, thin stalks bear sprays of 2-inch yellow-orange flowers marked with red-purple dots. As the flowers fade, the seed pods ripen to reveal clusters of shiny black seeds that look like blackberries.

Flower stems may be cut for fresh use, while the seed pods can be used in dried arrangements. Easy to grow, with no appreciable pests. Why not try it?

Growing Guide
Full sun to partial shade. Average to humus-rich, well-drained soil.

Propagation
Division, seed. Self-sows, but is not invasive.

Uses
Middle of beds and borders. Meadow and dappled woodland gardens. Cut flowers.

Species, Varieties, Cultivars, Hybrids
B. chinensis (chin-*nen*-sis). Blackberry lily. East Asia. Grows to 3 feet tall and 1 foot wide. Sword-shaped leaves and yellow-orange, six-petaled flowers on zigzagged stems in summer, followed by seeds resembling blackberries. Yellow-flowered forms are available. Zones 5 to 10.

Belamcanda chinensis *seeds*.

BERGENIA
(ber-*jen*-ee-uh)
Bergenia
Saxifragaceae—saxifrage family

Bergenias are noted for the bold-textured effect of their foliage, variously described as cabbage-like, leathery, waxy or thick, with leaves growing up to 10 inches long. Although the leaves are evergreen, sometimes changing to burgundy in the winter, they can become tattered-looking during the colder months. Even so, the foliage is attractive for many months of the year. The leaves are also prized for use in flower arrangements. As another bonus, thick stems rise up in the spring, topped by clusters of bell- or cup-shaped pink, red or white flowers.

Growing Guide
Full sun in cooler climates to partial shade in hotter ones. A wide range of soils are tolerated, except in hot climates, where the soil must be moist but well drained. Remove faded flowers.

Propagation
Division, with each start having at least a 4-inch piece of rhizome. Seed.

Uses
Front of beds and borders, massed along paths, groundcover under shrubs and trees.

Species, Varieties, Cultivars, Hybrids
The best selections for the garden are the hybrids between species. The differences between the various ones are the flower color and winter or summer coloration of the leaves. Most grow 12 to 18 inches tall and as wide. Some to look for include 'Bressingham White', 'Evening Glow', 'Morning Red', 'Red Bloom', 'Silver Light' and 'Sunningdale'. Zones 4 to 8.

Bergenia.

Boltonia asteroides *'Snowbank'*.

BOLTONIA
(bol-*ton*-ee-uh)
Boltonia, false starwort
Compositae—daisy family

Rather like an aster on steroids, boltonias produce profuse quantities of small, starry flowers in late summer and fall. The most widely available species is a North American native, usually seen with white flowers, but lilac also occurs. Although its 7-foot height is a bit intimidating, to say nothing of floppy, a selection called 'Snowbank', at 4 feet, adds lightness and grace to the fall garden. It is an especially good choice for hot climates, where other fall-blooming plants may not fare so well.

Growing Guide
Full sun. Adapts to a wide range of soils that are well drained.

Propagation
Division.

Uses
Backs of bed and borders.

Species, Varieties, Cultivars, Hybrids
B. asteroides (as-ter-*roy*-deez). White boltonia. Eastern North America. Grows to 7 feet tall and 4 feet wide. Willow-like, blue-green leaves to 5 inches long. Airy, open sprays of white or lilac, daisy-like, 1-inch flowers. Selections include 'Snowbank', 4 feet tall with white flowers; 'Pink Beauty', 4 feet tall with pink flowers; and one most often listed as *B. a. latisquama* var. *nana*, 3 feet tall with larger, purple flowers. Lower stems may become bare, so place boltonias behind other plants. Zones 4 to 9.

BRUNNERA
(*brun*-ah-rah)
Siberian bugloss
Boraginaceae—borage family

The common name may be a bit off-putting, but the effect of Siberian bugloss, particularly when planted in masses beside a pool or along a stream, is one of pure romance. When the conditions are right, brunnera are long-lived and easy to grow.

Growing Guide
Partial to half shade. Humus-rich, moist but well-drained soil. Remove faded flowers unless self-sowing is desired.

Propagation
Seldom necessary, but possible by division, seed or, preferably, root cuttings.

Uses
Any moist, shady area, but especially around water features in the garden; groundcover.

Species, Varieties, Cultivars, Hybrids
B. macrophylla (makro-*fill*-uh). Siberian bugloss. Caucasus. Grows 12 to 18 inches tall and as wide. Mounding, with light green, roughly textured, heart-shaped leaves. Sprays of blue flowers resembling forget-me-nots in spring. Selections are offered with different types of leaf variegation; these must be propagated by division, and reversions to plain green leaves must be weeded out. Zones 3 to 7.

Brunnera macrophylla.

C

Campanula glomerata.

CAMPANULA
(kam-*pan*-yew-luh)
Bellflower
Campanulaceae—bellflower family

Campanulas are among the most beloved of perennials, partly because there are so many species and selections, but also because campanulas are strikingly beautiful. Liberty Hyde Bailey has written, "They are for those who love to grow plants for the joy of growing them." Most often thought of for their blue, bell-shaped flowers, colors are also available in lavenders and purples, pinks and whites. This is not an easy group to typify, since the ones for the garden range from tiny species for the rock garden to behemoths over 5 feet tall. The showiest campanula, Canterbury bells (*C. medium*), is a biennial.

Growing Guide
Full sun, with partial shade preferred in hotter climates. Humus-rich, moist but well-drained soil. Deadhead regularly for recurrent bloom. Apply protective winter mulch.

Propagation
Division, seed, stem cuttings, root cuttings.

Uses
Because of the many sizes and forms of campanulas available, they can fit in just about anywhere in the garden except deep shade. Plant in clumps of at least three. Taller forms are good cut flowers.

Campanula lactiflora.

Species, Varieties, Cultivars, Hybrids

C. carpatica (kar-*pa*-ti-kuh). Carpathian harebell. Eastern Europe. Grows 8 to 12 inches tall and 12 inches wide, forming trailing clumps of small heart-shaped leaves. The 1- to 2-inch violet-blue or white cup-shaped flowers bloom throughout the summer on wiry stems. Use in the rock garden or the front of the border. Zones 3 to 8.

C. glomerata (glom-er-*rah*-tuh). Clustered bellflower. Eurasia. Grows 12 to 18 inches tall and 12 inches wide. Leaves are dark green and coarsely textured. Tightly packed clusters of 1-inch purple or white flowers at the ends of erect stems bloom from early to midsummer. Zones 3 to 8.

C. lactiflora (lak-ti-*floh*-ruh). Milky bellflower. Caucasus. Grows 3 to 5 feet tall and 3 feet wide. Small leaves on bushy plants. Pale blue, violet-blue, pink or white 1-inch, bell-shaped flowers borne on long stiff spikes in summer. Readily self-sows. Especially easy to grow, but may need staking. Zones 5 to 7.

C. latifolia (lah-tee-*fo*-lee-uh). Great bellflower. Europe. Grows 3 to 5 feet tall and 3 feet wide. Rapidly spreading clumps with large leaves at the base of plants. Blooms in summer with 2-inch purple-blue or white flowers. Readily self-sows. May need staking. Zones 3 to 7.

C. persicifolia (per-si-ki-*foh*-lee-uh). Peach-leaf bellflower. Europe, Asia, North Africa. Grows 2 to 3 feet tall and 2 feet wide. Clump-forming plants with narrow, leathery leaves that are evergreen in mild-winter regions. Borne on spikes, the open, upward-facing, 1- to 2-inch flowers are available in shades of blue or white, as singles or doubles. Zones 3 to 8, with best growth in Zones 3 to 6.

C. portenschlagiana (por-ten-shlag-ee-*ah*-nuh). Dalmatian bellflower. Southern Europe. Grows to 6 inches tall and 18 inches wide. Smooth, kidney-shaped leaves on mat-forming plants. Funnel-

Campanula portenschlagiana.

shaped, lilac-blue or white, 1-inch flowers cover the plants in late spring and early summer. Self-sows. Zones 4 to 8.

C. rotundifolia (roh-tun-di-*foh*-lee-uh). Harebell. Europe. North America. Grows to 12 inches tall and as wide. Famous as the "bluebells of Scotland." Rounded, 1-inch leaves on dainty, tufted plants. Slender flower stems bear lavender-blue or white, 1-inch, nodding, bell-shaped flowers in summer. Zones 2 to 7.

Campanula latifolia.

Campanula persicifolia.

Campanula carpatica.

Centaurea montana.

CENTAUREA
(sen-*taw*-ree-uh)
Knapweed
Compositae—daisy family

Of the over 500 species of centaurea in the wild, only about a dozen are useful garden plants. These include such familiar annuals as cornflower, or bachelor's buttons. Among the perennial garden plants, they distinguish themselves with a tolerance of neglect and freely produced, thistle-like flowers that tend to strong colors and an excellence for cutting. The genus was named after the centaur Chiron, who is said to have been healed by the plant and went on to heal others.

Growing Guide
Full sun. Almost any well-drained soil. Deadhead for repeat flowering and to prevent self-sowing. Staking may be necessary.

Propagation
Division; seed, particularly when fresh; root cuttings.

Centaurea montana.

Uses
Middle of beds and borders. Cut flowers.

Species, Varieties, Cultivars, Hybrids
C. dealbata (dee-al-*bah*-tuh). Persian cornflower. Asia Minor. Grows 2 feet tall and as wide. Small, coarsely cut leaves, dark green above and downy white beneath. For about 4 weeks in summer, stiff stems bear pinkish purple to deep rose flowers 2 to 3 inches across. May need staking. Zones 5 to 7.

C. hypoleuca (hye-po-*loo*-kuh). Knapweed. Asia Minor. Grows 2 feet tall and 18 inches wide. Very similar in appearance to *C. dealbata*, except that growth is more compact, foliage more gray-green and flowers are centered with white. Rarely needs staking, but spreads rapidly. The variety 'John Coutts' may be listed under either *C. dealbata* or *C. hypoleuca*, but wherever, it is an excellent, long-blooming plant with deep rose flowers. Zones 4 to 7.

C. macrocephala (mak-roh-*sef*-ah-luh). Globe knapweed. Caucasus. Grows 4 feet tall and 2 feet wide. Bold plants with large, hairy leaves with wavy edges. Bright yellow flowers 3 to 4 inches across attract butterflies. Bloom period is shorter in areas with hot, humid summers. Use the flowers both fresh or dried.

C. montana (mon-*tah*-nuh). Mountain bluets, Montana cornflowers, mountain knapweed. Europe. Grows 18 inches tall and as wide. Downy, silver-gray leaves. Deep violet-blue, dark pink or white flowers in late spring and early summer. Spreads very rapidly by underground stems and self-sowing. Excellent for meadow gardens. Zones 3 to 8.

Centaurea macrocephala.

CENTRANTHUS
(sen-*tran*-thus)
Valerian
Valerianaceae—valerian family

Best for areas with cool summers, centranthus is adaptable enough to make it worth the effort in hotter climates. The lure is the large, showy spires of small, fragrant red, pink or white flowers. These are excellent for cutting and attract butterflies as well. The bushy plants of blue- or gray-green leaves have their own appeal.

Growing Guide
Full sun. Poor to average, well-drained soil that is neutral to alkaline. Deadhead to encourage repeat blooming.

Propagation
Division, seed, stem cuttings.

Uses
Sunny borders or rock walls. Cut flowers. Butterfly gardens.

Centranthus ruber.

Species, Varieties, Cultivars, Hybrids
C. ruber (*rue*-ber). Red valerian, Jupiter's beard, keys of heaven. Europe. Grows 2 to 3 feet tall and 18 inches wide. Branching, woody-stemmed plants with pointed, oval leaves. Branching, pointed clusters of ½-inch flowers in shades of pink, red or white. Zones 5 to 8.

CERASTIUM
(ke-*ra*-stee-um)
Snow-in-summer
Caryophyllaceae—pink family

"One person's weed is another's treasured plant" certainly applies to cerastium. It is also one of those plants that grows rapaciously in England, but that struggles with heat and humidity. But even a small mound of "snow" can bring pleasure, so where summers are not too stressing, the creeping cerastium should be included.

Growing Guide
Full sun. Poor to average, well-drained soil. Shear plants after flowering to prevent self-sowing.

Propagation
Division, seed, stem cuttings.

Uses
Groundcover, cascading over stone walls, edging.

Species, Varieties, Cultivars, Hybrids
C. tomentosum (toe-men-*toe*-sum). Snow-in-summer. Italy. Grows 6 inches tall and spreads to 24 inches. Forms dense mats of downy, silvery gray, fine-textured foliage. Masses of ¾-inch, white, star-shaped flowers in early summer. Zones 2 to 7.

Cerastium tomentosum.

CERATOSTIGMA
(ser-at-oh-*stig*-muh)
Leadwort, plumbago
Plumbaginaceae—plumbago family

Where hardy, leadwort is an easily grown, widely adaptable groundcover. As an added bonus, there are deep blue flowers from late summer into fall and glorious bronze-red foliage color, as well. Just be patient for it to leaf out in the spring.

Growing Guide
Full sun to light shade. Average, well-drained soil.

Propagation
Division, stem cuttings.

Uses
Front of the border, groundcover, especially good interplanted with small spring bulbs.

Species, Varieties, Cultivars, Hybrids
C. plumbaginoides (plum-bah-gi-*noi*-deez). Leadwort, plumbago. China. Grows 12 inches tall and 18 inches wide. Small, pointed, oval, dark green leaves on woody stems; leaves turn bronze-red in fall. Small clusters of gentian-blue flowers in late summer and fall. Zones 5 to 9.

Chelone.

CHELONE
(kee-*loh*-nay)
Turtlehead
Scrophulariaceae—figwort family

Maybe you have to use a lot of imagination to see the turtle's head, but, even so, these are attractive perennials that adapt to both sun and some shade. Native to moist woodlands and prairies of North America, chelones bring color to the garden in summer and fall.

Growing Guide
Full sun to light shade. Humus-rich, moist but well-drained soil. Full sun tolerated if soil is constantly moist. Tolerant of acid soil. Pinch the growing tips in the spring for best growth and flowering.

Propagation
Division, seed, stem cuttings.

Uses
Shaded beds and borders, native areas, near pools and streams.

Species, Varieties, Cultivars, Hybrids
C. glabra (*glay*-bruh). White turtlehead. North America. Grows 3 feet tall and 2 feet wide. Clumps of sturdy stems with narrow, lance-shaped leaves to 6 inches long. Spikes of 1-inch, white or rose-tinted flowers for 3 to 4 weeks in late summer. Zones 3 to 8.

C. lyonii (lye-*oh*-nee-eye). Pink turtlehead. Higher elevations of the southeastern United States. Grows 3 feet tall and 18 inches wide. Dark green, broadly lance-shaped, serrated leaves to 6 inches long. Tight clusters of 1-inch pink flowers produced for about 4 weeks in late summer to early fall. Zones 4 to 8.

C. obliqua (oh-*blee*-kwuh). Rose turtlehead. Wetlands of eastern North America. Grows 3 feet tall and 2 feet wide. Very similar in appearance to *C. lyonii*, but the flowers are a deeper rose color. The flowers and handsome appearance make it a good companion to other fall-blooming plants. Zones 6 to 9.

Ceratostigma plumbaginoides.

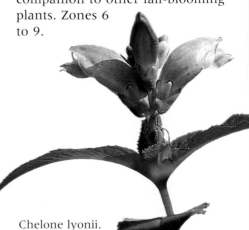

Chelone lyonii.

Chrysanthemum *(Leucanthemum)*.

CHRYSANTHEMUM
(kris-*anth*-ah-mum)
Chrysanthemum
Compositae—daisy family

Among the oldest of cultivated plants, chysanthemums are usually thought of in terms of those plants that fill the garden with fall blooms as well as the florist's flowers and plants. Hundreds of different forms have been developed, but there are dozens of other species and selections for the garden. With their daisy-like flowers, albeit in many forms and all colors but blue, and ease of growth, the entire clan constitutes an important addition to the sunny garden. In recent years, taxonomists have scattered this group to the winds; their new names are given on page 96.

Growing Guide

Full sun. Humus-rich, moist but well-drained soil, with a few exceptions as noted below. The ubiquitous garden chrysanthemum transplants easily, even when in full bloom. Plants set out in the spring or grown from year to year in the garden should have the growing tips of the stems pinched out several times until mid-July. The types referred to as cushions don't need this pinching. Taller or weaker-stemmed types must be staked. Deadhead regularly. A summer mulch is beneficial to keep the soil moist, and a winter mulch is needed for protection.

Propagation

Division, stem cuttings. Painted and Shasta daisies and feverfew from seed.

Uses

Depending on the form and size, chrysanthemums can be used singly, in groups, massed in beds and borders or used as an edging. Cut flowers.

Chrysanthemum *(Dendranthema)* zawadski *'Clara Curtis'* *(x* rubella*)*.

Chrysanthemum *(Tanacetum)* coccineum.

Species, Varieties, Cultivars, Hybrids

Dendranthema grandiflora (den-*dran*-thuh-muh gran-duh-*flor*-uh). Chrysanthemum. China, Japan. Thousands of selections developed over the centuries, ranging in size from 1 to 4 feet tall and up to 3 feet wide. Shape varies from short, fat mounds to tall and thin. The 1- to 6-inch flowers may be single or double, with special shapes like button, spoon, quill or spider. Special care includes extra feeding, pinching back the growing tips and staking the taller varieties. Hardiness varies greatly among selections, but the overall range is Zones 5 to 9.

Dendranthema rubella (rue-*bell*-uh). Red chrysanthemum. Probably a hybrid of Asian origins. Grows 2 to 3 feet tall and as wide. Compact, branching, free-flowering plant with 2- to 3-inch, muted red or deep pink, single, fragrant flowers held singly or in small clusters. Flowering starts in late summer. Most commonly found in the pink-flowered form 'Clara Curtis'. Zones 5 to 9.

Leucanthemum pacificum (lew-*kan*-thuh-mum pah-*sif*-uh-cum). Grows 2 feet tall and 18 inches wide. Grown mainly for its unusual foliage, which is small and rounded with silvery edges. Clusters of tiny, yellow, button-like flowers in mid- to late fall. Zones 6 to 9.

Leucanthemum x superbum (sue-*pur*-bum). Shasta daisy. Of hybrid origin, originally produced by Luther Burbank. Grows 18 to 30 inches tall and as wide. Produces a great quantity of stems with white, 2- to 3-inch daisies throughout summer. Is not long lived. Zones 5 to 8.

Tanacetum coccineum (tan-ah-*see*-tum cok-sin-ee-um). May also be listed as *Pyrethrum roseum*. Pyrethrum, painted daisy. Western Asia. Grows 1 to 3 feet tall and 1 to 2 feet wide. Ferny, dark green leaves. Single or double, 3-inch, daisy-like pink, red or white flowers with yellow centers on tall, single stems from early to midsummer. Best planted in groups of three. Most suited for areas with cooler summers, but with light shade, can do well in hotter areas. Use dwarf cultivars to eliminate the need for staking. This plant is the source for the insecticide pyrethrum. Zones 3 to 7.

Tanacetum parthenium (par-*thin*-ee-um). May also be listed as *Matricaria parthenium*. Feverfew. Europe. Grows to 2 to 3 feet tall and 1 to 3 feet wide. Strongly aromatic, deeply divided leaves. Masses of long-blooming, 1-inch, daisy-like flowers are white or yellow, single or double, and superb for cutting. Cut plants back by half when 12 inches tall to lessen sprawling. Single-flowered forms readily self-sow. A number of selections are available. Zones 5 to 8.

Chrysanthemum *x* superbum *'Shasta Snow'*.

Tanacetum parthenium.

Chrysogonum virginianum.

CHRYSOGONUM
(kris-*sog*-oh-num)
Goldenstar, green-gold
Compositae—daisy family

A local plant makes good, at least in the eastern United States, where this yellow-flowered edging plant or groundcover sells out quickly for use in shaded gardens and woodland plantings.

Growing Guide
Partial to full shade. Humus-rich, moist but well-drained soil.

Propagation
Division, seed.

Uses
Edging or groundcover for shady beds and borders, woodland gardens, near pools or streams. Does not become invasive. A winter mulch is necessary in Zone 5.

Species, Varieties, Cultivars, Hybrids
C. virginianum (vir-jin-ee-*ay*-num). Goldenstar, green-gold. Eastern United States. Grows to 8 inches tall and 12 inches wide. Dark green, rounded triangular, 1- to 2-inch-long leaves with serrated edges. Bright yellow, 1-inch flowers mainly in the spring, but some flowering off and on all season. A number of selections have been made, with somewhat indistinguishable differences. Zones 5 to 9.

CHRYSOPSIS
(kris-*op*-sis)
Golden aster, goldaster
Compositae—daisy family

For those in hot climates looking for an adaptable, easily grown, late-blooming plant, the golden aster fills the bill to a "T". The only problem is in following the name trail left by taxonomists; if chrysopsis doesn't turn up anything, try *Heterotheca*.

Growing Guide
Full sun. Any well-drained soil. When the first frost blackens plants, immediately cut back almost to the ground.

Propagation
Division, seed.

Uses
Back of beds or borders, meadow gardens.

Species, Varieties, Cultivars, Hybrids
C. villosa (vil-*loh*-suh). Hairy golden aster. North America. Grows 3 to 6 feet tall and 2 to 4 feet wide. A coarse plant with woody, branched stems and lance-shaped leaves. Multi-branched clusters of 1-inch, yellow, daisy-like flowers from late summer until frost. The cultivar 'Golden Sunshine' grows 3 to 4 feet tall, with 2-inch flowers. Zones 4 to 9.

Other species to consider include *C. mariana*, growing 1 to 3 feet tall and *C. bakeri*, growing 12 inches tall.

Chrysopsis villosa.

CIMICIFUGA
(sim-*mi*-suh-*few*-guh)
Bugbane
Ranunculaceae—buttercup family

Graceful and dramatic, bugbanes offer low maintenance for a wide range of garden sites. Although the long-lived plants are large, the foliage is fine-textured. White flowers resembling bottle brushes top the plants in summer and autumn. These may be used as fresh or dried flowers, and the seed spikes are good for dried arrangements. Both the genus and common names refer to the scented leaves of some species, said to repel insects.

Growing Guide
Best in light shade, although more or less light is tolerated. Deep, humus-rich, moist but well-drained

Cimicifuga racemosa.

soil. May need staking when in bloom. Plants take several years to become established.

Propagation
Division.

Uses
Beds and borders or woodland gardens. Effective combined with blue-leaved hostas and rodgersias and other bold-textured plants or when planted in masses.

Species, Varieties, Cultivars, Hybrids
C. racemosa (ray-sem-*oh*-suh). Black cohosh. North America. Grows 6 feet tall and 3 feet wide. Clump-forming plant with dark green, deeply cut leaves. Thin spikes of tiny ivory-white flowers may reach 2 feet in length. Depending on the climate, flowering may start in mid- to late summer, lasting 4 weeks. Must have even, constant moisture. Zones 3 to 8.

C. simplex (*sim*-plex). Kamchatka bugbane. Siberia, Japan. Grows 3 to 4 feet tall and 2 to 3 feet wide. Clump-forming plant with dark green, deeply cut leaves and purplish stems. Thin, arching spires of tiny, slightly fragrant white flowers in late summer and fall. The cultivars 'White Pearl' and 'Elstead Variety' are definite improvements over the species. Zones 3 to 8.

Clematis heracleifolia *var.* davidiana.

CLEMATIS
(*klem*-ah-tis)
Clematis
Ranunculaceae—buttercup family

The vining clematis may be more familiar, but there are also short, bushy varieties that fit right in among the perennials. Easy to grow and long-lived, most types also have plumed seeds that are showy, prolonging the garden display. Both the flowers and seed heads may be used in arrangements.

Growing Guide
Full sun to partial shade. Humus-rich, moist but well-drained soil. Additional lime may be necessary. Cool soil is a must,

so mulch in summer. Roots are easily damaged, so cultivate around them carefully. Place them next to tall plants that can provide some support or surround by twigs. Trim perennial clematis back to 6 inches in late fall or early spring.

Propagation
Division, terminal stem cuttings.

Uses
The slightly sprawling nature of perennial clematis makes them useful as a textural contrast in beds and borders.

Species, Varieties, Cultivars, Hybrids
C. heracleifolia (he-ra-klee-i-*foh*-lee-uh). Tube clematis. China. Grows 2 to 3 feet tall and as wide. Dark green, three-parted, slightly hairy leaves. Clusters of 6 to 12, tubular, blue, 1-inch flowers in late summer and fall are followed by fluffy seedheads. Several selections are available. Zones 3 to 8.

C. integrifolia (in-teg-ri-*foh*-lee-uh). Solitary clematis. Southern Europe. Grows 2 to 4 feet tall and as wide. Prominently veined, pointed leaves to 4 inches long.

Flowers bloom in late summer, with each borne singly at the end of a stem, hence the common name. They are 1- to 2-inch, nodding, bell-shaped blooms of lavender to violet-blue. Plumy seed heads follow. The most popular cultivar is 'Hendersonii', with larger, dark blue flowers; its proper name is *C.* x *eriostemon*. Zones 3 to 8.

C. recta (*rek*-tuh). Ground clematis. Southern Europe. Grows 3 to 4 feet tall and as wide. Slender, twining stems with finely divided leaves. Clouds of 1-inch, fragrant, star-shaped white flowers cover the plants in summer, followed by silken fruits. 'Flore-pleno' is a double-flowered variety, and 'Purpurea' has purple foliage. Zones 3 to 8.

CONVALLARIA
(kon-val-*lah*-ree-uh)
Lily-of-the-valley
Liliaceae—lily family

What would spring be without the heavenly scent or a simple bouquet of the small, perfectly formed white bells of lily-of-the-valley? This is one of the easiest plants to grow, providing a quickly spreading groundcover in shade. The name comes from the Latin *convallis*, for valley.

Growing Guide
Any type of shade. Humus-rich, moist but well-drained soil. Growth is considered rampant only by those with no taste or character.

Propagation
Division.

Uses
Groundcover. Cut flowers. Fragrant garden.

Species, Varieties, Cultivars, Hybrids
C. majalis (ma-*jah*-lis). Lily-of-the-valley. Europe, Asia, North America. Grows 12 inches tall and as wide. Single, dark green, broad, pointed leaves arise from creeping rhizomes. Arching flower stems carry drooping white bells along one side. Intensely fragrant. Among the selections are those that are slightly taller, double- or pink flowered or with palely striped leaves. Zones 2 to 7.

Convallaria majalis.

Coreopsis verticillata *'Moonbeam'*.

Coreopsis lanceolata.

COREOPSIS
(koh-ree-*op*-sis)
Coreopsis, tickseed
Compositae—daisy family

The ease of growth and production of sunshine-yellow, daisy-like flowers for much of the summer has endeared the perennial coreopsis to gardeners. The name is from the Greek *koris*, for bug and *opsis*, in that the seeds somewhat resemble a bug or tick. The flowers are long lasting when cut.

Growing Guide
Full sun. Average to humus-rich soil that must be well drained. Deadhead or cut plants back by one-third after the first flush of bloom.

Coreopsis lanceolata.

Propagation
Division, seed.

Uses
Beds and borders, either as specimens or massed. Cut flowers.

Species, Varieties, Cultivars, Hybrids
C. verticillata (ver-ti-sil-*lah*-tuh). Threadleaf coreopsis. North America. Grows 1 to 3 feet tall and as wide. Very finely divided, almost threadlike, 2- to 3-inch leaves on clump-forming, spreading plants.

In various shades of yellow, 2-inch flowers are produced in masses for a long time during the summer. If the plants are deadheaded or sheared back, a second flush of bloom occurs in the fall. The best selections include 'Golden Showers', growing 18 to 24 inches tall with bright yellow flowers; 'Moonbeam', growing 18 to 24 inches tall with yellow flowers in a soft, muted shade (it even does well in the South); and 'Zagreb', growing 12 to 18 inches tall with deep yellow flowers. Zones 3 to 9.

Other coreopsis to consider include *C. auriculata*, mouse-eared coreopsis (Zones 4 to 9); *C. grandiflora*, tickseed (Zones 5 to 9); *C. lanceolata*, lance-leaved coreopsis (Zones 3 to 8); and *R. rosea*, pink tickseed (Zones 4 to 9).

Coreopsis verticillata *'Zagreb'*.

Coreopsis verticillata.

CORYDALIS
(kor-*ri*-dah-lis)

Fumaria

Fumariaceae—fumitory family

Low-growing plants with finely divided leaves, fumarias add a graceful note to lightly shaded areas of the garden. The flowers resemble those of the smaller forms of bleeding heart, but are in shades of yellow, white or blue. It is the blue form that has particularly caught the attention of gardeners, especially since the availability of 'Blue Panda'. The generic name is derived from the Greek word meaning lark, in reference to the spurs on both the flowers and European larks.

Growing Guide

Partial to light shade. Humus-rich, moist but well-drained soil with a neutral to alkaline pH.

Propagation

Division, seed. Readily self-sows; old seed is difficult to germinate.

Uses

Shaded beds and borders, as groundcovers under shrubs or trees, in rock walls, among steppingstones. Cut flowers.

Corydalis flexuosa *'Blue Panda'*.

Species, Varieties, Cultivars, Hybrids

C. flexuosa (flex-*yew*-oh-suh). Blue corydalis. China. Grows 15 inches tall and as wide. Forms clumps with finely divided leaves. Electric-blue, ¾-inch flowers produced off and on throughout the growing season. Several named varieties, with different shades of blue flowers as well as one with purple blotches on the leaves. Zones 5 to 7.

C. lutea (*lew*-tee-uh). Yellow corydalis. Europe, Britain. Grows 1 foot tall and as wide. Clumps of lacy, cool-green leaves. Bright yellow, ¾-inch flowers produced throughout the growing season. *Ochroleuca* is similar but with white flowers. Zones 5 to 7.

Corydalis lutea.

CRAMBE
(*kram*-bee)

Colewort

Cruciferae—mustard family

As might be suspected from a plant related to cabbage, the leaves of crambe are bold. What may be unexpected are the enormous clouds of fragrant, starry white flowers in early summer. Some find the fragrance sweet, while others call it malodorous. One member, *C. maritima*, or sea kale, is edible and, what a surprise, does well in seaside locations.

Growing Guide

Full Sun. Poor to average, very well drained soil. Deadhead. Susceptible to the same pests as any cabbage-family member, especially caterpillars, so treatment with Bt may be necessary.

Propagation

Seed, root cuttings. Self-sows.

Uses

Back of beds or borders, meadow gardens.

Species, Varieties, Cultivars, Hybrids

C. cordifolia (kor-di-*foh*-lee-uh). Colewort. Caucasus. Grows to 6 feet tall and 4 feet wide. Forms mounds of hairy, crinkled, coarsely toothed, dark green leaves growing up to 2 feet across. Airy, open-branched stalks of ¼-inch white flowers in early summer, giving an appearance like a behemoth baby's breath. Zones 6 to 8.

Crambe cordifolia.

CROCOSMIA
(krow-*kos*-mee-uh)
Crocosmia, montbretia
Liliaceae—lily family

Except in warm and damp climates where croscosmia literally grows like a weed, it is little known. Yet it has proven to be a widely adapted plant and not invasive in colder areas. The benefits are vertical iris-like foliage and many arching stems of bright, funnel-shaped, scarlet, orange or yellow flowers for a long period in late summer and fall. These are excellent as cut flowers.

Growing Guide
Full sun to partial shade. Moist but well-drained soil.

Propagation
Division, necessary every 2 or 3 years or plants may become overcrowded and stop producing flowers.

Uses
As a vertical element in beds and borders. Where the color can be worked in, the form offers a pleasing diversion to all the daisy-like flowers of late summer and autumn. Combines well with yellow-flowering plants.

Species, Varieties, Cultivars, Hybrids
C. x *crocosmiiflora* (krow-kos-mee-eh-*floh*-ruh). Montbretia. Hybrid origin. Original crosses made by Lemoine in France in the 1880s. Grows 2 to 3 feet tall and to 12 inches wide. Bright green, grassy leaves and arching, branching stems of funnel-shaped flowers in shades of red, orange, orange-red, apricot and yellow in late summer and early fall. Zones 6 to 9.

C. x *curtonus* (kur-*tone*-us). Crocosmia. Hybrid origin. From crosses made of the two genera by Alan Bloom. Grows 2 to 3 feet tall and 1 foot wide. Bright green, grassy leaves and arching, branching stems of funnel-shaped flowers in shades of scarlet, orange-red and yellow. The most widely available one is 'Lucifer', with scarlet-red flowers. Zones 6 to 9.

Crocosmia *'Lucifer'*.

CYNARA
(si-*nah*-ra)
Cardoon
Compositae—daisy family

For those who want to have their perennials and eat them, too, cardoon is the plant of choice. This is a "statement" plant, with a decided boldness and elegance with its large mounds of long, gray-green, thistle-like leaves.

Growing Guide
Full sun. Well-drained soil a must. Benefits from winter protection.

Propagation
Division, seed, root cuttings.

Cynara cardunculus.

Uses
As an architectural focal point in beds or borders.

Species, Varieties, Cultivars, Hybrids
C. *cardunculus* (kar-dun-*kew*-lus). Cardoon. Europe. Grows to 6 feet tall and 3 feet wide. Mounds of foliage are created from the arching, 3- to 4-foot-long, silvery-gray, pointed and divided leaves. In late summer, stout gray stems bear large purple flowers resembling thistles. Zones 6 to 8.

Cynara cardunculus.

D

DELPHINIUM
(del-*fin*-ee-um)
Delphinium, larkspur
Ranunculaceae—buttercup family

Delphiniums are reminiscent of the rhyme about the little girl who "when she was good, she was very, very good, but when she was bad, she was horrid." So it is with these breathtaking flowers when they are in the right climate and grown with the best care. But, otherwise, why bother? Well, because of the striking spires of blossoms in shades from sky blue to lavenders, purples,

Delphinium elatum.

pinks and white. Okay, so where's the compromise for those of us who don't live in England, the Pacific Northwest, or the Maine coast? Basically, either treat them as annuals or grow the ones that give you the best bet for at least a modicum of success.

Growing Guide
Full sun to partial shade in the hottest climates. Humus-rich, moist but well-drained, slightly alkaline soil. Mulching in the summer and fertilizing in early spring and again in early summer is almost compulsory, as is staking and protection from the wind. Remove faded flowers to encourage reblooming. Cut all stems back to the ground in the fall. Susceptible to slugs and an assortment of fungal diseases. Even in the best of situations, they are usually replaced every 2 to 3 years.

Propagation
D. x *belladonna*—division, seed; *D. elatum*—seed, stem cuttings.

Uses
Middle to back of beds and borders. Cut flowers.

Delphinium.

Species, Varieties, Cultivars, Hybrids
D.* x *belladonna (bell-uh-*don*-uh). Belladonna delphinium. Hybrid origin, first introduced in 1900. Grows 3 to 4 feet tall and 2 feet wide. Large, many-branched plants that are relatively heat tolerant and that produce blooms for much of the summer in various shades of blue or white. Zones 3 to 7.

D. elatum (ee-*lay*-tum) hybrids. Hybrid delphinium. Western Europe to East Asia. This is the most frequent parent of the plethora of hybrid delphiniums available, including 'Pacific Hybrids', 'Mid-Century Hybrids', 'Giant Imperial Series', 'Connecticut Yankee Series' and others. Height ranges from 30 inches to 6 feet and to 3 feet wide. The full range of flower colors and forms, including singles, doubles and those with "bees." Zones 3 to 7.

DIANTHUS
(dye-*an*-thus)

Pinks

Caryophyllaceae—pink family

Beloved through the centuries for their delicious, spicy fragrance, long life as cut flowers and easy cultivation, dianthus remain integral to gardens today. From the 300 or so species, hundreds more selections have been hybridized, with much confusion over proper classification, but the essence of the best ones for the garden remains the same. Most of them form mounds or mats of grassy, gray-green to dark green leaves. Flowers may vary from only a half-inch to 2 inches across, be single, semi-double or double, with fringed or toothed petals either in a solid color or marked with a contrasting color, and in shades of pink, red or white. Although dianthus may be short-lived, propagation is easy, adaptability is wide and growth rapid but not rapacious. From the Greek words *dios*, divine, and *anthos*, flower, the name says it all.

Dianthus barbatus.

Dianthus gratianopolitanus 'Bath's Pink'.

Growing Guide

Full sun to partial shade. Best growth is in a humus-rich, sandy, slightly alkaline soil, but they do admirably well in any well-drained soil. The important aspect to avoid is poor drainage in winter. Winter protection may be necessary in colder regions. Deadhead regularly to prolong blooming or prevent self-sowing. Slugs, aphids, spider mites and fungal diseases may occasionally be a problem.

Propagation

Readily from division, but also stem cuttings and seed.

Uses

Front of beds and borders, edging, cascading over walls. Cut flowers.

Dianthus x allwoodii 'Clove Pink'.

Species, Varieties, Cultivars, Hybrids

D. x allwoodii (all-*wood*-ee-eye). Allwood pinks. Hybrid origin. Original crosses made by Montague Allwood in the 1920s. Size is highly variable, depending on the selection, with a range of 6 to 18 inches tall and up to 18 inches wide. Compact mats of gray-green, grassy leaves. Usually 2 flowers per stem, mostly doubles, and fragrant, for up to 8 weeks. Many selections. Zones 4 to 8.

D. barbatus (bar-*bah*-tus). Sweet William. Europe, Asia. Grows to 18 inches tall and 1 foot wide. Dark green leaves and leafy stems

Dianthus plumarius.

bearing tight 3-inch clusters of ½-inch flowers with no scent.

Officially a biennial, but it readily self-sows, keeping it coming back year after year; in warmer climates, it acts as a true perennial if faded flowers are removed. Many selections, with 'Newport Pink' among the favorites. Zones 3 to 9.

D. deltoides (del-*toy*-deez). Maiden pinks. Europe, temperate Asia. Grows 6 to 12 inches tall. Forms spreading mats of grassy, bright, semi-evergreen leaves. Most selections have fragrant, single flowers of white or red, usually 2 to a stalk. Plants bloom for many weeks in early summer, with some repeat bloom if faded flowers are removed. Many selections, with 'Zing Rose' most widely available. Zones 3 to 9.

D. gratianopolitanus (grah-tee-ah-na-pah-leh-*tah*-nus). Cheddar pinks. West and Central Europe. Grows to 12 inches tall and as wide. Gray-green, grassy leaves form compact mounds. The fragrant, 1-inch flowers are borne singly or 2 to a stem, mainly in shades of pink, rose and red. Can bloom from spring to late summer if faded flowers are removed. Many selections, with 'Bath's Pink' one of the oldest and best. Zones 3 to 9.

D. plumarius (plew-*mah*-ree-us). Cottage pinks, grass pinks. Eastern Central Europe. Grows 18 inches tall and 12 inches wide. The parent of many of today's hybrids. Grassy, gray-green leaves forming mounds. Selections have fragrant flowers up to 1½ inches wide with just about every flower form and color possible with the genus. Deadhead to prolong bloom. Many selections. Zones 3 to 9.

Dianthus deltoides.

Dicentra eximia *'Luxuriant'*.

DICENTRA
(dye-*sen*-truh)
Bleeding heart
Fumariaceae—fumitory family

How bereft shaded gardens would be without both the large and small bleeding hearts, with their unique flowers and fine-textured, blue-green foliage. These popular, easy-to-grow plants deserve all the credit they receive. For those who want to create a native woodland garden, be sure to include the related squirrel corn (*D. canadensis*), Dutchman's breeches (*D. cucullaria*) and golden eardrops (*D. chrysantha*), hardy in Zones 4 to 8.

Growing Guide
Partial to full shade. Humus-rich, moist but well-drained soil. Provide a summer mulch to keep the soil cool and moist. Deadhead regularly to prolong blooming of *D. exima* and *D. formosa* and their cultivars.

Propagation
Division, seed. Some self-sowing but not invasive.

Uses
Shaded beds and borders; cottage, rock and wildflower gardens.

Species, Varieties, Cultivars, Hybrids
D. eximia (ex-*im*-ee-uh). Fringed bleeding heart. Eastern United States. Grows to 18 inches tall and as wide. Forms neat mounds of gray-green, feathery foliage. Sprays of 1-inch, rose-pink, heart-shaped flowers borne on slender, branched stalks. Most of the blooming is in late spring and early summer, but there is some all summer long. *D. formosa*, native to the Pacific Northwest, is very similar. Cultivars and hybrids of these two species have created several improved selections. These include 'Adrian Bloom', 'Bountiful', 'Luxuriant' and 'Zestful', all with flowers in various shades of red or pink. There are also white-flowering forms. Zones 3 to 9.

D. spectabilis (spek-*tab*-i-lis). Common bleeding heart. Siberia, Japan. Grows 2 feet tall and 18 inches wide. Forms irregular mounds of divided leaves. Bears branching arches of pink, heart-shaped, 1½-inch flowers in late spring. A white-flowered form is available. Plants go dormant by midsummer, so they must be surrounded by other plants. Zones 2 to 9.

Dicentra spectabilis *'Alba' and* Dicentra spectabilis *(pink)*.

Dictamnus albus.

DICTAMNUS
(dik-*tam*-nus)
Gas plant
Rutaceae—rue family

Long-lived and low-maintenance, gas plant has a shrubby form with glossy, dark green leaves that are attractive all summer. The highlight of the early summer is the numerous spikes of 1- to 2-inch white flowers. The star-shaped seed pods are useful in dried arrangements. Both flowers and foliage produce a volatile oil with the scent of lemons. On a hot summer night, a lighted match at the base of the flower spike will send a flame shooting up, gratefully without harming the flowers. Some people have an allergic reaction to this oil.

Growing Guide
Full sun or partial shade. Humus-rich, moist but well-drained soil. Will tolerate some drought once well established. Plants are slow to sprout in the spring, so mark the site.

Propagation
Seed, root cuttings. Deep roots make it difficult to divide.

Uses
Sunny beds and borders.

Species, Varieties, Cultivars, Hybrids
D. albus (*al*-bus). Gas plant. Europe, Asia. Grows 3 feet tall and 2 feet wide. Glossy, dark green, aromatic leaves divided into leaflets up to 3 inches long. Spikes of fragrant, white flowers in early summer, each having 5 petals and 10 showy stamens.

'Purpureus' and 'Rubra' have mauve-purple flowers with darker veins. Zones 3 to 8.

Digitalis.

DIGITALIS
(di-gi-*tah*-lis)
Foxglove
Scrophulariaceae—figwort family

With tall spires of velvety, dotted bells rising from low clumps of large, rough, oval leaves, foxgloves provide drama to the early summer garden. A necessity for cottage gardens, they are equally lovely in formal beds and borders. Although most are either biennials or short-lived perennials, they can be easily started from seed, allowed to self-sow or divided. They are also long-lasting as cut flowers. Various tales go with the common name, but each flower resembles a glove finger and "fox" probably started out as "folks,"or the fairies. The drug digitalis is obtained from one species.

Growing Guide
Partial to light shade. Humus-rich, moist but well-drained soil. Remove the central flower spike when faded to encourage side shoots to grow and bloom.

Propagation
Division, seed.

Uses
Shady beds and borders, open woodlands, cottage gardens. Cut flowers.

Species, Varieties, Cultivars, Hybrids
D. ferruginea (feh-roo-*jin*-ee-ah). Rusty foxglove. Europe, Asia. Grows 5 feet tall and 2 feet wide. Two-foot spikes of rusty-red and white flowers in midsummer. Zones 4 to 8.

D. grandiflora (gran-duh-*flor*-ah). Also listed as *D. ambigua*. Yellow foxglove. Europe. Grows 3 feet tall and 18 inches wide. From late spring to early summer, produces yellow flowers with brown-speckled throats. Other yellow foxgloves include *D. lanata*, growing 2 feet tall with creamy yellow flowers in mid- to late summer, and *D. lutea*, growing 3 feet tall with pale yellow flowers in early summer. Zones 3 to 8.

D. x mertonensis (mer-toe-*nen*-sis). Strawberry foxglove. Hybrid origin. Original hybrid raised in Merton, England, in 1925. Grows 4 feet tall and 2 feet wide. Foliage remains particularly fresh. Large, bright pink flowers in early summer. Divide every year or two to maintain vigor. Zones 5 to 8.

D. purpurea (pur-pur-*ee*-ah). Common foxglove. Europe. Grows 3 to 5 feet tall and 2 to 3 feet wide. A true biennial; leave flower stalks on long enough to produce seed for a new crop, then pull out the original plant. Many selections available, with 'Foxy' growing only 30 inches tall and producing many blooming side shoots in the first year from seed. Zones 4 to 9.

Digitalis.

Digitalis grandiflora.

DORONICUM
(doh-*ron*-i-kum)
Leopard's bane
Compositae—daisy family

Of the 35 or so species, only one is widely used in gardens. It is prized for the early-spring, yellow, daisy-like flowers that are good for cutting, even though they close up at night. Plants go dormant during the summer, but return with the cooler days of autumn. The common name is said to come from the use of the juice of a particular species on the tips of arrows when hunting leopards. Perhaps that explains the paucity of leopards in the garden.

Growing Guide
Full sun in cooler climates to partial shade in hotter ones. Humus-rich, moist but well-drained soil. Deadhead faded flowers to prolong blooming. Remove faded leaves when plants go dormant in the summer.

Propagation
Division, seed.

Uses
Spring border, rock garden, cut flowers. Interplant with spring bulbs.

Species, Varieties, Cultivars, Hybrids
D. orientale (oh-ree-en-*tay*-lee) May also be listed as *D. columnae, D. cordatum* or *D. caucasicum*. Leopard's

Doronicum orientale.

bane. Europe. Asia. Grows 18 inches tall and 2 feet wide. Forms neat mounds with heart-shaped, deeply toothed leaves. Single or double daisy-like, 2- to 4-inch yellow flowers in early spring. Several selections available. Zones 4 to 8.

E

ECHINACEA
(e-kee-*nah*-kee-ah)
Purple coneflower
Compositae—daisy family

Purple coneflower is another case of local plant makes good. A wildflower of the central United States, it is one of the finest plants for sunny gardens. Tough, long-lived plants with a wide range of adaptability, they produce pink, daisy-like flowers for a long period during summer. The name is derived from the Greek word echinos, or hedgehog, because the base of the plant is rather prickly. Extracts from the thick, black roots are used for their efficacious properties, while the flowers are excellent for cutting and attracting butterflies.

Growing Guide
Does best in full sun but tolerates partial shade. Any humus-rich, well-drained soil. Staking is sometimes needed with the taller-growing forms when grown in very rich soil. Deadhead regularly to prolong blooming.

Propagation
Division, seed.

Echinacea purpurea 'White Swan'.

Uses
Middle to back of beds and borders. As specimens or massed. Butterfly gardens. Cut and dried flowers.

Species, Varieties, Cultivars, Hybrids
E. purpurea (pur-pur-*ee*-uh). Purple coneflower. Central

Echinacea purpurea.

United States. Grows 2 to 4 feet tall and 2 feet wide. Coarse, hairy stems and leaves. Tall, leafless stalks bear 4- to 6-inch flowers in summer. A number of selections are available, mainly differing either in size of plant or flower, with colors ranging from light to dark pink or white. There are also several other similar species native to other parts of the United States. Zones 3 to 8.

ECHINOPS
(*ek*-eh-nops)
Globe thistle
Compositae—daisy family

Globe thistles are easily grown, eye-catching plants, both for their gray-green, spiny-looking foliage and the globes of tiny lavender to blue flowers produced for a long period during the summer. Bees buzz around them during the day, while moths visit at night and flower arrangers prize them anytime, either fresh or dried. Because of their bristly appearance, the generic name is derived from the Greek word *echinos*, for hedgehog. There is much confusion not only as to the correct naming, but also in that two plants with the same name can appear very different. The search for a good one is worth it.

Growing Guide
Full sun. Almost any well-drained soil. Because of their deep root, heat and drought are tolerated once the plant is established. Staking may be required if the soil is rich.

Propagation
Division, root cuttings, seed.

Uses
Middle to back of beds and borders. Specimen among shrubs. Meadow gardens. Cut or dried flowers.

Species, Varieties, Cultivars, Hybrids
E. ritro (*rit*-roh). Also listed as *E. bannatus*. Globe thistle. Europe, Western Asia. Grows to 4 feet tall and 3 feet wide. The deeply serrated gray-green leaves grow to 8 inches long and are downy-gray on the underside. The 1- to 2-inch-diameter globes of tiny blue flowers form on branching stems during summer. The most popular cultivars are 'Taplow Blue' and 'Veitch's Blue'. Zones 3 to 8.

Echinops ritro.

Epimedium *x* versicolor *'sulphereum'*.

EPIMEDIUM
(ep-eh-*mee*-dee-um)
Barrenwort
Berberidaceae—barberry family

When only a few of these plants are grown, barrenworts can be easily overlooked. Plant them in masses as a groundcover and they come into their own. Delicate-looking yet sturdy, the low-growing, deciduous or evergreen, heart-shaped leaves provide a foil for the small but unusually shaped, columbine-like flowers borne in spring. Depending on the species and cultivar, these can range from white or cream to yellow, pink, red or violet. Leaves often have a pinkish cast in the spring, and may turn yellow, red or bronze in the fall. The common name is from the early herbal use as a contraceptive.

Growing Guide
Partial to full shade. Can be grown in full sun in cooler climates with plenty of moisture. Humus-rich, moist but well-drained soil. Slow to establish and spread. To better appreciate the flowers, some gardeners clip the leaves low to the ground very early in spring.

Epimedium rubrum.

Propagation
Division.

Uses
Groundcover.

Species, Varieties, Cultivars, Hybrids
E. alpinum **'Rubrum'** (al-*pine*-um *rue*-brum). Alpine barrenwort. Europe. Grows to 9 inches tall and 12 inches wide. Loose clusters of 12 to 20 flowers of red and yellow. Vigorous and spreads rapidly. Zones 3 to 8.

E. grandiflorum (gran-di-*flor*-rum). Longspur barrenwort, Bishop's hat. Japan. Grows to 15 inches tall and as wide. Among the largest of the species, with leaves to 3 inches long. Long-spurred flowers are cream and reddish purple, with about a dozen 1-inch flowers in a cluster. Cultivars include 'Rose Queen', 'White Queen' and 'Violaceum'. Zones 5 to 8.

E. pinnatum (pin-*nay*-tum). Persian epimedium. Caucasus. Grows to 12 inches tall and as wide. Foliage is red-bronze in spring and fall. Bright yellow flowers in loose clusters of 12 to 30 blooms. *E. p.* var. *colchicum* has larger yellow flowers. Crosses between it and *E. grandiflorum* produce *E.* x *versicolor*, with either solid yellow flowers or flowers of both rose and yellow. It is one of the toughest epimediums. Zones 5 to 8.

E. **x** *rubrum* (*rue*-brum). Red barrenwort. Hybrid origin. Grows to 12 inches tall and as wide. Vigorous offspring of *E. alpinum* and *E. grandiflorum*. Produces clusters of 15 to 20 1-inch, bicolored flowers of red and yellow. Leaves are tinged with red in spring and fall. Zones 4 to 8.

E. **x** *youngianum* (yung-ee-*ah*-num). Young's barrenwort. Hybrid origin. The result of a series of crosses. Grows 8 inches tall and as wide. Compact plants with reddish leaves in spring, turning to green in summer. Clusters of 3 to 8 ¾-inch, pink or white flowers on each stem. Zones 5 to 8.

Epimedium x youngianum *'Niveum'.*

Erigeron *'Azure Fairy'.*

ERIGERON
(ee-*rij*-er-on)
Fleabane
Compositae—daisy family

Resembling small-growing asters with their 2-inch daisy-like, yellow-centered flowers of blue, pink or white, fleabanes are easily grown and bloom well even in hotter climates. They are a source of cut flowers for many weeks in summer. Perhaps because most of the species are roadside natives in North America, they are not readily appreciated, but the many cultivars offer choice, low-maintenance plants. The early British herbalist Culpepper wrote that the name fleabane refers to the appearance of the seeds.

Growing Guide
Full sun in cooler climates to partial shade in hotter ones. Almost any well-drained soil, preferably enriched with humus.

Propagation
Division.

Uses
Front to middle of beds and borders. Lower-growing types as edging. Cut flowers.

Species, Varieties, Cultivars, Hybrids
E. speciosus (spee-see-*oh*-sus). Fleabane, Oregon fleabane. Western United States. Grows 2 feet tall and as wide. Well-branched, upright, clump-forming plants. Spoon-shaped, 3- to 6-inch leaves with hairy edges. Numerous clusters of 1- to 2-inch flowers. A number of cultivars are available, varying in size from 12 to 30 inches tall and flowers ranging from shades of pink to lavenders, violets or white. Among these, 'Darkest of All' grows 2 feet tall with deep violet-blue flowers; 'Dimity' grows 12 inches tall with light pink flowers; and 'Foerster's Leibling' grows 18 inches tall with double pink flowers. Zones 4 to 8.

Eryngium yuccifolium.

ERYNGIUM

(er-*rin*-jee-um)

Sea holly

Umbelliferae—carrot family

For a genus with over 220 members distributed widely around the world, including a number of highly distinctive, attractive perennial members that are undemanding and heat-loving, sea hollies don't make enough garden appearances. Go search them out, for their silvery-blue flowers surrounded by a spiny ruff are highly prized for their appearance in the garden and their use for both fresh and dried arrangements. The long-lived, thistle-like, gray-green foliage and flowers contrast well with fine-textured plants, especially ornamental grasses.

Growing Guide

Full sun. Adaptable to a wide range of well-drained soils. Deadhead to prevent self-sowing, unless desired.

Propagation

Because of the deep taproot, plants do not divide easily. If absolutely necessary, take root cuttings in spring. Seed sown outdoors as soon as ripe will germinate the following spring.

Uses

Use as an accent in bed or borders.

Species, Varieties, Cultivars, Hybrids

There are a great many species and cultivars with garden value. Most are relatively similar in appearance, with a few noted exceptions. There is much disagreement about proper naming by the taxonomists, a problem that is compounded by the discrepancies in which plants are actually being sold. Most grow about 2 to 3 feet tall and 2 feet wide. Among those worth searching out are *E. alpinum* and its cultivars 'Amethyst', 'Opal' and 'Superbum'; *E.* x *zabelii*, *E. bourgatti* and cultivars of *E. planum*. All of these are hardy in Zones 5 to 8. For colder areas, *E. amethystinum* is hardy in Zones 2 to 8. For those who like the truly unusual, there is the gray-white biennial *E. giganteum*; growing to 6 feet tall in Zones 4 to 8, it is commonly called 'Miss Wilmott's Ghost' in Britain, where the Victorian gardener, Ellen Wilmott, supposedly scattered seeds in gardens she visited. For a North American native, there is *E. yuccifolium*, or rattlesnake master, that, surprise, looks like a yucca; Zones 3 to 8.

EUPATORIUM

(yew-pah-*toe*-ree-um)

Boneset, mist flower, Joe-Pye weed

Compositae—daisy family

Of the 600 or so species of eupatorium, many of which are native to North America, only a handful are valued as ornamentals. Even among these, they are more prized by the English than in their own country. Although they vary widely in size, all are noted for the billowy clusters of tiny flowers in shades of blue or pink during late summer and fall. The name commemorates Mithridates Eupator, physician and king of Pontus, acknowledging the medicinal

Eupatorium fistulosum.

qualities of certain members of the genus.

Growing Guide

Full sun to partial shade in a wide range of average to moist soils, preferably well drained. Pinch or cut back *E. coelestinum* several times during the summer to encourage branching.

Propagation

Division.

Uses

Beds and borders, meadow gardens, butterfly gardens. Cut flowers.

Species, Varieties, Cultivars, Hybrids

E. coelestinum (see-less-*tye*-num). Mist flower, hardy ageratum. Eastern North America. Grows 2 feet tall and as wide. Roundly triangular, coarsely toothed leaves to 3 inches long. Most branches bear 1- to 3-inch-wide, fluffy-looking clusters of pale blue-violet flowers in late summer or early fall. These resemble the annual ageratum, hence one common name. White and dwarf forms are available. Can rapidly spread. Zones 6 to 10.

E. fistulosum (fis-tew-*loh*-sum). Joe-Pye weed. Eastern North America. Grows up to 10 feet tall and 3 to 4 feet wide. Thin, narrow, lance-shaped leaves up to 12 inches long on clump-forming plants with stout, sometimes speckled, stems. Large, rounded or flat heads of reddish purple flowers in late summer and early fall. Much confusion exists among several species, confounded by natural hybridization, so plants may also be listed as *E. maculatum* or *E. purpureum*. Several selections are offered, with either white flowers, purple foliage or shorter growth. Zones 3 to 8.

EUPHORBIA
(yew-*for*-bee-uh)
Spurge
Euphorbiaceae— spurge family

A diverse genus with over 1,800 species, including the Christmas poinsettia and sharp-spined crown-of-thorns, the euphorbias offer fewer than 18 perennials for the temperate garden. Of these, only four are widely adapted. Most spurges are noted for having colorful bracts and minuscule true flowers.

Growing Guide

Full sun. Average to poor, well-drained soil.

Propagation

Division, using care not to damage the fleshy roots. Seed.

Uses

Bed, borders or edging, depending on the species.

Species, Varieties, Cultivars, Hybrids

E. corollata (kor-oh-*lah*-tah). Flowering spurge. North America. Grows 3 feet tall and 18 inches wide. Open, loose growth with jade-green leaves on wiry stems. Airy, open clusters of tiny white flowers resembling baby's breath in summer. Good for cut flowers. Zones 3 to 9.

Euphorbia polychroma.

E. griffithii (gri-*fith*-ee-eye). Griffith spurge. Asia. Grows 2 to 3 feet tall and 2 feet wide. Spreading plant with thick stems and spear-shaped leaves with pink midribs. Coppery to orange bracts 2 to 4 inches long in early summer. Best known cultivar is 'Fire Glow', with red-orange bracts and red midveins. Zones 4 to 8.

E. myrsinites (mur-sin-*ee*-teez). Myrtle euphorbia. Europe. Grows 6 inches tall and 12 inches wide. Trailing plant with pointed, blue-green, evergreen leaves spiraling on woody stems. Bright yellow bracts in spring and early summer. Cut back faded flower stems. Zones 5 to 9.

E. polychroma (pol-luh-*kroh*-muh). Also listed as *E. epithymoides*. Cushion spurge. Europe. Grows 18 inches tall and as wide. Forms evenly rounded mounds of bright green, egg-shaped leaves topped with golden yellow to chartreuse bracts in spring. Does best with partial shade. Zones 4 to 8.

Other species to consider in Zones 7 to 9 include *E. amygdaloides, E. characias, E. palustris,* and *E. wallichii.*

Euphorbia myrsinites.

F

Filipendula rubra.

FILIPENDULA
(fil-eh-*pen*-dew-luh)
Meadowsweet, false spiraea
Rosaceae—rose family

With plumy clusters of tiny pink or white flowers and lush, dark green, divided leaves, filipendula are large, yet graceful plants found growing naturally along streams and in marshy areas. When picked before they are fully open, the flowers are good for cutting, with meadowsweet being hauntingly fragrant. The source of the genus name is the Latin words for "hanging threads," in reference to the thin, threadlike tubers hanging on the fibrous roots of *F. vulgaris*.

Growing Guide
Partial to light shade, with more sun tolerated in areas with cool summers. Humus-rich, moist but well-drained, neutral to alkaline soil. Plants are susceptible to mildew and leaf scorch if grown in full sun and dry soil.

Propagation
Division.

Uses
Middle to back of beds and borders. Among shrubs, beside streams and pools, wet meadows, bog gardens.

Filipendula palmata *'Elegans'*.

Filipendula vulgaris *'Flore-Pleno'*.

Filipendula ulmaria *'Variegata'*.

Species, Varieties, Cultivars, Hybrids

F. palmata (pal-*may*-tuh). Siberian meadowsweet. Siberia. Grows 3 to 4 feet tall and 2 to 3 feet wide. Clump-forming plants with dark green, 5- to 9-lobed leaves to 8 inches wide and white hairy beneath. Flat, 6-inch plumes of pale pink flowers in midsummer, ultimately fading to white. 'Nana' grows only 10 inches tall. The species *F. purpurea* , the Japanese meadowsweet, is similar, but with deeper pink flowers and red stems. Zones 3 to 8.

F. rubra (*rue*-bruh). Queen of the prairie. Eastern United States. Grows 6 to 8 feet tall and 4 feet wide. Clump-forming plants with jagged-edged, 5- to 9-lobed leaves to 8 inches wide on sturdy stems. Branching stems bear frothy pink flower clusters to 9 inches wide in summer, with some repeat flowering in fall. Impressive accent plant. 'Venusta', also listed as 'Magifica', has deeper pink flowers and is considered more vigorous. Zones 3 to 8.

F. ulmaria (ul-*mah*-ree-uh). Queen of the meadow. Europe, Asia. Grows 3 to 6 feet tall and 3 feet wide. Spreading plant with dark green, 3- to 5-lobed leaves, hairy white underneath. Flat, 4- to 6-inch wide clusters of sweetly fragrant white flowers in midsummer. Best grown in masses in wet soil. 'Aurea' has golden foliage, with the flowers removed to increase foliage vigor. 'Flore-Pleno' has double white flowers. Zones 3 to 9.

F. vulgaris (vul-*gah*-ris). Also listed as *F. hexapetala*. Dropwort. Europe, Asia. Grows 2 to 3 feet tall and 18 inches to 2 feet wide. Delicate-looking, with fern-like leaves to 10 inches long in ground-hugging clumps. Flat heads to 6 inches across of fragrant, creamy white flowers in summer. Tolerates drier soil than other species. Readily self-sows. Use at the front of the border or in a woodland garden. Zones 3 to 8.

FOENICULUM
(fee-*nik*-yew-lum)
Fennel
Umbelliferae—carrot family

Wispy threads of bronze-purple weave magic among the perennials when bronze fennel is used in the garden. Usually thought of for the kitchen or herb garden, fennel's delicately textured foliage has advantages beyond its anise-tinged flavor. Use the smoky appearance to soften and blend colors and forms.

Growing Guide
Full sun. Any well-drained soil, preferably enriched with humus. Remove the faded flower heads before the seeds ripen if self-sowing is not desired. Swallowtail butterfly larvae are partial to fennel foliage so grow enough for you and them.

Propagation
Easily from seed.

Uses
Middle to back of beds and borders.

Species, Varieties, Cultivars, Hybrids
F. vulgare var. *purpureum* (vul-*gah*-ree pur-pur-*ee*-

um). Also listed as *F. vulgare* var. *consanguineum*. Bronze fennel. Grows 3 to 5 feet tall and 2 feet wide. Thick, celery-like, angular stems. Airy sprays of threadlike, bronze-purple leaves. Flat heads of dull yellow flowers in summer. Zones 5 to 9.

Foeniculum vulgare *var.* purpureum.

Fragaria *'Pink Panda'*.

FRAGARIA
(fra-*gah*-ree-uh)
Strawberry
Rosaceae—rose family

Runnerless alpine strawberries have long been used as edging or groundcover plants in ornamental gardens, but with the advent of the Pink Panda strawberry, gardeners have had a new plant with a new look. The Pink Panda is a cross between *Fragaria grandiflora* and *Potentilla palustris* by English plant-breeder Dr. Jack Ellisin 1966; subsequent backcrosses led to this pink-flowered plant. Readily produced runners quickly carpet an area.

Growing Guide
Full sun to partial shade. Humus-rich, moist but well-drained, slightly acid soil.

Propagation
Division, runners.

Uses
Groundcover, edging.

Species, Varieties, Cultivars, Hybrids
F. frel (fral). Pink Panda strawberry. Hybrid origin. Grows 8 to 12 inches tall and as wide. Clumps of bright green, 3-part leaves with toothed edges. Spreads by runners; use as groundcover. Deep pink flowers, $1\frac{1}{2}$ inches across, with yellow centers produced in spring and early summer, with some bloom all season. Occasional small edible berries. Zones 5 to 9.

F. vesca (*ves*-kuh). Woodland strawberry, fraises des bois. Europe. Grows 8 inches tall and as wide. Clumps of dark green, 3-part leaves with toothed edges. White flowers, $\frac{1}{2}$ inch across, produced intermittently throughout the growing season, with small edible berries. Use as an edging. A number of cultivars available, with red, yellow or white berries. Zones 5 to 9.

G

GAILLARDIA
(gah-*lar*-dee-uh)
Blanket flower
Compositae—daisy family

A favorite perennial for use in warm-color combinations, blanket flower has daisy-like, multicolored blooms that are good for cutting. It is popular because it is easy to grow, tolerates heat and blooms for a long period. The genus is named after the French botanist, Gaillard.

Growing Guide
Full sun. Poor to average, very well-drained soil. Gaillardia are short-lived in fertile, moist soils. Deadhead plants, then trim back in late summer for fall bloom. Stake taller cultivars.

Propagation
Division or root cuttings for named cultivars.

Uses
Beds and borders, meadow gardens, cut flowers. Excellent mixed with black-eyed Susans and perennial sunflowers.

Species, Varieties, Cultivars, Hybrids
G. x grandiflora (gran-di-*floh*-ruh). Blanket flower. Hybrid origin. A cross between annual and perennial species. Grows 2 to 3 feet tall and 2 feet wide. Sprawling plants with gray-green, toothed, hairy leaves 4 to 6 inches

Gaillardia *x grandiflora* 'Goblin'.

long. Daisy-like, 3-inch flowers borne one to a stalk for a long period during summer. Flowers are usually combinations of yellow, gold, orange, scarlet, crimson or wine-red, often with purple centers. Noted cultivars include 'Baby Cole' and 'Goblin', growing 8 to 10 inches tall; 'Burgundy', with wine-red flowers; 'Yellow Queen', with yellow flowers; and 'Dazzler', with crimson tips and yellow centers. 'Monarch Strain' is a seed-propagated color mix. Zones 3 to 10.

Gaillardia *x grandiflora*.

Galium oderatum.

GALIUM
(*gal*-lee-um)
Sweet woodruff
Rubiaceae—madder family

Providing an easy-to-grow groundcover for shaded areas, sweet woodruff is best known to herb gardeners, who use the vanilla-scented leaves to flavor May wine and make insect-repelling potpourri. Spreads, but not invasively. Woodruff's whorls of rich green leaves are crowned with tiny white flowers in spring.

Growing Guide
Partial to light shade. Humus-rich, moist but well-drained soil. Tolerant of acid soils.

Propagation
Division.

Uses
Groundcover under trees and shrubs, woodland gardens. Interplants well with lily-of-the-valley, spring-blooming anemones, ferns and spring-blooming bulbs, such as *Leucojum* and *Galanthus*.

Species, Varieties, Cultivars, Hybrids
G. odoratum (oh-doe-*rah*-tum). Sweet woodruff. Europe. Grows 6 to 9 inches tall and 12 inches wide. Spreading plant with whorls of 6 to 8 narrow, 1-inch leaves on wiry stems. Fragrant white flowers, ¼ inch across, in spring. Zones 4 to 8.

GAURA
(*gaw*-ruh)
Gaura
Onagraceae—evening primrose family

Now here's a plant for hot summers with water at a premium. No also-ran either, what with its large clumps of willowy leaves and quantities of tall, airy flower spikes with white flowers tinged with pink produced for much of summer.

Growing Guide
Full sun. Average to humus-rich, well-drained soil. Deadhead to prolong flowering. Takes several years to become established before it flowers best.

Propagation
Seed. Division is difficult because of the long taproot.

Uses
Sunny beds and borders, slopes. Pale flowers and airy appearance act as a blending agent among other perennials.

Species, Varieties, Cultivars, Hybrids
G. lindheimeri (lind-*hay*-mer-eye). White gaura. Texas, Louisiana. Grows 3 to 4 feet tall and 2 to 3 feet wide. Clumps of narrow leaves to 3 inches long. Spikes of 1-inch white flowers tinged with pink. Blooms progressively up the spike like gladiolus. Zones 5 to 9.

Gaura lindheimeri.

GERANIUM

(jeh-*ray*-nee-um)
Cranesbill
Geraniaceae—geranium family

Among the "must have" perennials for English gardeners, geraniums are making inroads stateside. A widely adaptable genus with over 400 species and many cultivars, geraniums offer mounding forms and long-blooming pastel flowers for sunny and partially shaded gardens. These perennial plants are not related to the annual geraniums, which are the genus *Pelargonium*.

Growing Guide

Bloom is best in full sun, but in hotter climates, geranium grows better with partial shade. Humus-rich, moist but well-drained soil. Do not overfertilize, as this encourages lanky growth. Deadhead to prolong flowering.

Propagation

Division, stem cuttings.

Uses

Front of beds and borders, edgings.

Species, Varieties, Cultivars, Hybrids

G. cinereum (si-*ner*-ee-um). Grayleaf cranesbill. Balkans. Grows 6 to 12 inches tall and 12 inches wide. Mounds of gray-green leaves finely divided into lobes. Cup-shaped, 1-inch, pale pink flowers with dark veins in spring, then off and on. A number of selections have vibrantly colored pink, rose or deep red flowers. Less adaptable than other species. Zones 5 to 8.

G. clarkei (*klar*-kee-eye). Clarke's Cranesbill. Nepal. Grows 15 to 20 inches tall and 18 inches wide. Loose, open mounds of deeply cut leaves 4 to 6 inches wide. Great quantities of 1-inch blue flowers with pink veins in spring and early summer. Deep blue or white forms. Zones 4 to 8.

G. dalmaticum (dal-*mah*-ti-cum). Dalmation cranesbill. Balkans. Grows 6 inches tall and 10 inches wide. Rapidly spreading, dense cushions of glossy, rounded, deeply divided leaves to 2 inches wide. Foliage turns red or orange in the fall. Clear pink, 1-inch flowers in clusters of 3, mainly in spring, then off and on during summer. White-flowered form. This is one parent of the hybrid *G.* x *cantabrigiense*, a trailing plant 12 inches tall and 18 inches wide with bright pink or white flowers. Zones 4 to 8.

Geranium dalmaticum.

G. endressii (en-*dress*-ee-eye). Endress's cranesbill. Pyrenees. Grows 12 to 18 inches tall and 18 inches wide. Mounds of evergreen leaves, deeply divided into 5 segments. Light pink, 1-inch flowers in early summer, with some repeat. 'Wargrave Pink' is the most popular cultivar among many. Zones 4 to 8.

G. himalayense (him-ay-*lay*-ense). Also listed as *G. grandiflorum* or *G. meeboldii*. Lilac cranesbill. Asia. Grows 12 inches tall and 18 inches wide. Spreading mounds of long-stalked, deeply divided leaves to 8 inches wide. Saucer-shaped, 2-inch flowers borne on long stalks are deep blue with dark purple veins. Early summer flowering for 4 to 6 weeks, with some repeat. A number of selections. A parent of the popular hybrid 'Johnson's Blue', growing to 18 inches tall with clear blue flowers for many weeks. Zones 4 to 8.

Geranium himalayense *'Johnson's Blue'*.

Geranium himalayense.

Geranium macrorrhizum.

G. macrorrhizum (mak-ro-*rise*-um). Bigroot cranesbill. Southern Europe. Grows 15 inches tall and 18 inches wide. Mounds of shallowly lobed leaves to 8 inches wide, and aromatic when crushed. Clusters of magenta-pink, 1-inch flowers in late spring and early summer, then occasionally until frost. The thick, fleshy roots allow more tolerance to dry soil. Excellent groundcover. Selections with white or pink flowers. Zones 4 to 9.

G. maculatum (mak-yew-*lay*-tum). Spotted cranesbill. North America. Grows 2 feet tall and 18 inches wide. Loose, open plants with deeply lobed segments. Pink flowers, 1½ inches wide, in spring and early summer. Also a white-flowered form. Use in lightly shaded woodland gardens with ferns and *Phlox divaricata*. Zones 4 to 8.

G. x magnificum (mag-*nif*-eh-kum). Showy cranesbill. Hybrid origin. Grows 2 feet tall and as wide. Rounded plants with hairy, deeply lobed leaves to 6 inches wide. Flower stems to 5 inches long bear saucer-shaped, violet-blue flowers in late spring and early summer. Zones 4 to 8.

G. pratense (*pray*-tense). Meadow cranesbill. Europe, Asia.

Grows 2 feet tall and as wide. Clump-forming plants with long-stalked, finely lobed leaves. Saucer-shaped, 1-inch violet-blue or white flowers in early summer. A number of selections, including double-flowered forms. Needs staking. Zones 4 to 8.

G. psilostemon (sil-*oh*-stem-on). Armenian cranesbill. Armenia. Grows 3 to 4 feet tall and 3 feet wide. Stately, upright plants with 8-inch-wide, deeply lobed, evergreen leaves. Luminous flowers, appearing in midsummer, are 2 inches wide and dark magenta with black veins and centers. Needs staking. The selection 'Ann Folkard' grows 18 inches tall. Zones 5 to 8.

G. sanguineum (san-*gwin*-ee-um). Bloody cranesbill. Europe, Asia. Grows 12 inches tall and 12 to 18 inches wide. Mounds of thick, deeply cut leaves, with red fall color. Flowers, 1½ inches wide, are magenta, but many cultivars available with better shades of pink as well as white. The most widely grown and adapted geranium is *G. s. striatum*, usually sold under the names 'Lancastriense' or 'Prostratum'. It grows to 8 inches tall, with light pink flowers veined red. Zones 4 to 9.

Geranium maculatum.

Geranium sanguineum.

GEUM
(*jee*-um)
Avens
Rosaceae—rose family

Geums are useful plants when designing a garden composed of hot colors, with their red, orange or yellow flowers, restrained growth and fine-textured sprays of flowers. The main disadvantage to them is that their growth requirements must be closely met.

Growing Guide
Partial shade except in climates with cool summers, where they can survive full sun. Humus-rich, moist but well-drained soil. Good winter drainage is a necessity. Often short-lived. Deadhead regularly to prolong blooming.

Propagation
Division.

Geum quellyon *'Mrs. Bradshaw'*.

Uses
Front of beds or borders. Rock garden. Combine with other hot colors or with dark blues or purples. Plant in groups for best effect.

Species, Varieties, Cultivars, Hybrids
G. quellyon (*kwell*-ee-on). Also listed as *G. chiloense* or *G. coccineum*. Avens. Chile. Grows 24 inches tall and 18 inches wide. Mound-forming plants with large, hairy, dark green, compound leaves. Thin, branching stems rise above the leaves and bear 1½-inch single or double flowers of red, yellow or orange in late spring and early summer. The hybrid *G. x borisii* grows only 12 inches tall, blooms for a longer period and is slightly hardier. Zones 5 to 8.

GYPSOPHILA
(jip-*sof*-eh-luh)
Baby's breath
Caryophyllaceae—pink family

Baby's breath is a plant for those who view gardens with innocent eyes. Like a billowing cloud, the sprays of tiny white flowers soften the landscape, as well as both fresh and dried bouquets. A must for cottage gardens; many a formal perennial garden has benefited from its long-lived presence, as well. The name is from the Greek *gypos*, for gypsum, and *philos*, for friend, a reference to the affinity of the genus for limey, or alkaline, soils.

Growing Guide
Full sun. Average, well-drained, neutral to alkaline soil. Tall-growing types need staking. Deadheading encourages a second bloom. Double-flowered forms may be grafted onto a rootstock and must be planted with the graft union below the soil surface.

Propagation
Thick, fleshy taproots make division difficult. Seed, stem cuttings.

Uses
Filling in or softening among other perennials. Cut and dried flowers. Use creeping baby's breath as an edging, in rock gardens, or spilling over walls.

Species, Varieties, Cultivars, Hybrids
G. paniculata (pan-ik-yew-*lay*-tuh). Baby's breath. Europe. Grows 2 to 3 feet tall and 3 feet wide. Thin, wiry branching stems with a

Gypsophila repens *'Rosea'*.

few narrow, gray-green leaves. Masses of 1/16-inch-wide white flowers in summer. A number of cultivars, mostly with double or pink flowers and either 18 inches or 3 to 4 feet tall. 'Bristol Fairy' is most commonly offered, but 'Perfecta' is considered superior. Zones 4 to 9.

G. repens (*ree*-penz). Creeping baby's breath. Europe. Grows 8 inches tall and 12 to 18 inches wide. Mats of small, gray-green leaves. Masses of white or lilac-tinged flowers. Easy to grow, less sensitive to pH and tolerates heat, but good drainage is essential. Cultivars with pink flowers. Zones 3 to 8.

Gypsophila.

H

Helenium *'Moerheim Beauty'*.

HELENIUM
(hel-*lee*-nee-um)
Sneezeweed
Compositae—daisy family

Easily grown and blooming for a long period in late summer and early fall, heleniums are another North American native that adapts well to the garden. The yellow to orange daisy-like flowers are good for cutting. Though the common name may seem a reference to an allergic reaction, it actually comes from the use of the dried leaves as a snuff substitute.

Growing Guide
Full sun. Average to humus-rich, moist but well-drained soil. Pinch out growing tips in spring and early summer to encourage branching. Staking may be needed. Prune back after flowering.

Propagation
Division.

Uses
Back of borders. Meadow gardens. Planted among shrubs.

Species, Varieties, Cultivars, Hybrids
H. autumnale (aw-tum-*nay*-lee). Sneezeweed. Eastern North America. Grows 3 to 5 feet tall and 3 feet wide. Clump-forming plants with stiff, branched stems and lance-shaped, serrated leaves to 6 inches long. Loose clusters of yellow or orange, 2- to 3-inch daisy-like flowers with black centers. Flowering starts in summer and lasts for 8 to 10 weeks. Many cultivars, mainly varying in height or flower color. *H. hoopesii* is similar but with shorter growth, larger leaves and less tolerance of summer heat. Zones 3 to 8.

HELIANTHEMUM
(hee-lee-*an*-thuh-mum)
Sunrose
Cistaceae—rock rose family

Short, shrubby plants with woody stems and fine-textured evergreen leaves, sunroses produce quantities of yellow, pink or coppery-red flowers in late spring and early summer. Popular in English rock gardens, they are also useful at the front of the border, edging and wall plantings.

Helianthemum nummularium.

Growing Guide

Full sun. Must have moist but *very* well-drained soil, preferably neutral to alkaline and humus-rich. Shear plants back after flowering to encourage new growth. Does not do well in hot, humid areas.

Propagation

Division, cuttings.

Uses

Front of borders, edging, rock gardens.

Species, Varieties, Cultivars, Hybrids

H. nummularium (num-yew-*lay*-ree-um). Sunrose. Mediterranean. Grows 1 to 2 feet tall and as wide. Sprawling plants with woody stems and 1- to 2-inch, narrow, grayish, evergreen leaves.

Loose clusters of 1- to 2-inch, yellow flowers with five petals. Many cultivars, mainly differing in flower color; some flowers are double. Zones 5 to 7.

Helianthemum nummularium *'Buttercup'.*

Helianthus *x* multiflorus *'Loddon Gold'.*

HELIANTHUS
(hee-lee-*an*-thus)
Sunflower
Compositae—daisy family

Besides the annual sunflowers grown for their seeds, oil and ornamental flowers, and the Jerusalem artichoke (*H. tuberosum*), grown for its edible roots, there are perennial species that can be used to good effect in the garden, even in hot areas. Blooming for a long period in the fall with yellow, daisy-like flowers good for cutting. Sunflowers' generic name is derived from the Greek *helios*, for sun, and *anthos*, flower.

Growing Guide

Full sun. Most well-drained soils. Extra watering and fertilizing is beneficial. Staking may be necessary. Can spread rapidly.

Propagation

Division, seed, stem cuttings.

Uses

Back of borders. Meadow gardens. Especially good combined with large ornamental grasses. Cut flowers.

Species, Varieties, Cultivars, Hybrids

H. angustifolius (an-gus-ti-*foh*-lee-us). Swamp sunflower. Grows 5 to 7 feet tall and 4 feet wide. Rough, hairy, well-branched stems with untoothed, narrow, lance-shaped leaves to 8 inches long. Clusters of 3-inch-wide, yellow, daisy-like flowers with dark brown centers in fall. *H. salicifolius,* willowleaf sunflower, is similar but hardy to Zone 4, while *H. angustifolius* is hardy in Zones 6 to 9. *H. maximilliani,* Maximillian sunflower, is another desirable variety; it grows to 10 feet tall and is hardy in Zones 4 to 9.

H. x multiflorus (mul-ti-*floh*-rus). Also listed as *H. decapetalus multiflorus.* Sunflower. Hybrid origin. Grows 4 to 6 feet tall and 2 feet wide. Hairy, egg-shaped leaves to 10 inches long and 6 inches wide. Single or double, yellow to yellow-orange, 5-inch flowers for at least a month in the fall. Several cultivars are available. Zones 4 to 9.

HELIOPSIS
(hee-lee-*op*-sis)
Sunflower heliopsis
Compositae—daisy family

Heliopsis is a sunflower look-alike, albeit smaller, with the translation of its generic name meaning "sun-like." Plants are noted for their long blooming period in summer, ability to grow in hot, dry climates and excellence as cut flowers. Cultivars are preferred over the species for their more refined growth and appearance.

Growing Guide
Full sun. Average to humus-rich, moist but well-drained soil. Deadhead regularly to prolong blooming. Staking may be necessary. May be short-lived.

Propagation
Division, seed. May self-sow.

Uses
Back of beds. Meadow garden. Cut flowers.

Species, Varieties, Cultivars, Hybrids
H. helianthoides (hee-lee-an-*thoy*-deez). False sunflower. North America. Grows 4 to 5 feet tall and 2 to 3 feet wide. Vigorous, erect, freely branching plant with toothed, egg-shaped leaves to 5 inches long. Abundant clusters of 2- to 4-inch, yellow, daisy-like flowers in summer and early fall. The subspecies *scabra*, often listed as *H. scabra*, is better than the species for the garden, and the cultivars are even better, with most growing to 3 feet tall. Two in particular to look for include 'Golden Greenheart', with double yellow flowers with a green center, and 'Summer Sun', which tolerates heat particularly well and blooms for 10 to 12 weeks. Zones 4 to 9.

Heliopsis helianthoides *'Sommesonne' or 'Summer Sun'*.

Helleborus argutifolius.

HELLEBORUS
(hel-luh-*bor*-us)
Hellebore, Christmas rose, Lenten rose
Ranunculaceae—buttercup family

Like the spring-flowering bulbs, the hellebores renew the spirit of gardeners just when it seems winter will never end. Depending on the climate, hellebores may start blooming as early as midwinter, with the nodding flowers blooming for a month or more, withstanding freezing temperatures and snow. Common names notwithstanding, hellebores are not related to roses. The cup-shaped flowers, in shades of green, white, pinks and dusty red-purples, have five petals centered with golden stamens. If the stem ends are seared in a flame immediately, the flowers are good for cutting.

Growing Guide

Does best with sun in the winter and shade in the summer, such as under shade trees or among deciduous shrubs or other perennials. Humus-rich, neutral to slightly alkaline, moist but well-drained soil. Provide a summer mulch to keep soil moist, and a winter mulch for protection. Plants need several years to become established. Where foliage becomes tattered during the winter, it may be removed before flowering.

Propagation

Division, but plants do not respond well to disturbance. Seed, sown outdoors. Self-sows.

Uses

Woodlands with dappled shade, deciduous shrub borders, or among large-leaved perennials. Wonderful when grown in masses. Cut flowers.

Species, Varieties, Cultivars, Hybrids

H. argutifolius (ar-gew-ti-*foh*-lee-us). Also listed as *H. corsicus* or *H. lividus corsicus*. Corsican hellebore. Corsica. Grows 2 feet tall and 18 inches wide. Prized for clumps of foliage with gray-green, three-parted, spiny-toothed leaves. Clusters of 15 to 30 pale green, 1-inch flowers in late winter or early spring. Tolerates drier soil than most hellebores. Best with cool summers. Zones 6 to 8.

H. foetidus (*feh*-ti-dus). Bearsfoot hellebore, stinking hellebore. Western Europe. Grows 18 inches tall and as wide. Vigorous clumps of dark green leaves deeply divided into four to nine segments. Branching stems bear many pale green, 1-inch, unpleasant-smelling flowers in late winter or early spring. Zones 4 to 9.

H. niger (*nye*-jer). Christmas rose. Southern Europe. Grows 12 inches tall and as wide. Clumps of dark green leaves divided into seven to nine egg-shaped segments. Red-spotted stems bear 2- to 3-inch-wide white flowers in late winter or early spring. Most plants offered for sale are seed grown and highly variable. A few vegetatively propagated cultivars can sometimes be found. More difficult to grow than other hellebores. Zones 4 to 8.

H. orientalis (or-ee-en-*tay*-lis). Lenten rose. Greece, Asia Minor. Grows 18 inches tall and as wide. Clumps of leathery, dark green leaves divided into seven to nine finely toothed segments; leaves may be over a foot wide. Nodding, cup-shaped flowers, 2 to 4 inches wide in late winter to early spring for up to 10 weeks. Colors range from white to deep plum, sometimes blotched or speckled with darker spots. The easiest hellebore to grow and does even better with fertilization in early spring. Many cultivars and hybrids becoming available. Zones 4 to 9.

Other hellebores to consider include *H. atrorubens*, bearing dark purple flowers in midwinter and *H. viridis*, green hellebore, a deciduous species with green flowers. Both are hardy in Zones 6 to 8.

Helleborus orientalis.

HEMEROCALLIS
(hay-me-roh-*ka*-lis)
Daylily
Liliaceae—lily family

What's there to say about the most ubiquitous perennial in the American landscape today? Obviously, daylilies are easy to grow and widely tolerant. Witness the stories of people who left them uprooted in a garbage bag in a garage or bare root on a bench outdoors overwinter, only to have them bloom the following summer. Or where to begin on the 30,000-plus cultivars, with hundreds more added every year? The size of these range from 12 inches to over 6 feet, with flowers 2 to 8 inches across borne on leafless stalks, blooming anywhere from late spring to fall. Flower colors run the gamut from ivory to deep red, although most are in the yellow range; there may also be contrasting stripes, edges or throats, single or double forms, with petal edges plain, frilled or ruffled.

A large field of mixed Hemerocallis.

Growth, somewhat mercifully, remains as grassy clumps, and flowers still last only a day, remaining true to the Greek derivation of *hemero*, day, and *kallos*, beauty. If you can't bear the sight of one more 'Stella D' Oro', why not go back to simpler times, and consider some of the original species.

Growing Guide

Full sun to partial shade. A wide range of soils are tolerated, but best growth is with humus-rich, moist but well-drained soil. Extra watering during the growing season is recommended, but not extra fertilizer.

Propagation

Division.

Uses

Anywhere in the landscape with enough sun. Depending on the height, the front, middle or back of beds and borders, edgings, among shrubs or massed.

Species, Varieties, Cultivars, Hybrids

H. citrina (kee-*tree*-na). China. Grows to 40 inches tall and 24 inches wide. Clumps of coarse, dark green, semievergreen leaves to 10 inches long. Fragrant, pale yellow, 6-inch-wide flowers. Zones 3 to 9.

Hemerocallis *'Chicago Scintillation'*.

Hemerocallis *'Quaker Aspen'*.

Hemerocallis *'Stella D' Oro'*.

Hemerocallis *'Treasure Shores'*.

H. dumortieri (dew-mor-tee-*e*-ree). Japan. Grows 2 feet tall and 18 inches wide. Mounds of arching leaves 18 inches long and ½ inch wide. Flower stems are shorter than the leaves, with each bearing two to four red-brown buds opening to fragrant, golden orange flowers in late spring or early summer. Zones 3 to 9.

H. fulva (*ful-va*). Tawny daylily. Asia. Grows to 4 feet tall and 3 feet wide. Naturalizing through many parts of the world, this is the daylily seen growing along roadsides, spreading rapidly. Bright green, arching leaves to 2 feet long. Erect stems bear up to 12 tawny orange flowers to 7 inches across in summer. 'Kwanso' has double flowers. Use for mass plantings. Zones 3 to 9.

H. lilio-asphodelus (lil-*ee*-oh-ass-*foh*-del-us). Lemon daylily. Siberia, China, Japan. Grows to 3 feet tall and 2 feet wide. Arching, dark green leaves to 2 feet long and ¾-inch wide. Branched, curving stems bear five to nine fragrant, lemon-yellow flowers in early summer. Slower to become established than other daylilies. Good for mass plantings. Zones 3 to 9.

H. middendorfii (mid-an-*dorf*-ee-ee). Middendorf daylily. Siberia, Japan. Grows 2 feet tall and as wide. Similar to *H. dumortieri*, but with longer flower stems and tightly clustered 2- to 3-inch-long, yellow-orange, fragrant flowers in late spring and early summer. More tolerant of shade and moisture than other daylilies. Zones 3 to 9.

H. minor (*mi*-nor). Dwarf daylily. Siberia, Japan. Grows to 2 feet tall and 18 inches wide. Arching leaves to 18 inches long. Bell-shaped, light yellow, fragrant flowers lasting 2 days. Zones 3 to 9.

Hemerocallis.

Hemerocallis *'Dragon's Mouth'*.

HESPERIS
(*hes*-per-is)
Dame's rocket
Cruciferae—mustard family

Among the quintessential cottage-garden plants, dame's rocket may be short-lived but it scatters itself about the garden with welcome abandon. Resembling phlox, the clusters of lavender, purple, mauve or white flowers bloom from late spring to midsummer, gracing gardens and bouquets. The generic name is an allusion to its way of perfuming the air at dusk, when Hesperus, the evening star, is in the sky.

Growing Guide
Full sun to partial shade. Moist but well-drained, neutral to alkaline soil. Deadhead regularly to prolong blooming.

Propagation
Seed. Self-sows.

Uses
Massed at woodland edges, informal gardens, cottage gardens, meadow gardens. White forms particularly glow in late afternoon sun. Cut flowers.

Species, Varieties, Cultivars, Hybrids
H. matronalis (mah-tro-*nah*-lis). Dame's rocket. Europe, Asia. Grows 2 to 3 feet tall and 2 feet wide.

Heuchera *x brizoides* 'Northern Fire'.

HEUCHERA
(*hew*-ker-uh)
Coral bells, alumroot
Saxifragaceae—saxifrage family

Even though there are almost 70 species of heuchera native to North America, only coral bells played much of a role in gardens for many years. With the advent of 'Palace Purple', with its wrinkled purple leaves, heucheramania is spreading. What heucheras offer are low-growing plants for shade with marbled, sometimes evergreen leaves and wiry, graceful spikes of tiny flowers from late spring to late summer. The airiness of the flowers provides texture to the garden and bouquets. The genus is named after the German botanist Johann von Heucher (1677–1747).

Growing Guide
Partial to half shade in most areas, with full sun only in cool-summer areas. Humus-rich, moist but well-drained soil. Good winter drainage is essential. Deadhead regularly to prolong blooming. Use a protective winter mulch to prevent heaving of roots.

Propagation
Division of species or cultivars; seed of species.

Uses
Front of beds and borders, edging, groundcover. Cut flowers.

Branching plant with toothed, lance-shaped leaves to 4 inches long. Elongated clusters of four-petaled, ½-inch-wide, fragrant flowers late spring and early summer. Double forms exist, and must be propagated by division or stem cuttings. Zones 4 to 8.

Hesperis matronalis.

Species, Varieties, Cultivars, Hybrids

H. americana (ah-mer-i-*kay*-nuh). Alumroot. Eastern North America. Grows 2 to 3 feet tall and 18 inches wide. Clump-forming plants with 6-inch, rounded, heart-shaped, evergreen leaves with toothed lobes. Young foliage is a mottled purple, that disappears with maturity; there is almost continuous new growth. Spikes of tiny, greenish white flowers on stalks to 20 inches long in early summer. Tough, sturdy, reliable, even in hot regions. Used in breeding hybrid coral bells. 'Sunset', with purple foliage, is the best cultivar. Zones 4 to 9.

H. x brizoides (brih-*zoi*-deez). Hybrid coral bells. Hybrid origin. Grows 12 to 30 inches tall and 12 to 18 inches wide, depending on the cultivar. Mounding plants with dark green, rounded leaves with scalloped edges. Large, open clusters of red, pink or white flowers in late spring and early summer. Many cultivars of various

Heuchera sanguinea *'Coral Bells'*.

sizes and flower colors. From crosses of certain of these hybrids with *Tiarella cordifolia*, foam flower, the genus x *Heucherella* was created; the resulting cultivars are noted for mottled, evergreen foliage, and flowers similar to hybrid coral bells with plants spreading by stolons. Zones 4 to 8.

H. micrantha (my-*kran*-thuh). Western alumroot. Western North America. Grows to 24 inches tall and 18 inches wide. Mounding plants with rounded, heart-shaped, gray-green leaves to 4 inches long with toothed, rounded lobes. Loose, open clusters of ivory, 1/8-inch flowers. Important in the development of garden cultivars, including *H. micrantha* and 'Palace Purple'. Zones 4 to 8.

H. sanguinea (san-*gwin*-nee-uh). Coral bells. Southwestern North America. Grows 12 to 18 inches tall and 12 inches wide. Low, rounded mats of rounded, heart-shaped leaves to 2 inches long with toothed, rounded lobes. Branched flower stalks to 20 inches tall with 1/2-inch, bright red, bell-shaped flowers for many weeks in late spring. Must have good drainage in neutral to alkaline soil. Contributes the color to the many cultivars of *H.* x *brizoides*. Zones 4 to 8.

H. villosa (vil-*loh*-suh). Hairy alumroot. Southeastern United States. Grows 1 to 3 feet tall and 18 inches wide. Hairy, rounded, heart-shaped, deeply lobed leaves to 6 inches long, marked with light and dark green. Large, open, airy clusters of 1/4-inch, white flowers from late summer to fall. Naturally adapted to hot weather. Zones 6 to 9.

Heuchera micrantha *'Palace Purple'*.

Heuchera sanguinea.

A variety of different hostas, including Hosta undulata *'Thomas Hogg'.*

HOSTA
(*hoss*-tuh)
Plantain lily, hosta
Liliaceae—lily family

What daylilies are to the sunny perennial garden, hostas are to the shade garden, with their adaptability, few maintenance requirements, long life and neat, symmetrical mounds of leaves with varying textures and colors. Although there are fewer than 20 species, thousands of cultivars have been developed, ranging in size from 6 inches to over 3 feet across and with foliage dark green, blue-green or yellow-green, plain or variegated with yellow, cream or white, surfaces varying from shiny to waxen and distinctly veined, wavy-edged or puckered. Mainly grown as foliage plants, hostas bear spikes of white, purple or lavender, lily-like flowers, sometimes fragrant, in summer or fall.

Growing Guide
Partial to full shade. Humus-rich, moist but well-drained soil. Good drainage is particularly important in winter. Slugs and snails can be a major pest. May take several years for a plant to get fully established.

Propagation
Division.

Uses
Specimens or small groups in beds or borders, edging or massed as a groundcover. Cut flowers, especially *H. plantaginea* and related cultivars.

Species, Varieties, Cultivars, Hybrids
H. crispula (*krisp*-yew-lah). Curled-leaf hosta. Japan. Grows to 3 feet tall and 2 feet wide. Very dark green with white edge, wavy and twisted leaves to 5 inches wide and 8 inches long. Large quantities of 2-inch, pale lavender flowers on stalks 2 to 3 feet tall in early summer. Zones 3 to 8.

H. fortunei (for-*tune*-ee-eye). Fortune's hosta. Japan. Grows 2 feet tall and as wide. Slightly gray-green leaves to 12 inches long and 4 to 8 inches wide. Distinctive wings on leaf stems. Pale lilac, 1½-inch flowers on stems held well above foliage. The species and its cultivars are adapted to a variety of growing conditions with little care. Among the related cultivars, several are particularly notable, include 'Francee', 'Gold Standard', 'Hyacintha' and 'Golden Haze'. Zones 3 to 8.

H. lancifolia (lan-si-*foh*-lee-ah). Lance-leaf hosta. Japan. Grows 2 feet tall and 18 inches wide. Glossy, lance-shaped leaves to 7 inches long and 1 inch wide. Long-lasting, trumpet-shaped, 1½-inch, lavender flowers on stiff green stalks to 18 inches tall in late summer. The oldest known hosta in cultivation,

Hosta albo-picta.

Hosta *'Golden Tiara'*.

with drawings dating to 1690. A parent of many modern hybrids. Somewhat tolerant of dry soil. Zones 3 to 8.

H. plantaginea (plan-*tage*-ih-nee-ah). Fragrant hosta. China. Grows to 30 inches tall and 3 feet wide. Large mounds of long-stemmed, heart-shaped leaves to 10 inches long. Waxy, fragrant, trumpet-shaped flowers to 4 inches long on strong stalks.

Grown in gardens since the late 1800s. The species and related cultivars tolerate more sun and heat than other hostas. 'Royal Standard' is a favored cultivar with white flowers, as is 'August Moon', with its golden leaves and white flowers, while 'Honeybells' and 'Sweet Susan' have lilac flowers, all with fragrance. Zones 3 to 9.

H. sieboldiana (see-bold-ee-*ah*-nah). Siebold's hosta. Japan. Grows 2½ to 3 feet tall and 4 feet wide. Thick, waxy, puckered, almost round, blue-green leaves to 15 inches long and 12 inches wide. Stems bearing tight clusters of pale lilac flowers barely rise above foliage in early to midsummer; some gardeners remove them before blooming. Among the cultivars, the variety 'Elegans' has been popular since the early 1900s, but 'Frances Williams', with its gold-rimmed edges, is considered the most popular hosta of all today. Many other cultivars with blue-green leaves are available, including hybrids with *H. tardiflora*, a small dark green species, and *H. tokudama*, another small plant, as well as with *H. fortunei* and others. Some of the better known blue-leaved cultivars include 'Hadspen Blue', 'Halcyon' and 'Krossa Regal'.

H. sieboldii (see-*bold*-ee-eye). Also listed as *H. albomarginata*. Japan. Grows to 20 inches tall and as wide. Lance-shaped, dark green leaves to 6 inches long and 2½ inches wide, with white margins and undulating edges. Plants spread quickly by creeping rootstock. Bell-shaped, lavender, 2-inch flowers in late summer, with up to 30 per stalk. Zones 3 to 8.

H. undulata (un-dew-*lah*-tah). Wavy hosta. Japan. Grows 18 inches tall and as wide. Strongly undulating and twisting, shiny, leaves to 6 inches long, with white interior and green edges and red-dotted, winged stems. These are the most common hostas; may also be listed as 'Variegata' or 'Medio-picta'. Flower stems to 3 feet tall bear 2-inch pale lilac flowers in summer. 'Albo-mariginata' has white-margined leaves.

H. ventricosa (ven-trih-*koh*-sah). Blue hosta. China. Grows 2 to 3 feet tall and 3 feet wide. Broad, glossy, heart-shaped, dark green leaves to 7 inches long and 5 inches wide with distinctive veining. Flower stems to 3 feet tall with flaring, bell-shaped, dark purple flowers in summer. Several variegated forms. Very sturdy plant. Zones 3 to 9.

H. venusta (ven-*yews*-tah). Dwarf hosta. Japan. Grows 4 inches tall and 8 inches wide. Pointed, oval leaves to 2 inches long and ¾ inch wide. The 8- to 12-inch flower stems bear 4 to 8 lilac flowers in early summer. Plants spread well by stolons. Variegated and gold-leaved cultivars. Best when grown in groups of at least five plants. Other good small hosta cultivars include 'Ginko Craig', 'Gold Edger' and 'Lime Mound'. Zones 3 to 9.

Hosta sieboldiana *'Frances Williams'*.

Hosta sieboldiana elegans.

I

IBERIS
(eye-*beer*-is)
Candytuft
Cruciferae—mustard family

Among the staples of the spring-blooming garden, candytuft provides dense mounds and luxurious cascades of small, long-lasting, fragrant white flowers as the days warm up. A dependable plant, candytuft is attractive the rest of the year because of its fine-textured, evergreen foliage. Many of the 40 or so species of iberis are from Spain, also known as Iberia, hence the generic name. As to the common name, Candie is an old English name for Crete, where other forms were found.

Growing Guide
Full sun. Humus-rich, neutral to alkaline, moist but well-drained soil. Prune stems back halfway after flowering to keep the plant bushy and possibly get some reblooming.

Propagation
Division, but best left undisturbed; seed, stem cuttings. Provide winter mulch in cold areas with little snow cover.

Uses
Front of borders, edging, rock walls and gardens.

Species, Varieties, Cultivars, Hybrids
I. sempervirens (sem-per-*vye*-renz). Candytuft. Southern Europe. Grows to 1 foot tall and 2 feet wide. Mounding, woody-stemmed plant with dark, evergreen leaves to 2 inches long and ¾ inch wide. Two-inch-wide clusters of white flowers for up to 10 weeks in spring to early summer. A number of cultivars, with variations in height, flower production and purity of color are available. 'Autumn Snow' and 'October Glory' are noted for their ability to rebloom. Zones 3 to 9.

Iberis sempervirens *'Little Gem'*.

IRIS
(*eye*-ris)
Iris
Iridaceae—iris family

Grown for centuries and the emblem of many kings, irises offer a wide range of blooming times, colors and sizes for the garden and cut flowers for the home. Named for the Greek goddess Iris, who traversed between heaven and earth on a rainbow, irises do bloom in every color except true red. The intricately formed flowers consist of three upright petals called standards and three drooping petals called falls, which may have a crest or beard on them. Flowers may be bicolored, with the petal edges frilled, ruffled

Purple bearded iris.

Iris cristata.

Mixed bearded iris.

Growing Guide

Full sun, with partial shade tolerated. Humus-rich, moist but well-drained soil. Deadhead. Pests include iris borer, bacterial soft rot, aphids and thrips. To reduce problems with borers, remove and destroy infected rhizomes at any time and old foliage and litter in the fall to prevent overwintering borer eggs.

Propagation

Division.

Uses

Beds and borders. Certain varieties best suited for specific situations, such as rock gardens or bog gardens. Cut flowers.

Species, Varieties, Cultivars, Hybrids

I. "Bearded hybrids." Bearded iris. Hybrid origin. Grows 8 to 36 inches tall and 10 to 24 inches wide. Complex hybrids with thousands of different named plants, with every possible iris color, but all have the typical sword-like leaves. The flowers have both large standards and falls. They have been divided into categories based on the size of the plants. **Dwarf Bearded** types are further divided into miniature dwarfs and standard dwarfs. The miniature dwarfs are 4 to 10 inches tall and are the earliest to flower in early to midspring, with blooms 2 to 3 inches wide and spotted falls. They must have excellent drainage. The standard dwarfs are more vigorous than the miniatures, with flowers about a week later and 3 to 4 inches wide. **Intermediate Bearded** types bloom between the times of the dwarf and tall types. They grow 1 to 2 feet tall with flowers 3 to 4 inches across. **Tall Bearded** types are the ones most people equate with irises. They are the last of the hybrid bearded types to bloom in late spring and early summer, with flowers to 6 inches wide. Tall bearded irises are more susceptible to pests than others, but this can be greatly prevented by growing them in loose soil with excellent drainage and by destroying foliage in the fall. Zones 3 to 10.

or a different color. Iris blooms may peep through the snow, only inches tall, or stand 3 feet tall, with flowers glowing in autumn's golden light, with most blooming in late spring and summer. Foliage is generally narrow, stiff and sword-shaped, usually growing from spreading, fleshy, rhizomatous roots. With the thousands of species, varieties, cultivars and hybrids, there are irises for every part of the sunny landscape.

Iris pumila.

Bearded iris.

Iris ensata *'Velvety Queen'*.

I. bucharica (buh-*kar*-ih-kah). Bokhara iris. Bokhara. Grows 12 to 18 inches tall and 1 foot wide. Tuberous roots planted 4 inches deep give rise to arching, 2-inch-wide leaves produced on either side of a central stem. Yellow and white flowers in spring. Zones 6 to 9.

I. cristata (kris-*tah*-tah). Crested iris. Eastern North America. Grows 6 to 9 inches tall and 12 inches wide. Fans of ribbed, light green leaves to 1 inch wide. Shallow rhizomes multiply the clump rapidly. Fragrant, 2-inch flowers in spring are lilac-blue, with the standards shorter and narrower than the fall,

yellow crests and a white center spotted purple. There is a white-flowered variety and 'Shenandoah Sky' has light blue flowers and 'Summer Storm' has deeper blue flowers. Native to woodlands. Protect from slugs. Zones 4 to 9.

I. danfordiae (dan-*ford*-ee-eye). Danford iris. Eastern Turkey. Grows 4 to 6 inches tall and 3 inches wide. Belongs to the group known as reticulated iris. Grows from a bulb. Square, hollow leaves develop after the bright yellow flowers in early spring. Standards are ¾ inch long and the falls have dark spots. Zones 5 to 9.

I. douglasiana (doug-las-ee-*an*-ah). Pacific Coast iris. Oregon, California. Grows 1 to 2 feet tall and 2 feet wide. Arching, evergreen, 1-inch-wide, dark green leaves with a red base. Branched stalks bear many beardless flowers in spring and early summer. Colors range from reddish purple to pale blue, with dark blue veins and a yellow center. A parent of the 'Pacific Coast Hybrids', which are superior. Many hybrids. Zones 8 to 10.

I. ensata (en-*sah*-tah).

Also listed as *I. kaempferi*. Japanese iris. Eastern Asia. Grows 2 to 3 feet tall and 18 to 24 inches wide. Stiffly arching, 1-inch-wide, bright green leaves with a prominent midrib. Flower stalks bear three to four flat flowers to 6 inches wide in early to midsummer. Flower colors include deep violet, blue, red-purple and white, often with yellow-tinged falls. Many cultivars and hybrids. Crowns are planted 2 to 3 inches deep in humus-rich, acid, moisture-retaining but not necessarily boggy soil. *I. laevigata* is similar, but without the prominent midrib on the blue-green leaves. It is more tolerant of wet soil and lime. Several cultivars. Zones 5 to 9.

I. foetidissima (foi-tih-*dis*-ih-mah). Stinking iris, gladwyn iris. Europe, North Africa. Grows 2 feet tall and 18 inches wide. Dark, evergreen leaves to 1 inch wide. The odor of these when crushed is the source of the common name. Flattened, branching stalk bears one to three 2½-inch flowers in late spring and early summer. Flowers are gray-lilac with dark violet veins and a tinge of yellow. Mainly grown for the seeds, which are bright red and remain on the plant for a long time in winter; these may be dried for arrangements. Needs partial shade. Several varieties with yellow flowers and one with variegated leaves. Zones 6 to 9.

I. fulva (*ful*-vah). Copper iris. Southern and Central United States. Grows 2 to 3 feet tall and 2

Iris sibirica.

Iris pumila *'Sapphire Jewel'*.

Iris 'Skyfire'.

feet wide. Leaves are 1 inch wide, with drooping tips. Spring-blooming flowers have drooping petals of copper-red to orange-pink. Excellent for the bog garden. Notable for being a parent with *I. brevicaulis* of the 'Louisiana Hybrids', with many fine named cultivars. Zones 7 to 10.

I. x germanica (jer-*man*-ih-cah). German iris. Hybrid origin. Grows 2 to 4 feet tall and 2 feet wide. Gray-green leaves and yellow-bearded flowers of violet-blue in late spring and early summer. Of historical value for its contributions to "Bearded Hybrids." 'Florentina', orris root, with bluish white flowers, is grown for the perfume industry because of the fixative quality of its roots. Zones 4 to 9.

I. pallida (*pah*-lih-dah). Dalmatian iris, sweet iris. Southern Europe. Grows 2 to 4 feet tall and 2 feet wide. Silvery-gray leaves to 1½ inches wide and 2 feet long. Branched stalks bear fragrant, lilac-blue flowers with a yellow beard. 'Argentea Variegata' has leaves variegated with white; 'Variegata' has leaves variegated with yellow; 'Dalmatica' has larger, more silvery leaves. All are

excellent in the garden. Zones 5 to 8.

I. pseudacorus (sood-*ah*-koh-rus). Yellow flag. Europe, North Africa. Grows 2 to 4 feet tall and 2 feet wide. Stiffly upright, deep green leaves to 1 inch wide. Branched stalks bear bright yellow, 2-inch flowers with brown veins in late spring and early summer. 'Flore Pleno' has double flowers; 'Variegata' has leaves variegated with chartreuse. Widely naturalized in wet sites, but tolerates dry soil. Self-sows. Has been used as a medicinal herb for centuries. Seed capsules are dried and used in arrangements. Zones 5 to 9. *I. versicolor*, blue flag, is similar, but hardier (Zones 3 to 9) and with blue-purple flowers.

I. pumila (*pew*-mih-lah). Dwarf iris. Grows 4 to 6 inches tall and 12 inches wide. Gray-green leaves and unbranched flower stalks bearing fragrant yellow, purple or blue flowers, with yellow beards, in spring. Notable for its use in producing hybrid dwarf bearded irises. Zones 4 to 9.

I. reticulata (reh-tik-*yew*-lah-tah). Reticulated iris. Grows 4 to 6 inches tall and 4 inches wide. Netted-veined bulbs produce four-angled, pointed leaves and fragrant, purple flowers in early spring. Leaves go dormant by summer. Grows best with dry soil. Several cultivars, with flowers in various shades of blue or reddish purple. Zones 5 to 9.

I. sibirica (sih-*bih*-rih-kah). Siberian iris. Central Europe, Russia. Grows 2 to 4 feet tall and 2 to

3 feet wide. Erect to slightly arching, bright green leaves to ¾ inch wide. Stalks bear one or three violet-blue, 2-inch, flat flowers in late spring or early summer. May take several years to become established. Not susceptible to pests. Does best with even moisture. Elegant, excellent plants for the garden, with many cultivars, many with larger flowers, and more being offered every year. Related species include *I. chrysographes*, with dark maroon flowers marked with gold on the falls, and *I. orientalis*, with white flowers. Zones 4 to 9.

I. tectorum (tek-*tor*-um). Roof iris. China, Japan. Grows 1 to 1½ feet tall and 12 to 18 inches wide. Thick rhizomes with fans of light, evergreen, ribbed leaves to 2 inches wide. Branched stalks bear 3-inch, flat, dark-veined, lilac flowers with a white crest in early summer. Grown on thatched roofs in Japan. Prone to slug damage. White-flowered form and variegated-leaf form. Zones 5 to 9.

I. "Xiphium hybrids" (izih-fee-um). English, Spanish, Dutch iris. Grows 12 to 18 inches tall and 12 inches wide. Closely related plants offered as hybrid bulbs which should be planted 4 to 6 inches deep. Rush-like, blue-green leaves. Blooms in early to midsummer, with a broad range of colors, including bronze tones. Zones 6 to 9.

Iris sibirica.

K

Kirengeshoma palmata.

KIRENGESHOMA
(kih-reng-geh-*show*-mah)
Yellow waxbells, kirengeshoma
Saxifragaceae—saxifrage family

Relatively new to American gardens, yellow waxbells is a large, shrubby plant for the moist, shaded garden. Mainly grown for the form and foliage, the shrubby plants contribute a somewhat exotic but graceful look with large, maple-like leaves. The nodding, yellow flowers in late summer and early autumn, followed by horned seed capsules, are a bonus.

Growing Guide
Partial to full shade. Fertile, humus-rich, acid, moist but well-drained soil. Protect from strong winds.

Propagation
Division, but best left undisturbed for at least three to five years.

Uses
Back of shaded borders, woodland walks.

Species, Varieties, Cultivars, Hybrids
K. palmata (pahl-*may*-tah). Yellow waxbells. Japan. Grows 4 feet tall and as wide. Upright to arching, purplish stems with hairy, maple-like leaves to 6 inches wide. Waxy, 1½-inch, pale yellow, bell-shaped flowers borne near the top of the plant in late summer and early fall. Brownish green seed capsules with three pointed horns. The species koreana is similar but slightly taller and hardier, with wider-opening flowers. Zones 5 to 7.

KNAUTIA
(*naw*-tee-ah)
Pincushion flower, knautia
Dipsacaceae—teasel family

Resembling scabiosas, to which they're closely related, knautias contribute an airy effect to gardens with their summer-blooming flowers.

Growing Guide
Full sun. Average to humus-rich, moist but well-drained soil. Deadhead to prolong blooming. Staking may be necessary.

Propagation
Division, seed, stem cuttings.

Uses
Front to middle of beds and borders. Particularly effective with ornamental grasses and silver-foliaged plants.

Species, Varieties, Cultivars, Hybrids
K. macedonica (mah-*see*-doh-nik-a). Also listed as *Scabiosa rulmelica*. Crimson pincushion flower. Europe. Grows 2 feet tall and as wide. Sprawling plants with lyre-shaped to feathery leaves. Masses of 2-inch, rounded, crimson flowers on twisting stems in summer. Zones 5 to 8.

Knautia macedonica.

KNIPHOFIA
(nee-*fof*-ee-ah, nip-*hoh*-fee-ah)
Red-hot-poker, torch lily
Liliaceae—lily family

Invaluable for their long blooming season and architectural presence in warm-color gardens, kniphofias are best known for their orange-red flowers, but there are cultivars with ivory, yellow, red, scarlet, coral or even green blooms. Flowering proceeds from the base to the top of the narrow flower spike arising from the clumps of sword-like leaves.

Growing Guide
Full sun. Humus-rich, moist but well-drained soil. Winter moisture is particularly deleterious; some gardeners resort to bending the foliage over the plant crown, then tying it down to exclude water. Deadhead to prolong blooming. When flowering is finished, cut foliage back by half.

Propagation
Division, seed.

Uses
Middle to back or center of beds and borders. Also effective planted in masses.

Species, Varieties, Cultivars, Hybrids
K. uvaria (yew-*vay*-ree-ah). Common torch lily. South Africa. Grows 4 feet tall and 3 feet wide. Clumps of gray-green, sword-like leaves to 3 feet long and 1 inch wide with abrasive edges. Tall, narrow spikes of small, tubular flowers in summer. Species generally superseded by numerous cultivars and hybrids with other species, varying in plant size, flower color and blooming season. Zones 6 to 9.

Kniphofia uvaria.

L

LAMIUM
(lay-*mee*-um)
Spotted nettle
Labiatae—mint family

From a group of plants mainly considered as weeds comes an easily grown, attractive groundcover for shaded areas of the garden. Without the pain-inducing hairs of the related stinging dead nettle, *Urtica dioica*, spotted dead nettle is favored for its frequently variegated forms and small flowers throughout summer. The yellow-flowered form, variously listed under the genus *Lamiastrum*, *Galeobdolon* or *Lamium* is less well mannered, often becoming highly invasive.

Growing Guide
Partial to half shade. Most soils that are moist but well drained. Trim plants back after flowering to encourage new growth.

Propagation
Division, stem cuttings.

Uses
Groundcover in shaded areas or under trees and shrubs.

Species, Varieties, Cultivars, Hybrids
L. maculatum (mak-yew-*lah*-tum). Spotted dead nettle. Europe, Asia. Grows to 12 inches tall and 18 inches wide. Heart-shaped, toothed, prominently veined leaves with central, greenish white stripe. Whorls of magenta, 1-inch, hooded flowers from late spring well into summer. Species has been superseded by cultivars, especially 'White Nancy', with white flowers and silver leaves edged in green, and 'Beacon Silver', with rose-pink flowers and silver leaves edged in green. Zones 3 to 8.

Lamium maculatum *'White Nancy'*.

LAVANDULA
(lav-*van*-dew-lah)
Lavender
Labiatae—mint family

Besides being a beloved, indispensible herb for its fragrant flowers and foliage, lavender is effective as a specimen plant,

Lavandula angustifolia.

edging or low hedge in ornamental gardens. The gray-green, finely textured foliage softly blends other plants, while the flowers bloom for a long period and are useful in fresh or dried arrangements.

Growing Guide
Full sun. Best in sandy, alkaline, well-drained soil, but other well-drained soils tolerated. Good winter drainage is essential and a winter mulch may be necessary. Deadhead to encourage a second blooming.

Although spring pruning is almost universally recommended for shaping, it can have a deleterious effect, so proceed with caution.

Propagation
Stem cuttings, seed.

Uses
Beds and borders, edging, low hedge. Fresh or dried cut flowers.

Species, Varieties, Cultivars, Hybrids
L. angustifolia (an-gust-ih-*foh*-lee-ah). Common lavender, English lavender. Mediterranean. Grows 2 to 3 feet tall and as wide. Mounding to sprawling clumps of woody stems with abundant gray-green leaves to 2½ inches long and ¼ inch wide.

Leafless flower spikes rise 4 to 10 inches above foliage with whorls of tiny lavender, purple, pink or white flowers at the top in summer. For drying, cut flowers when showing color but before fully open. Several cultivars, varying in size and flower color. Zones 5 to 9. Other perennial species are usually grown as annuals, except in Zones 8 to 9.

LIATRIS
(lye-*ay*-tris, *lye*-ah-tris)
Blazing star, gayfeather
Compositae—daisy family

A most undaisy-like member of the daisy family, liatris instead bears tall wands of small, fluffy, purple flowers. Very popular as cut flowers, they are unusual in that they start blooming at the top of the spike, working their way downward. The flowers are also very attractive to bees and butterflies. The vigorous, long-lived North American natives lend grace to the garden with their grassy dark green leaves.

Growing Guide
Full sun. Sandy to average, moist but well-drained soil. Tolerant of dry soil and must have good winter drainage. Staking may be required. Deadhead to prevent self-sowing.

Propagation
Division, seed.

Uses
Beds and borders, meadow gardens, butterfly gardens, massed. Cut flowers.

Species, Varieties, Cultivars, Hybrids
L. spicata (spih-*kah*-tah). Also listed as *L. callilepis*. Spike gayfeather. Eastern and Central United States. Grows 2 to 3 feet tall and 2 feet wide. Clumps of leaves to 12 inches long and ½ inch wide. Narrow, 6- to 15-inch spikes of magenta flowers in summer. Several cultivars with white, lavender or blue-purple flowers. Most widely available cultivar is 'Kobold', also sold as 'Gnome', growing 18 to 24 inches tall, with mauve-pink flowers. Zones 3 to 9.

Other species to consider include *L. pychnostachya*, Kansas gayfeather, growing to 5 feet tall with mauve-purple flowers; *L. aspera*, rough gayfeather, and its cultivars, growing 4 to 6 feet tall with lavender-purple or white flowers; *L. scariosa*, tall gayfeather, growing 3 feet tall with larger, more open magenta flowers.

Liatris spicata.

LIGULARIA
(lig-yew-*lay*-ree-ah)
Golden ray, ligularia
Compositae—daisy family

Bold, dramatic plants, ligularias are best suited for shady sites with moist or boggy soil and cool summer temperatures. The yellow to orange daisy-like flowers brighten the summer garden and readily attract butterflies.

Growing Guide
Partial to half shade, with afternoon shade a must. Humus-rich, moist to boggy soil. A favored food of slugs and snails. Leaves often wilt in the afternoon.

Propagation
Division.

Uses
Shaded beds and borders, near pools and streams. Contrast well with ferns and other fine-textured plants. Butterfly garden.

Ligularia dentata *'Desdemona'*.

Ligularia stenocephala *'The Rocket'*.

Species, Varieties, Cultivars, Hybrids
L. dentata (den-*tah*-tah). Also listed as *L. clivorum*. Bigleaf ligularia. China, Japan. Grows 3 to 4 feet tall and as wide. Clump-forming plants with toothed, heart-shaped, leathery leaves to 20 inches wide. Branched stems of 2- to 5-inch yellow-orange, daisy-like flowers in summer. Flowers often look like they are wilting even when not, so some gardeners cut them off when in bud. Cultivars 'Desdemona' and 'Othello' are similar to each other, with bright red new growth maturing from deep purple to green, and are considered more heat tolerant. Zones 5 to 8.

L. stenocephala (sten-oh-*seph*-ah-lah). Narrow-spiked ligularia. Japan, Northern China. Grows 3 to 5 feet tall and as wide. Dark purple stems with light green, toothed, heart-shaped leaves to 1 foot long. Spikes 12 to 18 inches long with many 1-inch, bright yellow flowers in early summer. Cultivar 'The Rocket' grows 3 to 4 feet tall, with lemon-yellow flowers; it may be listed as a form of *L. przewalskii*, which has deeply cut leaves and flowers with three instead of five ray florets in each flower. Zones 5 to 8.

Limonium latifolium.

LIMONIUM
(lye-*mon*-ee-um)
Sea lavender, German statice
Plumbaginaceae—plumbago family

Like its annual relatives, perennial statice is often grown for its easily dried flowers. In the perennial border, they contribute clouds of flowers that soften and fill in around other plants.

Growing Guide
Full sun, with afternoon shade in hotter climates. Any well-drained, neutral soil. May take several years to become established and bloom well. Poor drainage and air circulation may result in crown or root rot.

Propagation
Division, but difficult because of the long roots. Seed.

Uses
Front of beds and borders. Contrasts well with silver-foliaged plants. Cut flowers, fresh or dried.

Species, Varieties, Cultivars, Hybrids
L. latifolium (lah-tee-*foh*-lee-um). Sea lavender. Bulgaria, Southern Russia. Grows 2 feet tall and as wide. Basal rosettes of leathery, evergreen, spoon-shaped leaves to 10 inches long. Wiry, branching stems bearing masses of tiny, lavender-blue flowers. Cultivars available with pink, light blue, violet-blue and dark violet flowers in summer. Tolerant of salt spray. Zones 4 to 9.

L. tataricum (tah-*tah*-rih-kum). German statice. Southeastern Europe. Grows 15 inches tall and as wide. Basal rosettes of leathery, spear-shaped leaves to 6 inches long. Wiry but stiffer, branching stems bearing masses of even tinier, pale blue to white flowers in mid- to late summer. The variety 'Nanum' grows 9 inches tall, while the variety 'Angustifolium' has narrower leaves and silvery flowers. Zones 4 to 9.

Limonium tataricum.

LINUM
(*lye*-num)
Flax
Linaceae—flax family

Besides the annual plant that provides flax fiber for linen and linseed oil, the genus *Linum* also gives us several prolifically flowering perennials for the garden. Forming graceful, upright clumps with small, fine-textured leaves, they bloom with delicate-looking, five-petaled flowers of blue, yellow or white for up to 6 weeks during the summer. Each individual bloom lasts only a day, but many are produced. Plants may not live for many years, but they self-sow well.

Growing Guide
Full sun or partial shade in hotter climates. Sandy to average, moist but well-drained soil. Winter protection is beneficial in colder areas. Prune by two-thirds after flowering to keep growth from becoming leggy.

Propagation
Division, seed, stem cuttings.

Linum flavum *'Cloth of Gold'*.

Linum perenne.

Uses

Beds and borders, especially dry, sunny spots. Rock gardens. Blue flax in meadow gardens.

Species, Varieties, Cultivars, Hybrids

L. flavum (*flay*-vum). Golden flax. Europe. Grows 18 inches tall and 12 inches wide. Erect, woody stems with narrow, lance-shaped, blue-green leaves. Masses of 1-inch, golden yellow flowers for a long period in summer. Several superior cultivars, including 'Compactum', which grows to 9 inches tall, and 'Gemmel's Hybrid', growing to 12 inches tall. Both species and cultivars should be grown more. Zones 5 to 8.

L. narbonense (nar-bon-*en*-see). Narbonne flax. Southern Europe. Grows 1 to 2 feet tall and 18 inches wide. Erect stems with stiff, narrow, gray-green leaves to ¾ inch long. Funnel-shaped, 2-inch blue flowers with a white center in late spring and early summer. May require staking. The longest-lived perennial flax. There is a white-flowered form, and the cultivar 'Heavenly Blue', growing to 18 inches tall, with dark blue flowers. Zones 6 to 8, or farther north with winter protection.

L. perenne (peh-*ren*-ee). Blue flax. Europe. Grows 18 inches tall and 12 inches wide. Blue-green, narrow, 1-inch-long leaves. Nearly leafless arching stems bear branched clusters of 1-inch, pale blue flowers for up to 12 weeks in late spring and early summer. Tolerant of heat. Best when planted in groups of five or more. White-flowered forms available, along with several cultivars, mainly with shorter growth and more intensely blue flowers. Zones 5 to 9.

LIRIOPE
(leh-*rye*-oh-pee)
Lilyturf
Liliaceae—lily family

At the turn of the century, liriope was hardly grown. Today, it is the foremost heat-tolerant groundcover. The thickly spreading clumps of evergreen, grass-like leaves are adaptable to a variety of conditions and easily grown. The spikes of tiny lavender flowers bloom in late summer, followed by black fruits. The genus is named after the nymph Liriope.

Growing Guide

Full sun to full shade. Almost any soil that is well drained. Cut plantings to the ground in late winter or early spring to make way for the new year's growth.

Propagation

Division.

Uses

Groundcover, edging or for textural effect at the front of beds and borders.

Species, Varieties, Cultivars, Hybrids

L. muscari (mus-*kar*-ee). Blue lilyturf. China, Japan. Grows to 18 inches tall and 12 inches wide. Clump-forming plant with arching, evergreen leaves to 1 inch wide. Spikes of densely clustered, tiny lavender flowers in late summer, followed by black berries. Many cultivars, mostly with variegated leaves, but some with white flowers. Zones 6 to 9.

Creeping lilyturf, *L. spicata*, is hardy to Zone 4, has narrower leaves, shorter growth, much more invasive growth.

Liriope muscari.

LOBELIA
(loh-*bee*-lee-ah)
Cardinal flower
Campanulaceae—bellflower family

One can be easily smitten by the intensely colored, asymmetrical blooms of cardinal flower, only to have the heart ultimately broken by the short-lived affair. So every three years or so, the relationship must be started anew. This time you promise to provide just the right amount of shade, plenty of soil moisture and a light winter mulch. The affair won't last any longer, but the pleasure is worth the effort, while the hummingbirds attracted by the flowers are a bonus.

Growing Guide
Full sun in cool-summer climates if the soil is always moist. Otherwise, provide partial to light shade. Moist to wet, humus-rich soil. Summer mulch to keep soil moist, and a very light winter mulch for protection in all climates.

Propagation
Division, seeds, stem cuttings. With the right conditions, will self-sow.

Uses
Shaded beds and borders. Woodland, pool or streamside or bog gardens.

Species, Varieties, Cultivars, Hybrids
L. cardinalis (kar-din-*nah*-lis). Cardinal flower. Eastern and Central United States. Grows 3 to 4 feet tall and 2 feet wide. Basal rosettes of toothed, lance-shaped leaves to 4 inches long. Stout purplish stems bear spiked clusters of deep red, 1½-inch flowers with three-lobed lips, blooming in late summer. Cultivars with white or pink flowers and hybrids with other species, mainly with red flowers and bronze leaves, such as 'Bee's Flame' and 'Queen Victoria'. Zones 3 to 9.

L. x gerardii (jer-ard-*ee*-eye). Also listed as *L*. x *vedrariensis*. Hybrid purple lobelia. Hybrid origin. Grows 3 feet tall and 1 foot wide. Dark green, 6-inch-long, lance-shaped leaves. Spikes of two-lipped purple flowers in summer. Somewhat more tolerant of moist but well-drained soil and sun. Zones 5 to 8.

L. siphilitica (si-fih-*lih*-tih-kah). Blue lobelia. Eastern United States. Grows 3 feet tall and 18 inches wide. Clump-forming plants with stiff, unbranched stems and toothed, lance-shaped, light green leaves to 6 inches long. Spikes of 1-inch, light blue flowers in late summer, after *L. cardinalis*. There is a white-flowered form. Zones 4 to 8.

Lobelia cardinalis *'Queen Victoria'*.

Lobelia cardinalis.

Lobelia siphilitica.

LUNARIA
(lew-*nair*-ee-ah)
Perennial honesty
Cruciferae—mustard family

Few gardeners know that there is a perennial form of the plant that enriches them with papery "silver dollars." The perennial's seed pods are oval, 2 to 3 inches long and 1 inch wide; these can be used in flower arrangements, like those of the biennial money plant. Perennial honesty is easily grown in partially to lightly shaded gardens, naturalizing somewhat, and providing fragrant flowers in late spring and early summer, followed by the silvery seed pods.

Growing Guide
Partial shade. Average to humus-rich, moist but well-drained soil.

Propagation
Division, seed. Self-sows.

Uses
Beds and borders. Meadow, woodland or fragrance gardens. Dried arrangements.

Species, Varieties, Cultivars, Hybrids
L. rediviva (reh-dih-*veev*-ah). Perennial honesty. Europe. Grows 3 to 4 feet tall and 24 inches wide. Shrubby plants with finely-toothed, heart-shaped, dark green leaves to 5 inches long. Loose, open, branching clusters of pale lavender flowers in late spring and early summer, followed by persistent, silvery-white seed pods. Zones 4 to 8.

Lunaria.

LUPINUS
(lew-*pye*-nus)
Lupine
Leguminosae—pea family

Perfectly sculpted spikes of intense, brilliant colors are the hallmark of lupines. Their glory is often seen in masses, whether as a hybrid in a cottage garden or Texas bluebonnets carpeting a pasture, but even a single specimen can be stunning. Although there are more than 200 species, many of which are native to the United States, lupine history became inextricably intertwined with the English when gardeners began hybridizing them in the 1890s, culminating in the work of Yorkshire hobbyist George Russell in the early 1900s. Easily grown in the English climate, lupines do best in cool-summer areas of the United States. Gardeners in hotter climates still enjoy their beauty by growing them as short-lived perennials or as annuals planted out in the fall for bloom the following spring.

Growing Guide
Full sun to partial shade. Humus-rich, moist but well-drained, acid soil. Deadhead faded flowers to encourage repeat blooming. Use a summer mulch to keep soil moist, and a winter mulch for protection. Slugs and snails can be a problem.

Propagation
Stem cuttings or seeds, neither of which is easy. Do not disturb once established. May self-sow.

Uses
Beds and borders, cottage gardens. As specimen plant or in masses.

Species, Varieties, Cultivars, Hybrids
Hybrid lupines. Bushy plants with gray- to bright green, fan-like leaves divided into a dozen or so pointed leaflets. Bloom spikes 12 to 24 inches tall, densely packed with pea-like flowers in shades of blue, purple, yellow, red, pink, either solid or bicolored in late spring or early summer. Many cultivars, varying in height and color. Zones 4 to 8.

Lupines.

Lupines.

Lychnis chalcedonica.

LYCHNIS
(*lik*-nis)
Campion, catchfly
Caryophyllaceae—pink family

Although short-lived and diverging greatly in appearance, the various garden campions all have a long blooming season. Flowers are good for cutting, and they are easily grown.

Growing Guide
Full sun, with partial shade in hotter climates. Average to humus-rich, moist but well-drained soil.

Propagation
Division, seed.

Uses
Beds and borders. Cottage gardens. Cut flowers.

Species, Varieties, Cultivars, Hybrids
L. x *arkwrightii* (ark-*rye*-tee-eye). Arkwright's campion. Hybrid origin. Grows 18 inches tall and 12 inches wide. Bronze-green leaves. Clusters of 1½-inch scarlet-orange flowers in summer. Pinch plants in spring to encourage branching. Seed pods add visual interest to the garden. Zones 6 to 8.

L. chalcedonica (chal-see-*don*-ih-kah). Maltese cross. Eastern Russia. Grows 2 to 3 feet tall and 18 inches wide. Clump-forming plant with oval, 4-inch-long, dark green leaves. Dense clusters of numerous, 1-inch, cross-shaped scarlet flowers. May need staking. White, pink and double forms available. A favorite "old-fashioned" plant. Zones 4 to 9.

L. coronaria (kor-oh-*nay*-ree-ah). Rose campion. Southern Europe. Grows 2 to 3 feet tall and 18 inches wide. Basal rosettes of gray, woolly, oval leaves to 4 inches long. Branched, woolly stems bear bright magenta, 1-inch flowers profusely in summer. Grows well in dry, poor soils. Short-lived but readily self-sows. Varieties with white or carmine-red flowers and cultivars with soft pink flowers. Flower-of-jove (*L. flos-jovis*) is similar, but grows to 18 inches with rose-red flowers and is longer-lived. Zones 4 to 8.

L. x *haageana* (hah-jee-*ay*-nah). Haage campion. Hybrid origin. Grows 18 inches tall and 12 inches wide. Basal clumps of dark green, lance-shaped, 4-inch leaves. Clusters of 2-inch orange-scarlet flowers in summer. Needs full sun and consistent moisture; susceptible to slugs. Zone 4 to 9.

L. viscaria (vis-*kay*-ree-ah). German catchfly. Europe. Grows 12 to 18 inches tall and 12 inches wide. Basal clumps of grassy, dark green leaves to 5 inches long. Strong, sticky stems bear clusters of 1-inch, magenta flowers in early summer. Zones 3 to 8.

Lychnis coronaria.

Lychnis coronaria 'Alba'.

LYSIMACHIA
(lye-sim-*ahk*-ee-ah)

Loosestrife

Primulaceae—primrose family

If ever a need arises for calming angry oxen, grab some lysimachia, as the genus is named after King Lysimachus of Thrace, whose legend tells of his using loosestrife to calm a beast pursuing him. Otherwise, loosestrife is useful as a native plant beside streams or in other large, sunny or lightly shaded areas, as the roots tend to spread rapidly.

Lysimachia clethroides.

Growing Guide
Full sun to partial shade. Average to humus-rich, moist soil.

Propagation
Division, seed.

Uses
Moist meadow gardens, along streams. Cut flowers.

Species, Varieties, Cultivars, Hybrids

L. clethroides (kleth-*roi*-deez). Gooseneck loosestrife. China, Japan. Grows 2 to 3 feet tall and 3 feet wide. Spreading, shrubby plants with slightly hairy, oval leaves to 6 inches long. Dense, 12- to 18-inch curving spikes of ½-inch white flowers in late summer. Good for cutting. Zones 3 to 8.

L. ephemerum (ef-*fem*-er-um). Europe. Grows 3 feet tall and 1 foot wide. Noninvasive, upright plants with leathery, lance-shaped, gray-green leaves to 6 inches long. Narrow spikes of small white flowers from mid- to late summer. Zones 6 to 8.

L. nummularia (num-yew-*lah*-ree-ah). Creeping Jenny. Europe. Grows 4 to 8 inches tall and 2 feet wide. Prostrate stems with rounded, 1-inch leaves quickly carpet moist, shady areas. Fragrant yellow, 1-inch flowers in early summer. 'Aurea' has lime-green leaves. Zones 3 to 8.

L. punctata (punk-*tah*-tah). Yellow loosestrife. Central Europe, Asia Minor. Grows 2 feet tall and 1 foot wide. Whorled, spear-shaped leaves to 4 inches long, with each "layer" bearing whorls of 1-inch, yellow flowers with a brown throat throughout summer. Zones 4 to 8.

Lysimachia punctata.

M

MACLEYA
(mak-*lay*-ah)
Plume poppy
Papaveraceae—
poppy family

Sometimes a bold stroke is just what a garden needs to give it some élan. Plume poppy is one dramatically impressive candidate for the job. Both the flowers and seed pods can be used in arrangements.

Growing Guide
Full sun, with partial shade in hotter areas. Best if grown in a site sheltered from wind, otherwise staking may be necessary. May spread more than desired.

Propagation
Division, seed.

Uses
Large beds or borders where spreading roots won't cause problems. Cut flowers.

Species, Varieties, Cultivars, Hybrids
M. cordata (kor-*dah*-tah). Formerly listed as *Bocconia cordata*. Plume poppy. China, Japan. Grows

Macleya cordata.

5 to 8 feet tall and 4 feet wide. Spreading plant with strong, unbranched stem with deeply lobed, gray-green leaves to 8 inches across; the undersides are felty white. Airy plumes to 1 foot long bear ½-inch, petalless, ivory flowers in summer followed by attractive seed pods. Another species, *M. microcarpa*, is inferior and more invasive. Zones 3 to 8.

MALVA
(*mal*-vah)
Mallow
Malvaceae—mallow family

Mallows are part of a large group of related plants that offer upright growth and pink, hibiscus-like flowers. Their form, long blooming period and drought tolerance more than make up for their relatively short life and susceptibility to assorted pests.

Malva moschata *'Alba'*.

Malva moschata.

Growing Guide

Full sun, with partial shade in hotter areas. Average, neutral to alkaline, well-drained soil. Pests such as Japanese beetles, spider mites and fungal diseases are worse in hotter climates.

Propagation

Division, seed. Self-sows.

Uses

Beds and borders.

Species, Varieties, Cultivars, Hybrids

M. alcea (ahl-*see*-ah). Hollyhock mallow. Europe. Grows 2 to 4 feet tall and 18 inches wide. Erect, multi-branched stems with slightly hairy, five-lobed, toothed leaves.

Pink, lavender, or white 2-inch flowers borne in leaf axils along stems and in terminal clusters from summer into early fall. With very upright growth and rose-pink flowers, the variety 'Fastigiata' is grown most frequently. *M. moschata* is similar but not as showy. Zones 4 to 8.

MARRUBIUM
(mar-*rew*-bee-um)
Horehound
Labiatae—mint family

Because of the softening and blending effect of silver-foliaged plants, gardeners always want to add to the list of possibilities. Silver horehound with its round, wrinkled, woolly leaves, is among the best, as it is one of the few silver-gray perennials that does not rot in hot, humid climates.

Growing Guide

Full sun. Sandy to average well-drained soil. Drought tolerant. Tends to sprawl if soil is too fertile. Can be pinched or pruned to encourage bushiness. Can die off if soil is too wet in winter.

Propagation

Division, seed. Self-sows.

Uses

Beds and borders.

Species, Varieties, Cultivars, Hybrids

M. incanum (in-*kan*-um). Silver horehound. Southern Europe, Asia Minor. 2 to 3 feet tall and 2 feet wide. Shrubby plant with stems near the base becoming woody. The pointed, egg-shaped leaves are up to 2 inches long and covered with gray-white hairs. Whorls of tiny white flowers. The common horehound, *M. vulgare*, is similar but slightly less silver; you can make your own cough drops from it. Zones 3 to 9.

MECONOPSIS
(mee-koh-*nop*-sis)

Meconopsis
Papaveraceae—poppy family

Meconopsis ranks high on the fantasy-plant list, with gardeners diligently working to create just the right conditions. Why bother? Come across a planting bearing the sky-blue flowers just once .... Of course, gardeners in the Pacific Northwest have the best chance of success, with their cool, damp climate and moist, acid soil, but

Meconopsis betonicifolia.

gardeners elsewhere have been successful. The Welsh version, with golden flowers, is much easier to grow.

Growing Guide
Partial shade. Fertile, humus-rich, acid soil that is constantly moist but also well drained. Provide a summer mulch. Protect from wind or stake taller types.

Propagation
Division, fresh seed.

Uses
Woodland gardens. Associates well with other plants with similar requirements, such as rhododendrons, ferns, primulas and rodgersias.

Species, Varieties, Cultivars, Hybrids
M. betonicifolia (bet-on-iss-ih-*foh*-lee-ah). Himalayan blue poppy. Asia. Grows to 4 feet tall and 18 inches wide. Basal rosettes with toothed, heart-shaped leaves diminishing in size as they progress up the stems. Clusters of outward-facing, blue poppy-like flowers to 3 inches across in late spring and early summer. Zones 6 to 8.

M. cambrica (*kam*-brih-kah). Welsh poppy. Western Europe. Grows 12 inches tall and as wide. Ferny, deeply divided leaves with yellow or orange, 2-inch, poppy-like flowers in summer. The variety 'Flore-pleno' has double flowers. Zones 6 to 8.

M. grandis (*gran*-dis). Blue poppy. Asia. Grows 2 to 4 feet tall and 2 feet wide. Clump-forming plant with toothed, hairy, lance-shaped leaves. Upward-facing, sky-blue to purple, 4- to 5-inch flowers in early summer. Cultivars and hybrids with other species have been developed but are difficult to locate. Zones 6 to 8.

MERTENSIA
(mer-*ten*-see-ah)

Bluebells
Boraginaceae—borage family

Viewing drifts of Virginia bluebells glorying in the dappled shade at the edge of a woodland in spring can number among life's better moments. They are easily grown and should be added to any shady, moist area where they can be allowed to colonize slowly. As the plants go dormant and disappear by midsummer, some gardeners interplant them with ferns.

Growing Guide
Partial to full shade. Humus-rich, acid, moist but well-drained soil. Best if soil is drier when dormant. Slugs may be a problem.

Propagation
Division, fresh seed.

Uses
Woodland gardens.

Species, Varieties, Cultivars, Hybrids
M. virginica (vir-*jin*-ih-kuh). Virginia bluebells. Eastern United States. Grows 1 to 2 feet tall and 18 inches wide. Spreading clumps of blue-green, egg-shaped leaves to 6 inches long. Upright stems bear nodding clusters of small pink buds that open to 1-inch-long bluish purple bells. 'Alba' has white flowers, and 'Rubra' has pink flowers. Zones 3 to 9.

Mertensia virginica.

MONARDA
(moh-*nar*-dah)
Bee balm, bergamot, Oswego tea
Labiatae—mint family

Long-lived, easily grown, widely adaptable, long blooming season in summer, with uniquely shaped flowers that are edible with a minty flavor, good for cutting, attracting hummingbirds and butterflies, and drying, along with the leaves, for potpourri. Sound like the miracle perennial? The monardas, native to North America, certainly have become staples in the garden since their discovery in the seventeenth and eighteenth centuries, but they do have the tragic flaw of susceptibility to mildew. There are several ways to overcome this inconvenience, including keeping the soil evenly moist, growing disease-resistant varieties, and cutting the plants back severely after blooming. Monarda's claim with history is use of the leaves of *M. didyma* as a substitute for black tea during the Revolutionary War.

Growing Guide
Full sun to partial shade. Humus-rich, moist but well-drained soil. Deadhead regularly to prolong flowering.

Propagation
Division for cultivars; division or seed for species.

Uses
Beds and borders; naturalized in moist meadows or edges of

Monarda didyma *'Cambridge Scarlet'*.

Monarda fistulosa.

woodlands; near pools or streams; hummingbird and butterfly gardens. Cut flowers.

Species, Varieties, Cultivars, Hybrids
M. didyma (*did*-ih-mah). Bee balm, bergamot, Oswego tea. Eastern United States. Grows 2 to 4 feet tall and 2 to 3 feet wide. Spreading plants with upright stems. Dark green, aromatic leaves are pointed, toothed, hairy and egg-shaped, to 6 inches long. Clusters of flowers, each with numerous tubular red flowers surrounding a dense center. Grows naturally along stream banks under overhanging trees, spreading by underground stems. A number of cultivars and hybrids in various shades of red, pink, purple or white. Much effort to create mildew-resistant plants; look for 'Marshall's Delight' and hybrids from breeder Piet Ouldolf, among others. Zones 4 to 9.
M. fistulosa (fiss-tew-*loh*-sah). Wild bergamot. North America. Grows 2 to 4 feet tall and 2 to 3 feet wide. Similar to *M. didyma*, but with leaves slightly more hairy and less toothed. Flowers are lavender to pale pink, with a stem and flower sometimes growing out of previous flower heads. Tolerates drier soil and is less susceptible to mildew. Purple-flowered hybrids, such as 'Violet Queen', are usually listed under *M. didyma*, but usually have this species in the parentage, so drier soil is tolerated and plants have better mildew resistance.

MYOSOTIS
(mye-oh-*soh*-tis)
Forget-me-not
Boraginaceae—borage family

The romantic notion of prolifically blooming forget-me-nots far exceeds their role in the garden, but, nonetheless, they should be considered for the woodland or streamside garden. Although short-lived, they readily self-sow.

Growing Guide
Partial to light shade. Humus-rich, acid, moist but well-drained soil for *M. alpestris*; humus-rich, acid, moist soil for *M. scorpioides*. Thin foliage in summer to reduce leaf rot in *M. alpestris*.

Propagation
Division, seed. Self-sows.

Uses
Woodland gardens or near streams or pools.

Species, Varieties, Cultivars, Hybrids
M. alpestris (ahl-*pes*-tris). Also listed as *M. sylvestris*. Woodland forget-me-not. Europe. Grows 8 inches tall and as wide. Compact, clump-forming plants with hairy, oval leaves to 3 inches long. Tiny blue flowers with yellow centers open along coiling stems in early spring, with occasional blooming in summer. Several cultivars and hybrids, with flowers of white, pink, or various shades of blue. Zones 3 to 8.
M. scorpioides (skor-pee-*oi*-deez). Also listed as *M. palustris*. Water forget-me-not. Europe. Grows 6 inches tall and 12 inches wide. Prostrate stems with rough, hairy, lance-shaped leaves. Tiny blue flowers with yellow centers open along coiling stems in early spring. Can grow even in shallow water. The variety 'Semperflorens' is more compact and blooms longer. Zones 3 to 8.

N

Nepeta sibirica.

NEPETA
(*nep*-eh-tah)
Nepeta, catnip
Labiatae—mint family

The perennial catnips chosen for their ornamental qualities rather than their appeal to felines are easily grown, can bloom abundantly for a long period and provide fine texture in the garden. The town of Nepet, in Tuscany, is said to be the origin of the genus name.

Growing Guide
Full sun, with partial shade recommended for hot, humid climates. Sandy to average well-drained soil. Cut plants back by half after flowering to encourage bushy new growth and repeat flowering. In the spring, prune back dead growth.

Propagation
Division for both species; seed for *N. mussinii*, which can self-sow; stem cuttings.

Uses
Beds and borders, edging, mass plantings.

Nepeta mussinii.

Species, Varieties, Cultivars, Hybrids
N. x *faassenii* (fah-*sen*-ee-eye). Faaseen's nepeta. Hybrid origin. Cross between *N. mussinii* and *N. nepetella*. Grows 18 to 24 inches tall and 18 inches wide. Vigorous, clump-forming plants with branching stems. Gray-green, toothed, heart-shaped leaves to 1½ inches long. Six-inch spikes of ¼-inch lavender-blue flowers for a long period from early to mid-summer, repeating well in the fall if deadheaded. Sterile, so no seed is produced. Considered superior to *N. mussinii*, but many plants sold as *N.* x *faassenii* are probably *N. mussinii*. Many cultivars, including 'Six Hills Giant', which grows to 3 feet tall with dark violet flowers. Zones 4 to 9.

N. mussinii (muss-*seen*-ee-ye). Persian nepeta. Caucasus. Grows 1 foot tall and as wide. Sprawling stems with hairy, softly toothed, gray-green, heart-shaped leaves to 1 inch long.

Spikes of lavender-blue flowers in late spring or early summer, with some repeat if trimmed back. White-flowered form available. Zones 3 to 8.

Two other nepetas worth searching out are *N. nervosa* (Zones 6 to 8) and *N. sibirica* (Zones 4 to 8). They grow 2 to 3 feet tall, with larger, brighter green leaves and spikes of pale to bright blue flowers in summer. There are many other species, as well as new cultivars and hybrids of nepeta.

Nepeta *x* faassenii.

O

OENOTHERA
(ee-noh-*thuh*-rah)
Sundrops, evening primrose
Onograceae—evening primrose
family

Since they're not related to primroses, and the best types for the garden bloom in the daytime, let's speak of the oenothera as sundrops. Sunny, bright yellow flowers do predominate, but there are also pink-flowered ones. A large genus of many plant types, with several native to North America, the best oenothera for the garden are not necessarily the ones chosen. Still, most are undemanding, easily grown and generous with their flowers.

Growing Guide
Full sun. Average, well-drained soil, which should not be overly fertile.

Propagation
Division or seed.

Uses
Many are best allowed to carpet an area by themselves; use more restrained growing forms in beds and borders. Casual growth best for informal designs, cottage gardens and meadow gardens.

Species, Varieties, Cultivars, Hybrids
O. caespitosa (ses-pih-*toh*-sah). Tufted evening primrose. Western North America. Grows 4 to 8 inches tall and 12 inches across. Stemless plants with clusters of 4-inch, narrow, hairy leaves. Fragrant, 2- to 3-inch flowers are white, aging to pink, and open in the evening. Zones 4 to 7.

O. missouriensis (miz-ur-ee-*en*-sis). Ozark sundrops. Southern and central United States. Grows 12 inches tall and 18 inches wide. Sprawling, spreading plants with red-tinged stems and lance-shaped leaves to 6 inches long. Red-spotted flower buds open on summer afternoons to 5-inch, cup-shaped, yellow blooms. Zones 4 to 8.

Oenethera tetragona *'Yellow River'*.

O. speciosa (spee-see-*oh*-sah). Evening primrose. Southern United States. Grows 12 to 18 inches tall and 24 inches wide. Rapidly spreading, stoloniferous growth with lobed, lance-shaped leaves to 3 inches long. Cup-shaped, pale pink flowers borne in leaf axils open in evening in early summer. Give plenty of room. Zones 5 to 8.

Hybrid sundrops. A variety of hybrids and cultivars, of both certain and uncertain parentage, mainly with *O. fruticosa* and *O. tetragona*, which suffer taxonomic confusion in the trade. Most grow 1 to 2 feet tall and as wide. Lance-shaped, dark green leaves to 3 inches long. Terminal clusters of yellow, cup-shaped, day-blooming flowers. Look for 'Fireworks', 'Yellow River', 'Highlight', 'Summer Solstice' and 'Youngii', among others. Zones 3 to 8.

Nodding sundrops, *O. perennis*, is widely offered but short-lived and not as showy as the hybrid sundrops.

Oenothera missouriensis.

OPHIOPOGON
(oh-fee-oh-*poh*-gon)
Mondo grass
Liliaceae—lily family

A strong contender with liriope for most-used edging or groundcover in warmer regions, mondo grass differs in that it is less hardy, with narrower leaves and metallic blue fruits. The introduction of black mondo grass from England added a plant to the gardening repertoire that offers stunning, dark-purple foliage.

Growing Guide
Partial to light shade. Moist but well-drained soil. Drought tolerant. May take several years to become established.

Propagation
Division, seed.

Uses
Edging, groundcover, between paving stones.

Species, Varieties, Cultivars, Hybrids
O. japonicus (jah-*pon*-ih-kus). Mondo grass. Japan. Grows 12 inches tall and as wide. Spreading clumps with dark green, grassy leaves to ¼ inch wide and 12 inches long. Short clusters of pale lilac flowers in summer, often hidden by foliage, followed by metallic blue berries. Several variegated cultivars. Zones 7 to 9.
O. planiscapus var. 'Nigrescens' (plahn-ih-*skah*-pus nih-*gres*-enz). Black mondo grass. Grows 6 inches tall and 12 inches wide. Slowly spreading clumps of dark purple, grassy leaves. Short clusters of white to pale pink flowers in summer followed by metallic black berries. Contrasts well with Japanese blood grass, blue-leaved grasses, or plants with light green leaves. Zones 6 to 9.

Ophiopogon *var. 'Nigrescens'*.

P

Paeonia.

PAEONIA
(pay-*on*-ee-ah)
Peony
Paeoniaceae—peony family

No garden would be complete without the large, silken blooms of peonies in late spring and early summer. Ubiquitous in gardens but with good reason, peonies are among the longest-lived of perennials, widely adaptable, with flowers readily produced with little effort. Thousands of cultivars and hybrids are available, providing a wide range of flower forms and colors.

Growing Guide
Full sun, partial shade in hotter climates. Humus-rich, moist but well-drained soil. Important to set the eyes, or red sprouts, at the proper depth, about 1 inch below the soil line. Taller types may need staking. To prevent botrytis blight, cut off all stems and

Paeonia lactiflora.

leaves in the fall. Peonies need a certain number of chilling hours to break dormancy, so in hotter areas select cultivars proven in these areas; also it's better to grow early to mid-season and single or Japanese flower forms in these areas. Use a winter mulch where needed to prevent heaving. Use fertilizer cautiously, as too much results in foliage rather than flowers.

Propagation
Best left undisturbed, but can be divided in the fall, cutting roots apart with a knife, with each piece having three eyes.

Uses
Beds and borders, in front of shrubs, as a low hedge, or beside a wall or fence. Cut flowers.

Species, Varieties, Cultivars, Hybrids
P. lactiflora (lak-tih-*floh*-rah). Chinese peony. Most peonies offered for sale and grown in gardens are cultivars or hybrids, rather than the species. Many of the thousands of offerings are most closely related to the common, or Chinese, peony (*P. lactiflora*). These are bushy plants growing 2 to 3 feet tall with large, divided, dark green, shiny leaves. Plants bloom in late spring, with 3- to 6-inch flowers in shades of white, creamy yellow, pink or red and in one of five forms: single, with eight petals and a prominent cluster of yellow stamens; Japanese, with a carnation-like center and a saucer-shaped petal collar; anemone, similar to Japanese but shaggier; semidouble, with stamens apparent; and double, with stamens missing or hidden. Zones 3 to 8.

P. officinalis (oh-fis-ih-*nah*-lis). Common peony, Memorial Day peony. Similar to the Chinese peony with 4-inch single crimson flowers with yellow stamens. Several cultivars with various shades of red or double flowers. Zones 3 to 8.

Other peonies to consider include *P. veitchii*, *P. tenuifolia*, and *P. mlokosewitschii*. Tree peonies, *P. suffruticosa*, are woody plants.

PAPAVER
(pah-*pah*-ver)
Poppy
Papaveraceae—
poppy family

Papaver orientale.

Poppies are beloved for their papery translucent petals in pastels or brilliant reds and oranges. The Oriental poppy is the only species among the hundred or so in the genus that is reliably perennial and long-lived. Others, such as the Iceland poppy, are best grown as annuals, along with the other truly annual species. Flowers are good for cutting if picked just as the buds begin to open in early morning and the stem ends are seared in a flame.

Growing Guide
Full sun. Average, well-drained soil. Poor drainage in winter is usually fatal. Staking may be necessary with taller types. Both a summer and winter mulch is beneficial. Plants go dormant after flowering, so plant poppies where other plants will fill in around them.

Propagation
Division, root cuttings.

Uses
Beds and borders.

Papaver orientale.

Species, Varieties, Cultivars, Hybrids
P. orientale (oh-ree-en-*tah*-lee). Oriental poppy. Asia. Grows 2 to 4 feet tall and 2 to 3 feet wide. Silver-green, rough-textured stems and leaves, which are lobed and toothed. Cup-shaped flowers in early summer to 4 inches across, often with a black eye, in shades of scarlet, red, orange, apricot, salmon, pink or white. Zones 2 to 7.

Patrinia scabiosifolia.

PATRINIA
(pah-*tree*-nee-ah)
Patrinia
Valerianaceae—valerian family

The tiny, long-lasting flowers of patrinia are beautiful even when faded, so the airy effect, reminiscent of lady's mantle, benefits the garden for many weeks. The quality of fragrance is questionable, smelling somewhat of dogs. The genus is named after a French naturalist, E. L. Patrin (1724–1815).

Growing Guide
Partial to light shade. Humus-rich, acid, moist but well-drained soil.

Propagation
Division, seed.

Uses
Beds and borders, blending other flowers and plants together.

Species, Varieties, Cultivars, Hybrids
P. gibbosa (gib-*bose*-ah). Japan. Grows to 2 feet tall and 1 foot wide. Slowly spreading, clump-forming plants with shiny, toothed, egg-shaped leaves to 6 inches long. Branched clusters of tiny yellow flowers in summer. Zones 5 to 8.

P. scabiosifolia (scab-ee-oh-sih-*foh*-lee-ah). Eastern Asia. Grows 3 to 5 feet tall and 2 feet wide. Slowly spreading, basal clumps of toothed, egg-shaped leaves, with stem leaves divided. Erect, leafy stems with branched clusters of numerous tiny yellow flowers, followed by attractive seeds. Self-sows. Zones 5 to 8.

PENSTEMON
(pen-*stay*-mon)
Beard tongue
Scrophulariaceae—figwort family

Many species of penstemon are native to North America, with certain ones having gone to Europe to get "refinement." They returned as cultivars and hybrids, with great variation in flower color and plant size. Upright plants with spiky clusters of pastel to scarlet, snapdragon-like flowers, penstemons are not particularly long-lived, but are easily grown. The genus name comes from the Greek, for five stamens.

Growing Guide
Full sun. Fertile, humus-rich, moist but well-drained soil. Cannot survive poorly drained winter conditions. Light winter mulch prevents heaving.

Penstemon barbatus *'Prairie Dusk'*.

Propagation
Seed, stem cuttings.

Uses
Beds and borders.

Species, Varieties, Cultivars, Hybrids
P. barbatus (bar-*bay*-tus). Beard tongue. Southwestern United States. Grows 2 to 3 feet tall and 18 inches wide. Basal tufts of egg-shaped leaves to 6 inches long. In summer, erect stems bear spikes of slightly nodding, tubular, 1-inch-long scarlet flowers with a bearded lower lip. Most cultivars grow 12 to 18 inches tall with white, pink, orange or scarlet flowers. Zones 3 to 8.

P. campanulatus (kam-pan-yew-*lay*-tus). Harebell penstemon. Central America. Grows 2 feet tall and as wide. Toothed, lance-shaped leaves to 3 inches long and tubular purple, violet, or white flowers. One parent of a number of good garden plants, including 'Apple Blossom' and 'Evelyn', both with pink flowers. Zones 6 to 8.

P. digitalis (dij-ih-*tay*-lis). Foxglove penstemon. Eastern and Central United States. Grows 3 feet tall and 2 feet wide. Clump-forming plants with lance-shaped leaves to 7 inches long, becoming smaller up the erect stems. Spikes of bell-shaped whitish pink flowers in early summer. 'Husker Red', with purple-red leaves and stems and white-flushed purple flowers, is popular. Better for hot, humid climates than the western North American natives. Zones 3 to 9.

PEROVSKIA
(peh-*roff*-skee-ah)
Russian sage
Labiatae—mint family

Perovskias provide a feathery haze of fine-textured gray foliage and tiny purple-blue flowers in summer into fall. Native from Iran to northwest India, most of the plants grown in gardens are hybrid seedlings of *P. abrotanoides* and *P. atriplicifolia*. There is great variation among the plants sold as Russian sage, including foliage ranging from undissected to finely divided, plant form being highly branched and shrubby to sparsely stemmed. It is best to buy plants that are known to be vegetatively propagated from exceptional plants, no matter what the name.

Growing Guide
Full sun. Average, well-drained soil. Drought tolerant. Must have good winter drainage. Cut back plants in spring to encourage bushy growth.

Propagation
Stem cuttings.

Uses
Beds and borders, especially good paired with daylilies and any plant with daisy-like flowers.

Species, Varieties, Cultivars, Hybrids
P. atriplicifolia (ah-trih-plis-ih-*foh*-lee-ah). Russian sage. Most plants sold under this species name are seedlings of various parentage. Grows 3 to 5 feet tall and 4 feet wide. Shrubby plant with variably cut and toothed leaves to about 2 inches long and 1 inch wide. Branched spikes 12 to 15 inches long with tiny tubular lavender-blue flowers for up to 4 months from midsummer to early fall. Zones 5 to 9.

Perovskia atriplicifolia.

Phlomis fruticosa.

PHLOMIS
(*floh*-miss)
Jerusalem sage
Labiatae—mint family

A well-grown plant of Jerusalem sage is rather spectacular, with its rounded, bushy form punctuated with whorls of yellow flowers spaced along the stems from base to top. There are other species in this genus that are more tender and therefore useful in Zones 7 to 9, including the yellow-flowered *P. russeliana* and the pink-flowered *P. samia*.

Growing Guide
Full sun, with partial shade in areas with hot, humid summers. Humus-rich, moist but well-drained soil is best, but dry soil is tolerated.

Propagation
Division, seed.

Uses
Beds and borders.

Species, Varieties, Cultivars, Hybrids
P. fruticosa (frew-tih-*koh*-sah). Jerusalem sage. Bushy plants with upright stems. Coarse, wrinkled, and woolly oval leaves to 4 inches long. Plants are evergreen from Zone 7 south. Twenty to 30 flowers surround the stem at each whorl of leaves. Blooming time depends on the locale, with spring bloom in the South, summer bloom in the North, and winter bloom in Southern California. Zones 4 to 8.

Phlox subulata.

PHLOX
(flox)
Phlox
Polemoniaceae—phlox family

Among the plants native to Eastern North America, no other genus can compare with that of *Phlox* in contributing such important perennials to the garden. From the bright patches of creeping phlox in early spring to the last of the garden phlox blooming in summer, these plants provide gardeners with readily available, easily grown, long-blooming masses of color in both sunny and shaded areas. When choosing phlox for the garden, be sure to consider some of the lesser-known kinds, which are some of the most carefree. All phlox bear the distinctive, five-petaled, flat-faced flowers.

Growing Guide
Full sun to light shade, depending on the species. Fertile, humus-rich, moist but well-drained soil. Grow disease-resistant varieties to prevent problems with mildew, and thin out *P. paniculata* cultivars to four to six stems to increase air circulation and keep foliage dry when watering. With soil kept evenly moist, spider mite problems are lessened. Deadhead to maintain vigor and prevent self-sowing.

Propagation
Division, seed, stem cuttings.

Uses
The taller types are best for beds and borders; use the shorter, spreading types in wildflower and woodland gardens; the mat-forming ones are ideal for spilling over walls, the fronts of borders, edging walks or rock gardens. Cut flowers.

Species, Varieties, Cultivars, Hybrids
P. divaricata (dih-var-ih-*kah*-tah). Wild blue phlox, woodland phlox. Eastern North America. Grows 1 foot tall and as wide. Plants spread slowly by creeping rhizomes and trailing, non-flowering shoots that root at the nodes. Dark green, 2-inch, oblong leaves. Small, loose clusters of slightly fragrant, 1½-inch, light blue flowers. Several cultivars, most with flowers in various shades

Phlox stolonifera.

Phlox paniculata.

of blue or pink, but the best is 'Fuller's White' growing to 8 inches tall. *P.* x *chattahoochee*, often listed as a cultivar, is thought to be a cross between *P. divaricata laphamii* and *P. pilosa*; the pale blue flowers have a purple eye. Grow in partial shade with humus-rich, moist but well-drained soil. Zones 3 to 9.

P. maculata (mak-yew-*lah*-tah). Spotted phlox, wild sweet William. Eastern North America. Grows 2 to 3 feet tall and 2 feet wide. Erect plants with hairy stems often mottled red. Roundly lance-shaped, glossy, dark green leaves to 4 inches long. Cone-shaped clusters of fragrant, pink flowers in early summer. Cultivars often replacing garden phlox because of their mildew resistance. More and more new cultivars, mainly with white or pink flowers, some with a darker eye. Grow in full sun in humus-rich, moist but well-drained soil. Zones 3 to 9.

P. paniculata (pah-nik-*yew*-lah-tah). Garden phlox. Eastern North America. Grows 3 to 4 feet tall and 2 feet wide. Clump-forming plants with stiff, erect, leafy stems. Oblong leaves to 6 inches long. Pyramidal clusters of ¾-inch flowers from midsummer to early fall. Great number of cultivars, with some

Phlox stolonifera.

variation in flowering time and with flowers in many shades of purple, pink, red and white, often with darker-colored eyes. Susceptible to mildew and spider mites. Thin to four to six stems. Full sun with humus-rich, moist but well-drained soil. Provide afternoon shade in hotter climates. Zones 4 to 8.

P. stolonifera (stoh-loh-*nif*-er-ah). Creeping phlox. Eastern North America. Grows 6 to 9 inches tall and 12 inches wide. Spreading plants, with stoloniferous roots and nonflowering shoots rooting at the nodes. Spoon-shaped leaves to 1 to 3 inches long. Clusters of 2 to 3¾-inch, lavender-blue flowers in spring. A number of cultivars, mainly with flowers of white or various shades of pink or blue. 'Sherwood Purple' is noted for its purple-blue, highly fragrant flowers. Excellent groundcover for shade. Zones 2 to 8.

P. subulata (sub-yew-*lah*-tah). Moss phlox, creeping phlox. Eastern North America. Grows 6 to 9 inches tall and 12 inches wide. Creeping mounds with narrow, linear, ½-inch-long leaves. Great numbers of ½- to ¾-inch flowers with notched petals completely cover the plants in early spring. The predominant color is a bright magenta pink, but a number of cultivars are available, in shades of blue, purple, pink, red and white. There are a number of hybrids between it and *P. nivalis* and *P. bifida*, both also with creeping growth. Grow in full sun in well-drained soil. Zones 2 to 9.

Phlox divaricata.

Physalis alkekengi.

PHYSALIS
(fye-*sal*-lis)
Chinese lantern
Solonaceae—nightshade family

The brightly decorative, bladderlike pods of Chinese lanterns add interest to gardens using orange in their color scheme, and provide material for dried decorations in autumn. With sprawling growth, physalis also have spreading roots, so be ready to contain or share.

Growing Guide
Full sun. Humus-rich, moist but well-drained soil. For use in dried arrangements, harvest pods just as they enlarge and begin changing to orange.

Propagation
Division, seed.

Uses
Beds and borders. Dried arrangements.

Species, Varieties, Cultivars, Hybrids
P. alkekengi (al-ke-*ken*-jee). Also listed as *P. franchetii*. Chinese lantern. Japan. Grows 18 to 24 inches tall and 24 inches wide. Broad, pointed leaves to 3 inches long on loose, open, branching plants. White, 1-inch flowers with yellow stamens borne near the top, followed by orange pods. 'Gigantea' has pods to 8 inches across, while 'Pygmaea' grows to 12 to 15 inches tall. Zones 3 to 9.

PHYSOSTEGIA
(fye-so-*stee*-jee-ah)
False dragonhead, obedient plant
Labiatae—mint family

False dragonheads are easily grown, bushy plants with stiff spikes of pink, magenta, rose, lilac or white tubular flowers that bloom for a long period in summer and fall. Excellent for cutting, a flower will "obediently" stay at the angle where it is placed. Spreading growth can be rather vigorous, so the species is best sited in areas of the garden where less aggressive plants won't be harmed, such as in meadows or along streams. Named cultivars are the better choice for beds and borders.

Physostegia virginiana.

Growing Guide
Full sun. Average to humus-rich, acid, moist soil. Drier soil is tolerated if plants are grown in partial shade.

Propagation
Division, stem cuttings.

Uses
Beds, borders, meadow gardens, near streams or pools. Cut flowers.

Species, Varieties, Cultivars, Hybrids
P. virginiana (ver-jin-ee-*ah*-na). False dragonhead, obedient plant. Eastern United States. Grows 3 to 4 feet tall and 3 feet wide. Spreading, clump-forming plants with stiff stems and toothed, lance-shaped leaves to 5 inches long. Spikes to 12 inches long in late summer and early fall with 1-inch tubular, lipped, and lobed flowers. Among the cultivars, consider 'Summer Snow', with pure white flowers; 'Variegata', with handsome variegated leaves and rose flowers; and 'Vivid', growing only 20 inches tall, with long-lasting, dark pink flowers. Zones 3 to 9.

PLATYCODON
(plat-ih-*koh*-don)
Balloon flower
Campanulaceae—bellflower family

Children of all ages are fascinated by the balloon-shaped flower buds that open to broadly bell-shaped, five-pointed flowers. For a closer look, cut the flower stems and bring indoors for bouquets. Plants are long-lived and require little care. The genus name is from the Greek *platys*, broad, and *kodon*, bell.

Growing Guide
Full sun to partial shade. Sandy to average, well-drained soil; good drainage in winter is essential. Plant with the crown just below the soil surface. Plants are slow to sprout in spring, so mark location well. May take several years to become established. Staking may be needed with taller types. Deadhead regularly to prolong blooming.

Propagation
Division, seed.

Uses
Beds and borders, best when grown in groups of three plants.

Species, Varieties, Cultivars, Hybrids
P. grandiflorus (gran-dih-*floh*-rus). Balloon flower. Japan, China. Grows 3 feet tall and 2 feet wide. Whorls of toothed, egg-shaped, blue-green leaves to 3 inches long on stiff, upright stems. Clusters of 2- to 3-inch flowers near the top of the stem in summer. A number of cultivars, with plants varying in size from 12 to 36 inches, and single or double flowers of violet, blue, pink or white. Zones 3 to 8.

Platycodon grandiflorus.

Polemonium caeruleum.

POLEMONIUM
(pol-eh-*moh*-nee-um)
Jacob's ladder
Polemoniaceae—phlox family

Evenly arranged leaflets give the appearance of a ladder on these perennials for shaded sites. In late spring or early summer, graceful clusters of blue or white flowers brighten the garden.

Growing Guide
Partial to light shade. Humus-rich, moist but well-drained soil. Remove faded flower stems.

Propagation
Division, seed.

Uses
Beds and borders, woodland gardens.

Species, Varieties, Cultivars, Hybrids
P. caeruleum (see-*rew*-lee-um). Jacob's ladder. Europe, Asia. Grows 18 to 24 inches tall and 18 inches wide. Clump-forming, upright plants with leaves composed of up to 20 paired, narrow leaflets. Light to deep blue, 1-inch flowers, in drooping clusters at the ends of stems in late spring and early summer. Does best in areas with cool summers. White-flowered form and several cultivars with deeper blue flowers available. Zones 4 to 7.

P. reptans (*rep*-tanz). Creeping polemonium. Eastern North America. Grows 8 to 12 inches tall and 12 inches wide. Sprawling plant with seven to 15 pairs of rounded leaflets. Terminal clusters of $\frac{1}{2}$-inch, bell-shaped blue flowers in spring. White-flowered form available. Zones 2 to 8.

POLYGONATUM
(poh-lig-oh-*nay*-tum)
Solomon's seal
Liliaceae—lily family

More and more gardeners are discovering the architectural grace that the foliage of Solomon's seal can add to the shady garden. Grown mainly for its tall, unbranched, arching stems with pointed, oval leaves, the plant also bears drooping, tubular white flowers in late spring and early summer. Slowly spreading by rhizomatous roots, plants gradually form handsome colonies. A number of stories attempt to explain the common name; one is that the flat, round scars on the roots resemble the seals on ancient documents.

Polygonatum commutatum.

Polygonatum odoratum 'Variegatum'.

Growing Guide

Partial to heavy shade. Humus-rich, moist but well-drained soil. Dry soil is somewhat tolerated.

Propagation

Division, seed.

Uses

Beds and borders, woodland gardens, with trees and shrubs. Cut flowers (actually foliage).

Species, Varieties, Cultivars, Hybrids

P. biflorum (bye-*floh*-rum). Small Solomon's seal. Eastern North America. Grows 1 to 3 feet tall and 2 feet wide. Arching stems with 4-inch leaves. Pairs of greenish white flowers beneath the leaves in spring, with dark blue berries in fall. A variant is the giant Solomon's seal, sometimes listed as *P. commutatum, P. canaliculatum* or *P. giganteum*, it grows from 3 to 7 feet tall with 7-inch leaves and white flowers in clusters of three to eight. Hybrids include forms with double flowers or variegated leaves. Zones 3 to 9.

P. odoratum (oh-door-*ah*-tum). Fragrant Solomon's seal. Europe, Asia. Grows 2 feet tall and as wide. Angular to ridged, arching stems with 4-inch leaves. Fragrant, greenish white, bell-shaped flowers, produced either singly or in pairs. The cultivar *P. odoratum thunbergii* 'Variegatum', with creamy-white leaf edges, is among the most elegant plants for shaded gardens. Zones 3 to 9.

POLYGONUM
(poh-*lig*-oh-num)
Fleeceflower, knotweed
Polygonaceae—buckwheat family

Anyone who has ever fought knotweed in the garden may wonder why you'd actually try to grow it, but there are a few civilized members that can make a positive contribution, albeit with plenty of room. The genus *Polygonum* has been redirected to *Persicaria* and *Fallopia*, so both old and new names are given below.

Growing Guide
Full sun to partial shade. Humus-rich, moist but well-drained soil. Must have at least afternoon sun in hotter climates to prevent leaf scorching. May be bothered by Japanese beetles. Prune to control spreading growth.

Propagation
Division.

Uses
Beds and borders, groundcover.

Polygonum affine *'Donald Lowndes'*.

Polygonum amplexicaule *'Inverleith'*.

Species, Varieties, Cultivars, Hybrids
Polygonum affine (a-*fee*-nee). (*Persicaria affinis*). Himalayan fleeceflower. Himalayas. Grows 12 inches tall and as wide. Spreading, mat-forming plants with semiwoody stems. Lance-shaped, glossy, dark green leaves to 4 inches long. Leaves turn bronze in the fall and persist until spring. In summer to early fall, dense, 2- to 3-inch spikes of pinkish red flowers rise above the foliage. Several cultivars, but 'Donald Lowndes' is among the best. Zones 3 to 7.

P. amplexicaule (am-pleks-i-*kaw*-lee). (*Persicaria amplexicaulis*). Himalayas. Grows 4 feet tall and as wide. Large, leafy plant with dark green, egg-shaped leaves to 6 inches long. Numerous thin, 6-inch spikes of red flowers from summer into fall. Several cultivars with red, pink, or white flowers. Zones 5 to 8.

***P. bistorta* 'Superbum'** (biss-*tor*-tah soo-*perb*-um). (*Persicaria bistorta*). Europe, Asia. Grows 2 to 3 feet tall and 2 feet wide. Vigorous, clump-forming plants with oval leaves to 6 inches long and a prominently white midrib. Dense spikes, 4 to 6 inches long, of pink flowers in early summer, held high above the foliage. May rebloom in late summer if soil remains moist and cool. Zones 3 to 8.

PORTERANTHUS
(por-ter-*an*-thus)
Bowman's root
Rosaceae—rose family

Woodland gardens needn't be limited to spring-blooming plants. Bowman's root brings graceful growth and delightful starry flowers to the woodland garden in summer.

Growing Guide
Partial to half shade. Humus-rich, moist but well-drained soil.

Propagation
Division, seed.

Uses
Beds and borders, woodland gardens.

Species, Varieties, Cultivars, Hybrids
P. trifoliata (trih-foh-lee-*ah*-tah). Also listed as *Gillenia trifoliata*. Bowman's root. Eastern North America. Grows 2 to 4 feet tall and 2 feet wide. Bushy, clump-forming plants with reddish stems and dark green, lance-shaped, deeply cut leaves. Masses of star-shaped, white flowers to 2 inches wide in summer. Zones 4 to 8.

Porteranthus trifoliata.

POTENTILLA
(poh-ten-*till*-ah)
Cinquefoil, potentilla
Rosaceae—rose family

Potentillas are mainly thought of as woody shrubs for the garden, but a few of the 500 or so species are worthwhile perennials. Both the leaves and flowers resemble those of strawberries, with flower colors including white, pink, yellow and red. The genus name comes from the Latin *potens*, powerful, a reference to the medicinal properties of some species.

Growing Guide
Full sun, with partial shade in hotter climates. Average, well-drained soil. Drought tolerant.

Propagation
Division, seed.

Uses
Beds and borders, rock gardens.

Species, Varieties, Cultivars, Hybrids
P. x *menziesii* (men-*zeez*-ee-ee). Hybrid cinquefoil. Hybrid origin. Grows 12 to 18 inches tall and as wide. Open, clump-forming plants with silver-gray foliage held on long stems. Sprays of 1-inch, single or semidouble flowers in brilliant shades of red, orange or yellow. Zones 5 to 8.
P. nepalensis (nep-ah-*len*-sis). Nepal cinquefoil. Nepal. Grows 18 inches tall and 2 feet wide. Open, clump-forming plants with hairy leaves held on long stems. Produces sprays of 1-inch carmine or orange-scarlet flowers for a long period in summer. Zones 5 to 8.

Potentilla atrosanguinea.

Primula denticulata.

PRIMULA
(*prim*-yew-lah)
Primrose
Primulaceae—primrose family

It's hard to imagine spring without primroses, even if it only means setting out a few plants from the grocery. But with over 400 species and innumerable cultivars, primroses offer a vast array of forms and colors for the garden. Sometimes considered strictly plants for cool-summer climates, many of these spring-blooming plants are easily grown throughout the country with help from the specialist mail-order nurseries and the American Primrose Society.

Growing Guide
Growing requirements vary from species to species, but generally primroses are plants for partial shade and humus-rich, moist but well-drained soil. Provide both summer and winter mulch. Plants are susceptible to slugs, snails, black vine weevils, aphids, and rust and leaf spot diseases.

Propagation
Division, seed.

Uses
Varies with species, but basically for woodland gardens, planted under shrubs, near streams or pools, or rock gardens.

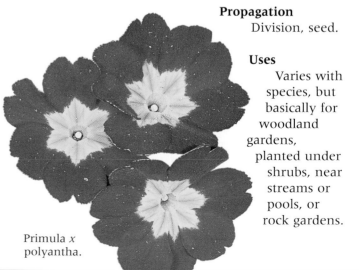

Primula *x* polyantha.

Primula japonica.

Primula *x* polyantha.

Species, Varieties, Cultivars, Hybrids

P. auricula (ow-*rik*-yew-lah). Auricula primrose. European Alps. Grows 6 inches tall and as wide. Thick, oval leaves to 6 inches long. Stems and flowers densely coated with the powdery substance called farina. Clusters of fragrant yellow flowers in early spring. The variety *ciliata* does not have farina and flowers are not fragrant. Cultivars with red or yellow flowers. Partial shade with alkaline, gritty soil. Zones 3 to 8.

P. denticulata (den-tik-yew-*lah*-tah). Drumstick primrose. Himalayas. Grows 12 inches tall and as wide. Spoon-shaped, finely toothed leaves, 4 inches long at flowering, maturing to 12 inches long. Globular clusters of lavender, white or pink flowers with yellow eyes in early spring. One of the easiest to grow. Many cultivars. Zones 5 to 8.

P. japonica (ja-*pon*-ih-kah). Japanese primrose. Japan. Grows 1 to 2 feet tall and 12 to 18 inches wide. Vigorous, spreading species for wet soil. Toothed, lobed, spoon-shaped leaves to 12 inches long. Sturdy flower stems bear successive whorls, called candelabras, of 1-inch purple, magenta, pink or white flowers in late spring. Many cultivars and related species. Zones 5 to 7.

P. x polyantha (pah-lee-*anth*-ah). Polyantha primrose. Hybrid origin. Grows 8 to 12 inches tall and 10 inches wide. Basal rosettes of textured, oval leaves. Clusters of 1½-inch flowers on 4- to 6-inch stems in early spring. Vast number of colors, either single or bicolor. Important plant for potted-plant market; these can be transplanted outdoors. Combines well with bleeding hearts, small hostas, hellebores, bloodroot and other spring-blooming perennials for partial shade with humus-rich, moist but well-drained soil. Zones 3 to 8.

P. sieboldii (see-*bold*-ee-eye). Siebold primrose. Japan. Grows 12 inches tall and as wide. Wrinkled, heart-shaped, scalloped-edged, downy leaves to 4 inches long. Flower stems to 12 inches tall with clusters of 1½-inch flowers of purple, pink or white. Foliage goes dormant in summer. Partial to half shade with humus-rich, moist but well-drained soil. Zones 4 to 8.

P. vulgaris (vul-*gah*-ris). English primrose. Europe. Grows 6 to 8 inches tall and as wide. Toothed, wrinkled, roundly lance-shaped, bright green leaves, 3 inches long when flowering, maturing to 6 inches long. Tubular, 1-inch-long, pale yellow flowers in spring. Subspecies with white or pink flowers. Naturally grows in woodlands and meadows, so tolerates a wider range of conditions than many primroses. Zones 5 to 8.

Primula sieboldii.

Primula vulgaris.

PRUNELLA
(pruh-*nell*-ah)
Self-heal
Labiatae—mint family

The name may imply something that looks like one of Cinderella's sisters, but in fact, self-heal is a rather pretty, though diminutive, spreading plant. Forming dense mats of foliage, the plants bloom profusely in summer. Both the common and botanical names refer to the medicinal uses of certain species, with the genus name derived from the German *brunellen*, for an inflammation thought to be cured by the plant.

Growing Guide
Full sun to partial shade. Any moist soil. Deadhead flowers to prevent self-sowing.

Propagation
Division, seed.

Uses
Groundcover, particularly near streams or pools.

Species, Varieties, Cultivars, Hybrids
P. x *webbiana* (web-ee-*ah*-nah). Hybrid self-heal. Hybrid origin. Grows to 8 inches tall and 18 inches wide. Mat-forming plants with dark green, egg-shaped leaves to 2 inches long. Whorled clusters of hooded and lipped ½-inch flowers in summer. Several cultivars with various flower colors, including white, purple-blue, lavender, red and pink, with 'White Loveliness' bearing larger flowers than normal. Zones 5 to 8.

Prunella x webbiana.

Pulmonaria *'Roy Davidson'*.

PULMONARIA
(pul-moh-*nar*-ee-ah)
Lungwort
Boraginaceae—borage family

Generally thought of as a subtle plant, pulmonarias can have a significant impact on the spring garden, particularly if some of the showier cultivars are planted in large drifts. Pulmonarias are characterized by spotted leaves and spring-blooming flowers that are often pink in bud but opening to blue. Both the genus and common names refer to the medicinal use of the plant for lung ailments in the sixteenth and seventeenth centuries, based on the "doctrine of signatures," or that the outward appearance of a plant suggested its medicinal uses.

Growing Guide
Partial to full shade. Humus-rich, moist but well-drained soil. Provide a summer mulch to keep soil moist. Plants spread by creeping roots, but are seldom invasive.

Propagation
Division.

Uses
Beds and borders. Among the best of groundcovers for shady areas, particularly under trees and shrubs or massed along a path.

Species, Varieties, Cultivars, Hybrids
P. angustifolia (an-gus-tih-*foh*-lee-ah). Blue lungwort. Europe. Grows 9 to 12 inches tall and 18 to 24 inches wide. Lance-shaped, unspotted, bristly, dark green leaves 8 to 12 inches long. Little sprays of funnel-shaped, nodding flowers, pink bud, open to deep blue in early spring. Makes a good groundcover under spring-blooming shrubs like forsythia and competes well with trees and shrubs for moisture and nutrients. Several cultivars, all very similar, with dark blue flowers. Zones 2 to 8.

P. longifolia (long-gih-*foh*-lee-ah). Long-leaf lungwort. Europe. Grows 9 to 12 inches tall and 18 to 24 inches wide. Narrow, pointed, spotted leaves 12 to 18 inches long. Dense sprays of vivid, purple-blue, funnel-shaped flowers in mid-spring. Holds up well in hot-summer climates. Zones 3 to 8.

P. rubra (*rew*-brah). Red lungwort. Europe. Grows 12 to 18 inches tall and 24 inches wide. Lance-shaped, velvety, pale green, unspotted leaves that are evergreen in milder areas. Sprays of coral-red, tubular flowers appear before the foliage in very early spring. Several cultivars, with flowers in various shades of red, pink and salmon. Zones 4 to 7.

P. saccharata (sah-kah-*rah*-tah). Bethelem sage. Europe. Grows 12 to 18 inches tall and 2 feet wide. Handsome leaves three times as long as wide, heavily spotted with silver, gray or white; evergreen in milder climates. Showy flower clusters in early spring, with pink buds opening to funnel-shaped blue flowers. Many excellent cultivars with various leaf markings and flower color, including shades of blue, pink or white. Zones 3 to 8.

Pulmonaria saccharata *'Sissinghurst White'*.

R

RANUNCULUS
(rah-*nun*-kew-lus)
Buttercup
Ranunculaceae—buttercup family

Buttercups are found growing around the world, with many being invasive weeds but a few providing

Ranunculus aconitifolius.

their cheerful flowers in a more restrained manner. The genus name is derived from the Latin *rana*, frog, alluding to the wet soil many species prefer.

Growing Guide
Full sun to partial shade. Moist, well-drained soil.

Propagation
Division, seed.

Uses
Beds and borders.

Species, Varieties, Cultivars, Hybrids
R. aconitifolius (ah-kon-ee-tih-*foh*-lee-us). Aconite buttercup. Europe. Grows 2 to 3 feet tall and as wide. Glossy, dark green, fan-shaped leaves divided into three to five parts. Large, open, branching sprays of 1-inch white flowers in late spring and early summer. The varieties are grown more than the species, including 'Flore Pleno', with double white flowers; 'Platanifolius' ('Pleniflorus'), with large, single flowers; and 'Luteus Plenus', with double yellow flowers. Zones 5 to 8.

R. acris 'Stevenii' (*ay*-kris steh-*ven*-ee-eye). Steven's buttercup. Grows 3 to 4 feet tall and 2 feet wide. Leaves divided into three to seven sections. Large, open, branching sprays of 1-inch yellow flowers in spring. Not invasive, as the species is. Zones 3 to 7.

RATIBIDA

(rah-*tih*-bih-dah)
Prairie coneflower,
Mexican hat
Compositae—daisy family

From the prairies and
plains of the southwestern
United States comes this
drought-tolerant plant with
colorful daisy-like flower
with prominent centers.
These high-domed centers
surrounded by drooping
yellow, red-brown or
mahogany rays provide the
source of the common name.

Growing Guide

Full sun. Any well-drained
soil.

Propagation

Division, seed.

Uses

Beds and borders, meadow
gardens, drought-tolerant gardens.

Species, Varieties, Cultivars, Hybrids

R. columnifera (col-um-*nif*-er-
ah). Mexican hat, prairie
coneflower. Central and
southwestern North America.
Grows 2 to 3 feet tall and 18 inches
wide. Coarse, hairy, gray-green
leaves divided into seven to nine
segments. Flowers borne singly on
long stalks; yellow ray flowers
surrounding 1½-inch-tall gray to
tan central cone. The variety
pulcherrima has mahogany-red and
yellow ray flowers. Zones 3 to 9.

R. pinnata (pin-*nay*-tah). Gray-
head coneflower, green coneflower,
drooping coneflower. North
America. Grows 4 feet tall and 18
inches wide. Coarse, hairy leaves
divided into three to five leaflets.
Long stems bear flowers with
golden yellow rays and a gray or
green ¾-inch-tall central cone.
Zones 3 to 9.

Ratibida pinnata.

Ratibida columnifera.

Ratibida columnifera.

Rheum palmatum.

RHEUM

(*ree*-um)
Rhubarb
Polygonaceae—buckwheat family

Few temperate plants are as
boldly exotic as the rhubarbs,
whether you choose a strictly
ornamental species or the edible
kind. The advantage of edible
rhubarb is that it is easy to grow,
and you get dessert. Care and
attention is the price to pay for the
striking ornamental types. Either
way, the adventurous spirit brings
rewards.

Growing Guide

Partial to light shade for
ornamental types; edible rhubarb
can withstand both full sun to
partial shade. Fertile, humus-rich,
constantly moist but well-drained
soil. Remove flower buds on
edible types prior to blooming;
remove faded flower spikes on
ornamental types. Both summer
and winter mulches are beneficial.
Takes several years to become
established.

Propagation
Division, seed.

Uses
Beds and borders for both types, or near streams and pools or bog gardens for ornamental types.

Species, Varieties, Cultivars, Hybrids
R. rhabarbarum (rah-bar-*bar*-um). Rhubarb. Manchuria. Grows 3 to 4 feet tall and as wide. Clump-forming plants with celery-like, green or red stems to 2 feet long. Heart-shaped, wavy, dark green leaves to 1½ feet long. 'MacDonald' and 'Cherry' have red stems. Zones 4 to 8.

R. palmatum (pahl-*may*-tum). Ornamental rhubarb. China. Grows 5 to 8 feet tall and 4 to 6 feet wide. Fan-like, deeply cut, toothed, heart-shaped, dark green leaves to 3 feet wide. Branched 2-foot spikes of white, pink or red flowers in early summer. Cultivars offer purple foliage that becomes green by summer, staying purple-red underneath. Zones 5 to 7.

RODGERSIA
(rod-*jer*-see-ah)
Rodgersia
Saxifragaceae—saxifrage family

Only a few rodgersias are needed to make a strong architectural statement near a stream or other water feature, for they are large, bold plants. With the right site, they are worth the effort needed to meet their requirements. The genus is named after Rear Admiral John Rodgers of the U.S. Navy, who was in charge of the expedition during which rodgersias were first brought to the States from Asia.

Growing Guide
Partial to light shade. Humus-rich, moist soil. Can tolerate moist but well-drained soil. Does not do well in areas with hot, humid summers. Subject to leaf scorch if it gets too much sun or soil becomes too dry. May take several years to establish.

Propagation
Division, seed.

Uses
Beds or borders, near woodland streams or pools. Combines well with hostas.

Species, Varieties, Cultivars, Hybrids
R. aesculifolia (ess-kih-li-*foh*-lee-ah). Fingerleaf rodgersia. China. Grows 3 to 5 feet tall and 4 feet wide. Clump-forming plants with fan-shaped, bronze-tinged, toothed leaves divided into seven leaflets, each to 10 inches long. Clusters to 2 feet tall of fragrant, ivory to pink flowers in summer. Bronzeleaf rodgersia, *R. podophylla*, is similar, but with five-parted leaves. Zones 5 to 6.

R. pinnata (pin-*nah*-tah). Featherleaf rodgersia. China. Grows 3 to 4 feet tall and as wide. Clump-growing plants with bronze-tinged leaves with five to nine toothed, lance-shaped leaflets to 8 inches long. Branched, dense clusters of rose-red flowers in late spring. Several cultivars with flowers in white or shades of red or pink, with 'Superba' among the best. Zones 5 to 7.

R. tabularis (tab-yew-*lay*-ris). Also listed as *Astilboides tabularis*. Shieldleaf rodgersia. China, Korea. Grows 2 to 3 feet tall and as wide. Leaves are circular, and shallowly lobed, 2 to 3 feet across, with the stem attached to the middle. Plumy spikes of creamy white flowers. Zones 5 to 7.

Rodgersia aesculifolia.

Rudbeckia fulgida *'Goldsturm'*.

RUDBECKIA
(rud-*bek*-ee-ah)
Black-eyed Susan, orange coneflower
Compositae—daisy family

Black-eyed Susans, brightening fields and roadsides in summer over much of the United States, are matched in tended gardens—private, corporate and governmental—with the cultivar 'Goldsturm', bred in Germany in 1937. Certainly, rudbeckias are easily grown, long-lived, long-blooming plants that deserve the attention. Their ubiquity can be accepted when well used, particularly in creating warm-color gardens. They also provide cut flowers, and the cones remaining after the flowers have faded provide interest in the winter landscape.

Growing Guide
Full sun. Average to moist but well-drained soil.

Propagation
Division, seed.

Rudbeckia laciniata *'Golden Glow'*.

Uses
Beds and borders, meadow gardens, massed in large drifts. Cut flowers.

Species, Varieties, Cultivars, Hybrids
R. fulgida (*full*-jih-dah). Orange coneflower. United States. Grows 2 to 3 feet tall and 18 to 24 inches wide. Erect, clump-forming plants with toothed, lance-shaped, hairy, dark green leaves to 6 inches long. Branching stems bear 2- to 3-inch orange-yellow daisy-like flowers with brown-black centers from summer to fall. The cultivar 'Goldsturm' grows to 2 feet tall with 4-inch flowers; it should come only from vegetatively propagated plants as seed-grown strains are highly variable. Zones 3 to 9.

R. laciniata (lass-in-ee-*ay*-tah). Cutleaf coneflower. North America. Grows 4 to 6 feet tall and 3 to 4 feet wide. Vigorous, clump-forming plants with hairy stems and lance-shaped, deeply cut, toothed leaves. Branching stems with 3- to 4-inch flowers with drooping yellow rays and green centers in summer. 'Golden Glow' grows 3 to 5 feet tall with double, golden yellow flowers. Zones 3 to 9.

R. nitida (*nit*-ih-dah). Shining coneflower. Southern United States. Grows 3 to 4 feet tall and 2 to 3 feet wide. Clump-forming plants with egg-shaped leaves. Branching stems with 3- to 4-inch flowers with drooping yellow rays and green centers in summer. Cultivars supersede species. 'Gold-quelle' grows 3 feet tall with double yellow flowers; 'Herbstonne' ('Autumn Sun') grows 4 to 6 feet tall with an abundance of green-centered yellow flowers in late summer and fall. Zones 4 to 10.

R. triloba (try-*loh*-bah). Three-lobed coneflower. United States. Grows 2 to 3 feet tall and 18 inches wide. Leaves have three lobes. Numerous 1½-inch yellow flowers with purple-black centers in summer. 'Nana' grows 2 feet tall and blooms from early to midsummer. Zones 3 to 10.

RUTA
(*rew*-tah)
Rue, herb of grace
Rutaceae—rue family

Rue is among the most ornamental of perennial "herbs." The glaucous blue, finely textured foliage enhances any number of color combinations in the garden. It has been cultivated in gardens for thousands of years (with the Romans bringing it to Britain), and utilized for any number of medicinal and magical reasons. The larvae of the black swallowtail butterfly find the foliage particularly to their liking.

Growing Guide
Full sun. Any well-drained soil. Cut back to old wood in spring. Some people are allergic to a volatile oil produced by the plant in hot weather.

Propagation
Stem cuttings.

Uses
Beds and borders. Butterfly garden.

Species, Varieties, Cultivars, Hybrids
R. graveolens (grah-vee-*oh*-lenz). Rue, herb of grace. Southern Europe. Grows 2 to 3 feet tall and 18 inches wide. Shrubby plant with finely divided, rounded, glaucous blue leaves with a pungent odor and bitter taste. Small clusters of yellow-green, four-petalled, ¾-inch flowers in summer. 'Blue Beauty' and 'Blue Mound' grow to an 18-inch mound. 'Jackman's Blue' grows 30 inches tall with waxen, very blue foliage. 'Variegata' has leaves dappled with white, but they revert to blue as they age. Zones 5 to 9.

Ruta graveolens.

S

SALVIA
(*sal*-vee-ah)
Sage
Labiatae—mint family

Travel to almost any temperate or tropical part of the world, and a salvia will be native there. With about 800 species of annual, perennial and woody plants, salvias rank as one of the most important contributors to the garden. Their reputation is enhanced by their ease of growth and long flowering period. The genus name is derived from the Latin *salvere*, to save, referring to the healing properties of certain species, especially common sage, *S. officinalis*, which has been used since ancient times. Generally, sages have the typical square stems of the mints, with pointed, egg-shaped, often aromatic leaves. The flowers tend to be tubular, with a hooded upper lip and a protruding lower lip. Often borne in spiked whorls, the flowers come in a great range of colors, but most of the perennial garden types are deep purples and blues.

Growing Guide
Full sun. Average to humus-rich, moist but well-drained soil. Good winter drainage is essential. Deadhead and trim plants back after flowering to keep growth compact and encourage reblooming. A loose winter mulch is beneficial.

Propagation
Division, seed, stem cuttings.

Uses
Beds and borders.

Salvia officinalis *'Purpurascens'*.

Species, Varieties, Cultivars, Hybrids
S. argentea (ar-*jen*-tee-ah). Silver sage. Europe. Grows 3 feet tall and 2 feet wide. Basal rosettes of thick, silver-woolly, wedge-shaped leaves to 8 inches long. Grown for its foliage rather than its white flowers, which should be removed. Some flowers may be allowed to bloom and go to seed for new plants, as silver sage is short-lived. Foliage will suffer in hot, rainy weather. Zones 5 to 9.

S. azurea (ah-*zoo*-ree-ah). Azure sage. Southeastern United States. Grows 3 to 4 feet tall and 2 to 3 feet wide. Basal growth with erect, branching stems. Lance-shaped leaves to 3 inches long, becoming smaller up the stem. Spikes of azure-blue flowers in whorled clusters from late summer to mid-fall. Tolerant of high temperatures. The variety *grandiflora* (*S. pitcheri*) has hairy stems and larger flowers of sky blue. Stake or allow to flop and bloom through other plants. Zones 5 to 9.

S. jurisicii (jur-ih-*sik*-ee-eye). Jurisici's sage. Yugoslavia. Grows 12 to 18 inches tall and 18 inches wide. Branching plants with hairy stems and hairless, toothed, oblong leaves; stem leaves are deeply divided. Branching 8-inch spikes of deep lilac, upside-down flowers in early summer. Deserves to be more widely grown. Zones 5 to 8.

Salvia argentea.

S. officinalis (oh-fis-ih-*nah*-lis). Common sage. Europe, Asia Minor. Grows 2 to 3 feet tall and 2 feet wide. Shrubby to sprawling plants with woody lower stems. Gray-green, oblong leaves. Spikes of purple flowers in summer. White-flowered form, cultivars showing variously colored foliage, including, 'Purpurascens' with reddish purple leaves, 'Aurea', with leaves variegated with green and yellow, and 'Tricolor', with leaves variegated with white, purple to pink, and green. There are also forms with extra-large leaves and others with smaller leaves and dwarf growth. Zones 4 to 9.

S. pratensis (prah-*ten*-sis). Also listed as *S. haematodes*. Meadow sage. Europe. Grows 2 to 3 feet tall and 2 feet wide. Basal growth with long-stemmed, hairy, wrinkled, oblong leaves 3 to 6 inches long. Branching, flowering stems with lavender-blue flowers in early summer, with repeat bloom if deadheaded. Self-sows. Subject to much taxonomic debate. A number of cultivars, including a white-flowered form and a variegated form, and others with flowers of dark violet, light violet, rich blue, rose-purple or rose-red. Zones 5 to 9.

S. x superba (soo-*per*-bah). May be sold as *S. nemerosa* or *S. sylvestris*. Hybrid sage. Hybrid origin. Grows 18 to 36 inches tall and 3 feet wide. Clump-forming plant with woody stems at the base; leafy stems bear gray-green, toothed, rough, oblong leaves to 3 inches long. Numerous spikes of densely packed violet-blue flowers in early to midsummer. If cut back hard after blooming, flowering is repeated in late summer or fall. Does best with cool nights and moist soil, but tolerates drier soil. Choose shorter cultivars for hot, humid summer. Many cultivars, with most varying in height. The best known are 'Blue Queen', 'East Friesland', 'Lubecca' and 'May Night'. There are also pink-flowered forms. Try to find vegetatively propagated rather than seed-grown plants. Zones 4 to 8.

Salvia x superba 'Blue Queen'.

SANGUINARIA
(san-gwi-*nar*-ee-ah)
Bloodroot
Papaveraceae—poppy family

Most often used in woodland wildflower gardens, patches of bloodroot are being seen with greater frequency in more formal shaded settings. And deservedly so, as the foliage and flowers both provide inspiration with their spring appearance. The yet-to-fully-open, folded leaves encircle the white flowers, which resemble miniature water lilies. Both genus and common names refer to the reddish yellow sap found in the fleshy roots, which was used as a dye by Native Americans.

Sanguinaria canadensis.

Growing Guide
Full sun in early spring, such as under deciduous trees and shrubs, followed by light to half-shade. Humus-rich, moist but well-drained soil. Foliage goes dormant by mid- to late summer.

Propagation
Division, seed. When buying, be sure the plants are nursery-propagated, not gathered from the wild.

Uses
Woodland gardens, beds and borders.

Species, Varieties, Cultivars, Hybrids
S. canadensis (kan-ah-*den*-sis). Bloodroot. Eastern North America. Grows 6 to 9 inches tall and 12 inches wide. Gray- to blue-green, wavy, lobed, kidney-shaped leaves. Single white flowers to 3 inches across in early spring. Flowers remain closed on cloudy days. Each flower lasts only a few days, but a number are produced over several weeks. 'Multiplex' has double flowers with up to 50 petals, that are longer lasting; it must be propagated by division. Zones 4 to 9.

SANGUISORBA
(san-gwi-*sor*-bah)
Burnet
Rosaceae—rose family

Herb gardeners enjoy burnet (*S. officinalis*) for its fine-textured appearance as well as the cucumber flavor it adds to food. For perennial gardeners, several other species in the genera offer handsome foliage and flowers in summer and early fall. The genus name comes the Latin *sanguis*, blood, and *sorbere*, to staunch or soak up, referring to its styptic ability.

Growing Guide
Full sun, with partial shade in hot-summer areas. Humus-rich, acid, moist soil. Deadhead to prolong flowering. Summer mulch is beneficial.

Propagation
Division, seed.

Uses
Beds and borders, bog gardens, near streams or pools. Cut flowers.

Species, Varieties, Cultivars, Hybrids
S. canadensis (kan-ah-*den*-sis). Also listed as *Poterium canadense*. Canadian burnet. Eastern North America. Grows 4 to 6 feet tall and 4 feet wide. Vigorous, clump-forming plants. Compound leaves to 12 inches long, divided into 10 to 15, toothed, oblong, 3-inch segments. Spikes of white flowers resembling bottle brushes, to 6 inches long, in summer. Zones 3 to 8.

S. obtusa (ob-*tew*-sah). Japanese burnet. Japan. Grows 2 to 4 feet tall and 2 to 3 feet wide. Graceful, clump-forming plants with compound leaves to 18 inches long, divided into seven to 13 segments with blue- to gray-green undersides. Nodding, bottle-brush spikes, 3 to 4 inches long of bright pink flowers in midsummer. White-flowered form available. Zones 4 to 8.

Sanguisorba canadensis.

Santolina chamaecyparissus.

SANTOLINA
(san-toh-*lee*-nah)
Lavender cotton
Compositae—daisy family

Among the possibilities for gray-foliaged plants, santolina offers finely textured, low-growing, mounding plants for the front of the border. Able to withstand shearing and shaping, santolinas are often used in knot gardens or as low hedges for borders. The foliage is aromatic and easily dried, traits much appreciated by those making winter arrangements.

Growing Guide
Full sun. Sandy to average, well-drained soil. Prune after flowering to encourage fresh new growth. Does best in dry climates. Winter mulch is beneficial.

Propagation
Stem cuttings.

Uses
Beds and borders, rock gardens, low hedges.

Species, Varieties, Cultivars, Hybrids
S. chamaecyparissus (ka-mee-sip-pah-*ris*-is). Lavender cotton. Mediterranean. Grows 1 to 2 feet tall and 2 feet wide. Shrubby, many-branching, rounded plants with woody lower stems. Numerous narrow, toothed, aromatic gray leaves to 1½ inches long. Summer-blooming, globular yellow flowers to ½ inch across. Cut them off if they're not to your liking. Green lavender cotton, *S. virens*, is similar but with bright green leaves. Zones 6 to 8.

SAPONARIA
(sap-oh-*nah*-ree-ah)
Soapwort
Caryophyllaceae—pink
family

Soap manufacturers don't have to fear competition from soapwort, although the plant sap certainly does have a soapy quality. Better to focus on the great splash of pink flowers tumbling among other flowers or over walls, rocks, or banks in midsummer.

Growing Guide
Full sun. Poor to average, well-drained soil. Cut back hard after flowering to encourage new growth and repeat bloom. Does not do well in hot-summer areas.

Propagation
Seed.

Uses
Edges of raised beds or walls, rock gardens.

Saponaria officinalis.

Species, Varieties, Cultivars, Hybrids
S. ocymoides (oh-kim-*oye*-deez). Rock soapwort. Alps. Grows 6 to 8 inches tall and 12 inches wide. Trailing plants forming loose mats of many-branched stems with hairy, oval, olive green leaves ½ to 1 inch long. Airy sprays of small pink to rose flowers in early summer. Several varieties, including 'Rubra Compacta', forming compact mounds, and 'Splendens', with large, intensely rose-pink flowers, and 'Alba' with white flowers. Zones 3 to 7.

S. officinalis (oh-fis-ih-*nah*-lis). Soapwort, bouncing bet. Southern Europe; naturalized in Eastern and Midwestern United States. Grows 1 to 3 feet tall and 18 inches wide. Erect, unbranched stems arising from spreading, stoloniferous roots. Egg-shaped, prominently veined, dark green leaves to 4 inches long. Summer-blooming, fragrant pink flowers are 1 to 1½ inches across, with five notched petals. Pinching growth or staking necessary to keep plants from straggling. The double-flowered forms, in white, rose-pink or crimson, are best for the garden, blooming for many weeks. They are good cut flowers. Zones 4 to 8.

Saponaria ocymoides.

Scabiosa caucasica *'Fama'*.

SCABIOSA
(skab-ee-*oh*-sah)
Pincushion flower, scabious
Dipsacaceae—teasel family

Blooming for weeks on end, mainly in shades of soft blue, scabiosas are deserving of the popularity as flowers for both the garden and in bouquets. The pincushion moniker relates most strongly to the annual *S. atropurpurea*, with its tufted flowers resembling a velvet pincushion. The genus name has a more prosaic origin, coming from the Latin *scabies*, itch, referring both to the rough leaves and problems early herbalists sought to relieve with it.

Growing Guide
Full sun, with partial shade in hot-summer areas. Sandy to average, neutral to alkaline, well-drained soil. Deadhead to prolong blooming. May be slow to establish.

Propagation
Division, seed.

Uses
Beds and borders. Cut flowers.

Species, Varieties, Cultivars, Hybrids
S. caucasica (kau-*kah*-si-kuh). Pincushion flower. Caucasus. Grows 18 to 24 inches tall and 2 feet wide. Basal leaves are lance-shaped, with a whitish surface covering. Stem leaves are lobed and divided into narrow sections. Slender stems bear flat, pale blue flowers to 3 inches across in summer. A number of cultivars, with blue or white flowers. 'Fama' is popular for its strongly blue, silver-centered flowers on 18-inch stems. 'Butterfly Blue' grows 12 inches tall and blooms from spring until fall. Zones 3 to 7.

S. graminifolia (gram-mih-nih-*foh*-lee-ah). Grassleaf pincushion flower. Southern Europe. Grows 18 inches tall and as wide. Grassy mats of silvery-green leaves. Stiff flower stems bear 2-inch, lilac-blue to pale pink flowers in summer. Must have well-drained soil. Zones 5 to 8.

S. ochroleuca (ok-roh-*lew*-kah). Yellow pincushion flower. Southeastern Europe. Hairy stems and leaves. Lobed to dissected leaves. Wiry mass of stems bearing 1-inch, lemon-yellow flowers in late summer. Short-lived. Zones 5 to 7.

Scabiosa columbaria ochroleuca.

Sedum aizoon.

SEDUM
(*see*-dum)
Stonecrop
Crassulaceae—orpine family

Sedums offer gardeners handsome succulent growth, showy flowers that are both long-lasting and attractive to butterflies, easy-care toughness, wide adaptability and drought tolerance. There are hundreds of plants from which to choose, with many creeping forms good for rock gardens, draping over walls or steps, or as edging plants. Taller, upright types are staples of beds and borders. The genus name is from the Latin *sedeo*, to sit, in reference to the low-growing habit of many species.

Growing Guide
Full sun. Any well-drained soil.

Propagation
Division, stem cuttings.

Uses
Beds and borders, edgings, rock walls, walks and rock gardens.

Species, Varieties, Cultivars, Hybrids
S. acre (*ah*-ker). Gold moss stonecrop. Europe, North Africa, Asia. Grows 2 inches tall and 12 to 18 inches wide. Spreading, mat-forming plant with fleshy, light green, overlapping, evergreen leaves ¼ inch long. Small clusters of bright yellow flowers from late spring into summer. Several varieties and cultivars, including 'Elegans', with silver-tipped leaves. Zones 3 to 8.

S. aizoon (*aye*-zoon). Aizoon stonecrop. Siberia, China, Japan. Grows 12 inches tall and 18 inches wide. Clump-forming plant with upright, unbranched stems and fleshy, shiny, toothed, lance-shaped, light green leaves to 2 inches long and ½ inch wide. Flat, 3- to 4-inch clusters of ½-inch yellow flowers in summer. 'Aurantiacum' has red stems, dark green leaves, yellow-orange flowers, and red fruits. Zones 4 to 9.

S. x 'Autumn Joy'. Autumn Joy sedum. Hybrid origin. Grows 1 to 2 feet tall and 2 feet wide. Hybrid between *S. spectabile* and *S. telephium*. Clump-forming plant with fleshy, oval, toothed, gray-green leaves to 3 inches long. Dense, rounded, 4- to 6-inch clusters of starry flowers changing

Sedum sieboldii.

Sedum *x 'Autumn Joy'*.

Sedum kamtschaticum.

Sedum spurium.

from pale pink in early summer to red-pink in late summer and to rust-red in fall. Staking may be necessary. Most widely grown sedum. Zones 3 to 10.

S. kamtschaticum (kamt-*shah*-ti-cum). Kamschatka stonecrop. Eastern Asia. Grows 6 to 8 inches tall and 12 to 15 inches wide. Spreading, sprawling plant with fleshy, lance-shaped, toothed leaves 1½ inches long and ½ inch wide. Yellow, ½-inch flowers in summer. The variety 'Floriferum' produces many more flowers. 'Weihen-stephaner Gold' has rust-red buds and golden yellow flowers. Zones 3 to 8.

S. sieboldii (see-*bold*-ee-eye). Also listed as *Hylotelephium sieboldii*. Siebold stonecrop. Japan. Grows 6 inches tall and 12 inches wide. Open-centered, spreading plant with whorls of three fleshy, rounded, finely toothed, blue-green, evergreen leaves to 1 inch long and edged in red. Clusters of star-shaped, bright pink flowers in late summer and fall. Several variegated cultivars are available. Zones 5 to 8.

S. spectabile (spek-tah-*bil*-ee). Showy stonecrop. Eastern Asia. Grows 18 to 24 inches tall and 18 inches wide. Clump-forming plant with upright stem and fleshy, oval, finely toothed, pale green leaves to 3 inches long. Dense, flat, 3- to 5-inch clusters of pale pink flowers in late summer. Several widely available cultivars, including 'Carmine', with soft salmon-pink flowers; 'Brilliant', with rose-pink

flowers; 'Star Dust', with pink-tinged white flowers; and 'Variegatum', with variegated leaves. Zones 4 to 10.

S. spurium (*spur*-ee-um). Two row stonecrop. Caucasus. Grows 2 to 6 inches tall and 12 to 18 inches wide. Spreading, mat-forming plant with red, hairy stems and fleshy, oval, toothed, red-edged semi-evergreen leaves to 1 inch long, appear in two rows. Clusters of ¾-inch magenta flowers with orange centers in summer. Several rather colorful cultivars, including 'Dragon's Blood', with purplish bronze leaves and brilliant red flowers; 'Red Carpet', with bronze

foliage and red flowers; and 'Ruby Mantle', with purplish red foliage and deep pink flowers; also cultivars with variegated foliage. Zones 3 to 8.

S. x 'Vera Jameson'. Vera Jameson stonecrop. Hybrid origin. Grows 9 to 12 inches tall and 12 inches wide. Sprawling, clump-forming plant with fleshy, rounded, deep purples leaves to 1 inch long. Clusters, 1 to 4 inches wide, of pink flowers in early fall. Very beautiful for the front of the border. Zones 5 to 9.

Sedum x 'Vera Jameson'.

SEMPERVIVUM
(sem-per-*veev*-um)
Hen and chicks, houseleek, liveforever
Crassulaceae—orpine family

Looking like some rare, exotic, desert plant, sempervivums instead are widely and easily grown plants from the Alps, Apennines and Pyrenees of Europe. The perfectly formed, ground-hugging rosettes of fleshy, red-tipped leaves have been grown in gardens since the time of ancient Romans, who used them as medicinal plants. Much folklore surrounds sempervivums, including Charlemagne's decree that they were to be grown on every roof to ward off lightning. The same use is said to keep witches away. The genus name comes from the Latin *semper*, always, and *vivo*, live, while the common name, houseleek, is from the Anglo-Saxon *leac*, or plant. Hen and chicks comes from the way young plants form around the central "mother" plant. After sending up a long, arching flower stem, the hen goes on to greener pastures.

Growing Guide
Full sun. Sandy to average, well-drained soil.

Propagation
Detach and replant young plants. Seed.

Uses
Creeping over raised beds, rocks, walls, among stone walks.

Species, Varieties, Cultivars, Hybrids
S. tectorum (tek-*toh*-rum). Hen and chicks, houseleek. Europe. Grows 8 to 12 inches tall and as wide. Dense, 3- to 4-inch rosettes of 50 to 60 evergreen, fleshy, red-tipped leaves. Stoloniferous offsets readily produced. Blooms infrequently with clusters of 1-inch magenta flowers on branching, leafy, hairy stems to 12 inches tall in summer. Over 30 other species, with one of the more interesting being *S. arachnoideum*, cobweb houseleek, with its dense cobweb-like hairs. Hundreds of hybrids and cultivars, many with red leaves. Zones 4 to 8.

Sempervivum tectorum.

SIDALCEA
(see-*dahl*-see-ah)
Prairie mallow, false mallow, checkerbloom
Malvaceae—mallow family

Looks somewhat like a miniature hollyhock, to which it is closely related. Sidalcea has been the subject of much selection and breeding resulting in a number of more widely adapted, long-blooming cultivars with mallow-like flowers of rich pinks and reds.

Sidalcea malviflora *'Party Girl'*.

Growing Guide
Full sun, with partial shade in hot, humid climates. Sandy, humus-rich, acid, well-drained soil. Must have good winter drainage. Particularly susceptible to Japanese beetles. Cut back faded flower stems for repeat bloom. Staking may be necessary. Does best in cool, dry climates.

Propagation
Division, seed.

Uses
Beds and borders. Good in combination with perennials with blue flowers or silver foliage.

Species, Varieties, Cultivars, Hybrids
S. malviflora (mal-vah-*floh*-rah). Checkerbloom. Western North America. Grows 2 to 4 feet tall and 2 feet wide. Clump-forming, upright plant with deeply lobed, blue-green leaves. Leafy spikes of 2- to 3-inch, five-petaled pink or rose-red flowers in summer. Among the cultivars, 'Elsie Heugh', with pale pink, fringed flowers, is the most widely available. Dwarf varieties, such as 'Oberon' and 'Puck', grow 2 feet tall and don't need staking. Zones 5 to 7.

SILENE
(sye-*lee*-nee)
Campion, catchfly
Caryophyllaceae—pink family

Campions are widespread throughout the temperate regions of the world; they are often disregarded as roadside weeds, but several species consistently find their well-mannered, long-blooming way into the fronts of borders, rock gardens or woodland gardens. The sticky stems of some species provide the source of one common name, catchfly.

Growing Guide
Full sun to partial shade. Average, well-drained soil.

Silene vulgaris *ssp.* maritima.

Propagation
Division, seed, stem cuttings.

Uses
Beds and borders, rock gardens, woodland gardens.

Species, Varieties, Cultivars, Hybrids
S. schafta (*shaf*-tah). Schafta campion. Caucasus. Grows 6 inches tall and 12 inches wide. Mat-forming plant with rosettes of narrow, oval, light green leaves. Magenta-pink, ¾-inch flowers with notched petals bloom from mid- to late summer. Must have well-drained soil. Zones 5 to 8.
S. vulgaris (vul-*gah*-ris). Also listed as *S. uniflora*. Bladder campion. Europe, Asia, Africa. Erect, branching stems with oval, gray-green leaves to 2 inches long. Deeply notched, pinkish white flowers in summer, with a bladder-like base. Several varieties and cultivars, including a trailing form, double-white form and nodding, tubular-flowered form. Zones 4 to 8.

SISYRINCHIUM
(sih-suh-*ring*-kee-um)
Blue-eyed grass
Iridaceae—iris family

Growing wild in meadows and prairies of the Western Hemisphere, sisyrinchiums are grassy, tufted plants with star-shaped flowers of blue, white, yellow or purple. The common name comes from the species widely found in the eastern half of North America, *S. angustifolium*. For the garden, a South American native with iris-like leaves provides a vertical effect with its foliage and spikes of small yellow flowers.

Growing Guide
Full sun. Moist, well-drained soil. Deadhead to prevent self-sowing and to keep the plants vigorous and attractive. Fertilize after flowering.

Propagation
Division, seed.

Uses
Beds and borders.

Species, Varieties, Cultivars, Hybrids
S. striatum (stree-*ah*-tum). Argentine blue-eyed grass. Grows 1 to 2 feet tall and 1 foot wide. Clump-forming plants with lance-shaped, gray-green leaves to 1 inch wide and to 18 inches long. Unbranched, winged stems bear 1-inch, creamy yellow flowers with purple veins on the outside and dark yellow throats. Creeping root-stocks form large clumps, but plants are not invasive. Variegated-leaf form is particularly attractive. Zones 5 to 8.

SMILACINA
(smy-lah-*see*-nah)

False Solomon's seal

Liliaceae—lily family

False Solomon's seal does actually resemble the "genuine" Solomon's seal, *Polygonatum biflorum*, with its arching stems of pointed, oval leaves. The two are also often found growing side by side at the edges of North American woodlands. It differs in flowering, with fluffy ivory clusters of flowers at the tips of the stems, rather than the hidden bells of *Polygonatum*, and the berries are red instead of

Smilacina racemosa.

black. The genus name denotes another resemblance, this time with *Smilax*, a genus of woody vines.

Growing Guide
Partial to half shade. Humus-rich, acid, moist but well-drained soil. May take several years to establish well.

Propagation
Division, seed.

Uses
Beds and borders, woodland gardens, fragrant gardens, near streams or pools.

Species, Varieties, Cultivars, Hybrids
S. racemosa (ray-seh-*moh*-sah). False Solomon's seal. North America. Grows 2 to 3 feet tall and 2 feet wide. Clumps of arching stems bear 10 to 15 pointed, oval, light green, prominently veined leaves 5 to 9 inches long. Feathery, pyramid-shaped clusters of tiny, fragrant, ivory flowers are borne at the ends of stems in spring. Red berries with purple spots, favored by animals. *S. stellata* is similar but grows 1 to 2 feet tall and has star-shaped white flowers in smaller, more open clusters in spring. Zones 3 to 8.

SOLIDAGO
(soh-lih-*day*-goh)

Goldenrod

Compositae—daisy family

Perhaps if goldenrod wasn't so widespread in the wild, we would consider it a glorious, fall-blooming perennial for the garden as Europeans do. Then, too, there's the negative press about goldenrod causing hay fever, when ragweed is the actual culprit. Anyway, it's time to re-think goldenrod, whether in traditional borders or in *nouveau* plantings with other North American natives. There are about 130 species, with most native to North America, but the best ones are the shorter hybrids, with the heritage generally a hopeless jumble. There is even a goldenrod-aster cross. The genus name is probably from the Latin *solidus* and *ago*, to make whole, referring to its use as an herb for healing wounds.

Growing Guide
Full sun. Almost any well-drained soil, from sandy to humus-rich. Staking may be necessary with taller types.

Propagation
Division or stem cuttings of named hybrids and cultivars.

Uses
Beds and borders, meadow gardens. Cut flowers.

Species, Varieties, Cultivars, Hybrids
Hybrids and cultivars. Clump-forming plants with upright stems with narrow, pointed, serrated leaves to 6 inches long. Flowers usually borne in somewhat one-sided, branching clusters of tiny, golden yellow flowers in late summer and fall. Spread by rhizomatous roots, but are not invasive. Among the many hybrids and cultivars, two of the shorter ones are 'Golden Thumb', growing 1 foot tall, and 'Cloth of Gold', growing 18 inches tall. Many other excellent choices grow 2 to 3 feet tall. A cultivar of *S. sphacelata* called 'Golden Fleece' is also very good for the garden. Zones 4 to 9.

Solidago canadensis *'Baby Gold'*.

SPIGELIA
(spy-*jee*-lee-ah)

Spigelia, pinkroot, Indian pink

Loganiaceae—logania family

A mass of spigelia, planted along a garden path, is a wondrous sight in early summer. With striking red-and-yellow flowers, it is also a good addition to perennial beds and borders with a warm color scheme. The genus is named after Adrian von der Spigel (1578–1625), a professor of botany at Padua University.

Growing Guide
Full sun to partial shade, with protection from hot afternoon sun important. Humus-rich, moist but well-drained soil.

Propagation
Division, seed.

Uses
Beds and borders. The edges of woodlands.

Species, Varieties, Cultivars, Hybrids
S. marilandica (mare-ih-*lan*-dih-kah). Spigelia, pinkroot, Indian pink. Southeastern United States. Grows 1 to 2 feet tall and as wide. Upright stems with oval, dark green leaves to 4 inches long. Borne at the tips of the stems in early summer, the 2-inch, trumpet-shaped flowers have a five-petaled, yellow "inner" flower. Zones 6 to 9.

Spigelia marilandica.

STACHYS
(*stah*-kis)

Betony, lamb's ears

Labiatae—mint family

Stachys byzantina *'Countess Helene von Stein'*.

Seldom are two members of one genus as dissimilar as betony and lamb's ears. The former is appreciated as much or more for its flowers as for the wrinkled, dark green leaves, while the latter is chosen specifically for its thickly woolly leaves, with plant breeders even going so far as to develop a non-flowering form. Both are long-lived, easy to grow, and attractive to butterflies. The genus name is derived from the Greek word for spikes, referring to the flowers, while the common name originates from the Celtic words for head and good, referring to its ancient herbal use.

Growing Guide
Full sun to partial shade for betony; full sun for lamb's ears. Poor to average, well-drained soil. Betony may be deadheaded to prevent self-sowing. Extended rainy summer weather may cause the foliage of lamb's ears to rot or disfigure, but plants often recover by summer's end.

Propagation
Division of species and cultivars; seed of species.

Uses
Beds and borders, groundcover. Also use lamb's ears trailing over raised beds and along paths. Butterfly gardens.

Species, Varieties, Cultivars, Hybrids
S. byzantina (bih-zan-*teen*-ah). Also listed as *S. lanata* and *S. olympica*. Lamb's ears. Turkey, southwestern Asia. Grows 12 to 18 inches tall and 12 inches wide. Spreading, mat-forming plants with gray-green, very white-woolly, oval leaves 4 to 6 inches long. Woolly spikes of magenta flowers borne in whorls in summer. Some gardeners remove them just as they begin forming. 'Silver Carpet' does not bloom. Both 'Sheila McQueen' and 'Countess Helene von Stein' have larger, less woolly leaves, and 'Primrose Heron' has chartreuse leaves in spring, slowly mellowing to yellow-green. Zones 4 to 8.

S. macrantha (mah-*kranth*-ah). Also listed as *S. grandiflora*. Betony. Asia Minor. Grows 1 to 2 feet tall and 18 inches wide. Mat-forming with upright stems of elongated, heart-shaped, coarsely serrated, wrinkled, hairy, dark green leaves. Several distinct whorls of 10 to 20 tubular, 1-inch, magenta flowers are held on spikes to 8 inches long above the foliage in late spring. Several varieties, including robusta, with 4 to 5 whorls of rose-pink flowers; rosea with rose-red flowers; and superba and violacea, both with deep violet flowers. Wood betony, *S. officinalis*, is similar but with larger leaves and smaller flowers. Zones 4 to 8.

Stachys byzantina.

Stokesia laevis.

STOKESIA
(stoh-*kee*-zee-ah)
Stokes' aster
Compositae—daisy family

Stokes' aster is a Cinderella plant, having been transformed by the magic of plant breeding from a nice but unassuming wildflower into one of the belles of the perennial garden. Plants are long-lived, long-blooming, and widely adaptable. Excellent for cutting, the blue or white flowers have a lacy, fringed look reminiscent of cornflowers. The genus is named after Jonathan Stokes, an English botanist.

Growing Guide
Full sun. Average to fertile, humus-rich, well-drained soil. Benefits from winter mulching in colder climates, but must have good drainage. Best planted in groups of at least three.

Propagation
Division of species or cultivars; seed of species.

Uses
Beds and borders.

Species, Varieties, Cultivars, Hybrids
S. laevis (*lay*-vis). Also listed as *S. cyanea*. Stokes' aster. Southeastern United States. Grows 1 to 2 feet tall and 18 inches wide. Stiff, branching stems with lance-shaped, dark green leaves to 8 inches long with a prominent white midrib. Foliage is evergreen in milder climates. Several 4-inch, lavender-blue flowers are borne on single stalks in summer. Each flower consists of both tubular inner florets and long, flat, five-lobed outer florets. Cultivars vary in flower color from lavender-blue to several shades of light to dark blue, pink, yellow and white. Zones 5 to 9.

STYLOPHORUM
(sty-*lah*-for-um)
Celandine poppy, lesser celandine poppy, wood poppy
Papaveraceae—poppy family

The celandine poppy has a way of drawing attention. Perhaps it is in the nature of any poppy, with so many family members having simple but striking flowers with ethereally translucent petals. Or, maybe it's the way it naturally carpets a woodland floor. Whatever the reason, celandine poppies capture hearts and adapt well to shaded gardens. The term celandine was originally applied to the greater celandine poppy, *Chelidonium majus*, from the Latin word *chelidonia*, swallow, for the correlation of appearance between the bird and flower in the spring.

Growing Guide
Partial to half shade. Humus-rich, moist but well-drained soil.

Propagation
Division, but difficult. Seed, self-sows.

Uses
Beds and borders, woodland gardens.

Species, Varieties, Cultivars, Hybrids
S. diphyllum (dih-*fill*-um). Celandine poppy, lesser celandine poppy, wood poppy. Eastern North America. Grows 12 to 18 inches tall and 12 inches wide. Clump-forming plants with light green, hairy leaves 10 to 15 inches long, deeply lobed into five to seven segments.

Stems bear clusters of three to five four-petaled, 2-inch, bright yellow, poppy-like flowers in spring, followed by silvery pods. Foliage goes dormant unless soil remains moist. Cut stems exude a yellow sap used as a dye by Native Americans. Zones 4 to 9.

Stylophorum diphyllum.

Symphytum *x* uplandicum.

wrinkled, shiny dark green, and 4 to 7 inches long. Tolerates shade and drought, but does best in moist soil. Spreads rapidly, so use as a groundcover. The cultivar 'Variegatum' has light green leaves with creamy white margins; other cultivars have pink or pale blue flowers. Zones 3 to 8.

SYMPHYTUM
(*sim*-fih-tum)
Comfrey
Boraginaceae—borage family

Anyone who has battled the rapacious common comfrey, *S. officinale*, will be questioning the presence of comfrey here, but other species, particularly in their variegated form, are somewhat less invasive and complement other perennials quite well, both with the foliage and sky-blue, red or yellow flowers. Both the common and genus names refer to comfrey's ancient herbal use of setting bones, with the Latin *con forma*, meaning to join together, and the Greek *symphyo* translating to unite. A more current use is on the compost pile, where it speeds decomposition.

Growing Guide
Full sun to partial shade. Humus-rich, moist but well-drained soil.

Propagation
Division.

Uses
Beds and borders, groundcover, sunny to partially shaded meadow gardens.

Species, Varieties, Cultivars, Hybrids
S. caucasicum (kaw-*kah*-sih-kum). Caucasian comfrey. Caucasus. Grows 18 to 24 inches tall and 2 feet wide. Clump-forming plants with rough, lance-shaped, pale gray-green leaves to 8 inches long. Spring-blooming clusters of nodding, ¾-inch, bell-shaped flowers opening pink then turning azure blue. Best in partial shade. Zones 3 to 8.

S. grandiflorum (gran-dih-*floh*-rum). Large-flowered comfrey. Caucasus. Grows 10 to 15 inches tall and and 12 to 18 inches wide. Basal clumps with sterile stems lying on the ground and pointing upward. Fertile stems bear tubular, red-tipped yellow flowers in spring. Oval leaves are

S. x rubrum (*rew*-brum). Red-flowered comfrey. Hybrid origin. Grows 18 inches tall and 2 feet wide. Similar to *S. grandiflorum*, but spreads more slowly. Drooping, tubular, dark red flowers in spring. Use as a groundcover. Zones 3 to 8.

S. x uplandicum (up-*land*-dih-kum). Also listed as *S. peregrinum* or *S. asperrimum*. Russian comfrey. Hybrid origin. Grows 3 to 4 feet tall and 3 feet wide. Clump-forming plant with upright stems bearing lance-shaped, hairy, gray-green leaves to 10 inches long. Clusters of nodding, tubular, 1-inch flowers are pink in bud and open to blue in late spring and early summer. The much-prized cultivar 'Variegatum' has broad, creamy yellow leaf margins and pale lilac-blue flowers. Remove plants that revert to solid green foliage. Zones 4 to 8.

T

TEUCRIUM
(*tewk*-ree-um)
Germander
Labiatae—mint family

Most often thought of for its use as a clipped low hedge, germander may be better served by capitalizing on its fine-textured, aromatic foliage and rose-purple flowers. Most gardeners overlook other species that can contribute to wildflower and rock gardens. The genus name is from King Teucer, the first king of Troy, who supposedly used teucrium medicinally. The common name
is from the Greek word for ground oak.

Growing Guide
Full sun. Poor to average, well-drained soil.

Propagation
Division, stem cuttings.

Uses
Beds and borders, wildflower gardens, rock gardens and rock walls.

Species, Varieties, Cultivars, Hybrids
T. canadense (kan-ah-*dense*). Canadian germander. North America. Grows 3 feet tall and 1 foot wide. Upright stems with oval to lance-shaped, serrated leaves to 3 inches long and hairy underneath. Spikes of pale, purplish pink, hooded, tubular flowers in summer. Grows naturally in humus-rich moist soil at the edges of woodlands. Zones 4 to 8.

T. chamaedrys (kah-*mee*-drees). Wall germander. Europe, South central Russia, North Africa, Asia Minor. Grows to 1 foot tall and as wide. Shrubby plant with woody stems. Scalloped-edged, oval, dark evergreen leaves to 1 inch long. Spikes to 6 inches long of whorled, rose-purple, hooded flowers, ½ to ¾ inch long, in summer. The cultivar 'Prostratum' or 'Nanum' is a spreading, carpet-forming plant to 8 inches tall. 'Variegatum' has leaves marked with white. Plants sold as *T. chamaedrys* may actually be *T. massiliense* or a hybrid with *T. lucidum*. Must have good drainage. Foliage is attractive to cats. Zones 4 to 9.

T. pyrenaicum (pih-ray-*nah*-ih-kum). Pyrenees germander. Spain, France. Grows 3 inches tall and 10 inches wide. Spreading plant with woody, trailing stem and toothed, round, gray-green leaves to 1 inch long. Loose clusters of white and purple flowers in summer. For rock gardens and rock walls. Zones 6 to 9.

T. scorodinia (skor-oh-*din*-ee-ah). Wood germander. Europe. Grows 1 to 2 feet tall and as wide. Shrubby plants with woody, branched stems. Toothed, heart-shaped to oval, rough leaves. Loose clusters of tiny, pale greenish yellow flowers in late summer. Native to moors, so does best on humus-rich, acid, moist but well-drained soil. Zones 6 to 9.

Teucrium.

THALICTRUM
(tha-*lik*-trum)
Meadow rue
Ranunculaceae—buttercup family

Diaphanous flowers of lavender, pink or yellow and graceful, delicate foliage grant the meadow rues status among the elite perennials. Easily grown with the right conditions, they bring much-needed texture and depth to shaded gardens. Good for cutting, the flowers are unusual in that there are no petals, only colorful stamens and sepals. The common name is derived from the similarity of the foliage to that of Ruta, rue.

Growing Guide
Partial to half shade; more sun is tolerated in areas with cool summers. Fertile, humus-rich, moist but well-drained soil. Does not do well in areas with hot, humid summers. Taller types may need staking.

Propagation
Division for species and cultivars; seed for species.

Uses
Beds and borders, near streams or pools, wildflower gardens. Cut flowers.

Species, Varieties, Cultivars, Hybrids
T. aquilegifolium (ah-kwi-*leeg*-ih-foh-lee-um). Columbine meadow rue. Europe, northern Asia. Grows 3 feet tall and 1 foot wide. Upright, hollow stems. Leaves form at the base and along the stems, resembling those of columbine, with many rounded, lobed, blue-green leaflets to 1½ inches wide. Somewhat flat-topped clusters to 8 inches wide of fluffy, lilac-purple flowers in spring and early summer, followed by drooping, winged seeds. Best meadow rue for hot climates. A number of cultivars, including some with white, dark purple or pink flowers. With

'Atropurpureum', stems and flowers are dark purple. Zones 5 to 8.

T. delavayi (deh-lah-*vay*-ee). Yunnan meadow rue. Western China. Grows 2 to 4 feet tall and 2 feet wide. Clump-forming, upright stems. Leaves divided several times, with each three-lobed leaflet ½ inch wide. Airy, branching clusters of nodding yellow and lilac flowers in summer. 'Hewitt's Double', with longer-lasting, double lilac flowers, is most often grown. Also a white form. Plants sold as *T. dipterocarpum* are usually *T. delavayi*. Lavender mist, *T. rochebrunnianum*, is similar but with purplish stems, blue-green leaves and lavender-pink flowers with yellow stamens, blooming from mid- to late summer. Zones 4 to 7.

T. flavum (*flay*-vum). Yellow meadow rue. Europe, Siberia, Caucasus. Grows 4 feet tall and 2 feet wide. Clump-forming plants with sturdy stems. Multiple-divided leaves, with rounded, three-lobed leaflets. Rounded clusters of yellow and white, fragrant flowers in early to mid-summer. More adaptable than other species. More often grown is the dusty meadow rue, *T. f. glaucum*, also known as *T. speciosissimum* or *T. glaucum*, with blue-green leaves and sulfur-yellow flowers. The cultivar

Thalictrum delavayi.

'Illuminator' grows 3 feet tall, with lemon-yellow flowers. Zones 5 to 8.

T. minus (*my*-nus). Lesser meadow rue. Europe, Asia, Africa. Grows 1 to 2 feet tall and as wide. A highly variable species, often given other names, with three-lobed leaflets resembling the maidenhair fern, *Adiantum pedatum*. Grown mainly for foliage; greenish yellow flowers fade quickly. Plants offered as 'Adiantifolium' usually have the best appearance. Stoloniferous roots, but not invasive. Zones 3 to 7.

THERMOPSIS
(ther-*mop*-sis)

False lupine

Leguminosae—pea family

With both flowers and foliage resembling those of the lupine, *Lupinus*, the false lupine has a most appropriate genus name taken from the Greek *thermos*, lupine, and *opsis*, like. Attractive, easily grown, and long-lived, thermopsis has deep, drought-resistant roots. Slowly spreading clumps of foliage are crowned with tall spikes of pea-like, yellow flowers in spring, which are good for cutting.

Growing Guide
Full sun, with partial shade preferred in hotter climates. Poor to average, well-drained soil. Staking may be necessary with a windy site or when grown in shade.

Propagation
Division, but difficult because of the deep roots; seed, if fresh; stem cuttings.

Uses
Beds and borders, meadow gardens. Cut flowers.

Species, Varieties, Cultivars, Hybrids
T. caroliniana (kar-oh-lin-ee-*ay*-nah). Also listed as *T. villosa*. Southern lupine. Eastern United States. Grows 3 to 4 feet tall and as wide. Clump-forming plants with three-parted, oval, blue-green leaves, each 2 to 3 inches long and softly hairy beneath. Erect stems, 6 to 12 inches long, of densely spaced, bright yellow, pea-like flowers in spring, lasting up to a month. The cultivar 'Album' has shorter growth and white flowers. Zones 3 to 9.

T. lupinoides (lew-pih-*noi*-deez). Also listed as *T. lanceolata*. Lanceleaf thermopsis. Alaska, Siberia. Grows 1 foot tall and 18 inches wide. Clump-forming plants with lance-shaped, blue-green leaves, each 1½ inches long and covered with silky hairs. Blooms in summer with whorled spikes of bright yellow, pea-like flowers, followed by curved seed pods. Best for cool-summer climates. Zones 2 to 7.

T. montana (mon-*tan*-ah). Mountain thermopsis. Western United States. Grows 2 to 3 feet tall and 18 inches wide. Similar to southern lupine, but with slightly shorter flower spikes and more linear leaves to 4 inches long. Zones 3 to 7.

Thermopsis caroliniana.

TIARELLA
(tee-ah-*rel*-ah)

Foamflower, false mitrewort

Saxifragaceae—saxifrage family

Tiarella cordifolia.

Gardeners seem always on the lookout for new plants for shady areas, and recent breeding with native foamflowers are certainly satisfying this need. Five of the six species of tiarella are native to North America and have evergreen leaves, often with burgundy variegation and turning bronze in winter. Short, foamy spikes of white flowers rise above the foliage for about 6 weeks in spring. These tiny flowers are the source of the genus name from the Latin, translating as little tiara.

Growing Guide
Partial to half shade. Fertile, humus-rich, moist but well-drained soil.

Propagation
Division of cultivars and species; seed of species.

Uses
Beds and borders, particularly with the less spreading cultivars and hybrids; groundcover.

Species, Varieties, Cultivars, Hybrids
T. cordifolia (kor-dih-*foe*-lee-ah). Allegheny foamflower. Eastern North America. Grows 12 inches tall and 18 inches wide. Spreading plants with hairy, heart-shaped leaves to 4 inches wide. Flower spikes, 3 to 4 inches tall, bear ¼-inch fluffy white flowers in spring. The variety *collinia*, also listed as *T. wherryi*, is slightly taller and more clump-forming with triangular leaves. A number of cultivars and hybrids have been developed, varying mainly in leaf shape and color, but some also having pinkish flowers. Zones 3 to 8.

TRADESCANTIA
(trah-des-*kant*-ee-ah)
Spiderwort
Commelinaceae—spiderwort family

Although there are a hundred or so species of tradescantia, only one has securely taken its place in the perennial pantheon. Certainly deserving, spiderworts are plants of graceful, grass-like foliage and unique, three-petaled flowers with prominent stamens and pistils. Each individual flower lasts only a day, but plants are prolific producers for 8 weeks in summer. Easily grown and long-lived, spiderworts are widely adaptable. All in all, a suitable tribute to the Tradescant father and son, both English botanists and gardeners to Charles I, with the son also traveling in 1637 to collect plants from the New World.

Growing Guide
Full sun to light shade. Poor to average, moist but well-drained soil.

Trim stems to 8 to 12 inches in midsummer to encourage new growth and fall blooming. Staking may be necessary, or surround with short, sturdy perennials.

Propagation
Division.

Uses
Beds and borders.

Species, Varieties, Cultivars, Hybrids
T. x andersoniana (an-der-soh-nee-*aye*-nah). Spiderwort. Hybrid origin. Grows 1 to 2 feet tall and 2 feet wide. Hybrid between *T. subaspera, T. ohiensis,* and *T. virginiana.* Clump-forming plants with narrow, linear leaves to 18 inches long, clasping the stems. Clusters of flower buds form in the leaf axils, opening to 1- to 3-inch blooms. Many cultivars, with flower colors including shades of blue, maroon, rose-purple, mauve and white. Flowers may also have veining or an eye of a different color. Zones 4 to 9.

Tradescantia *x andersoniana.*

TRICYRTIS
(try-*sir*-tis)
Toad lily
Liliaceae—lily family

Tricyrtis hirta.

The attraction of toad lilies may not be readily apparent to the casual observer, but ardent gardeners are drawn to them for their small but uniquely shaped and colored fall-blooming flowers. For the rest of the growing season, toad lilies offer gracefully arching stems and foliage. The source of the common name is open to some debate; although probably due to the spotted flowers, the juice of a species from the Phillipines is reported to be a bait for frogs.

Growing Guide
Partial shade, with more sun tolerated in cool-summer climates. Humus-rich, moist but well-drained soil. Taller types may need staking. Benefits from both summer and winter mulches.

Propagation
Division.

Uses
Beds and borders; best when planted in groups of at least three. Cut flowers.

Species, Varieties, Cultivars, Hybrids
T. formosana (for-*moh*-sah-nah). Also listed as *T. stolonifera.* Formosa toad lily. Taiwan. Grows 1 to 2 feet tall and as wide. Slowly spreading plant with arching stems. Shiny, pointed, oval, dark green leaves to 5 inches long, somewhat clasping the stem. Stems end in branching clusters of 1-inch, funnel-shaped flowers of white spotted with purple, blooming over a long period in autumn. The cultivar 'Amethystina' is taller, with more erect stems and bluish flowers with red spots. Zones 5 to 9.

T. hirta (*hir*-tah). Japanese toad lily. Japan. Grows 2 to 3 feet tall and 2 feet wide. Clump-forming plant with white-hairy, arching stems. Closely set, pointed, oval, hairy, stem-clasping, dark green leaves to 6 inches long. Star-shaped, 1-inch, white flowers with purple spots borne for about a month in autumn. Blooms appear in leaf axils and at the ends of stems, either singly or in small clusters. Many varieties, cultivars and hybrids are beginning to be offered, varying in growth and flower color and size. Zones 4 to 8.

With the burgeoning interest in tricyrtis, more species and cultivars are being offered every year; if intrigued, search them out.

TRILLIUM
(*tril*-lee-um)
Wake robin
Liliaceae—lily family

Trilliums are among the most revered and beloved of all native spring-blooming woodland wildflowers. Unfortunately, that has meant much destruction of natural stands, either by individuals or nurseries collecting in the wild. It is imperative that all plants grown in the garden be nursery-propagated. Trilliums are aptly named from the Latin *tri* because leaves, petals and sepals are in threes. Leaves may be mottled with burgundy or plain green, and the solitary white, pink, yellow or red flowers are either borne stalkless or short-stalked in the center of leaves.

Growing Guide
Partial to half shade. Humus-rich, acid, moist but well-drained soil. Plant rhizomes 2 to 4 inches deep. Foliage goes dormant by late summer.

Propagation
Division, with difficulty.

Uses
Woodland gardens.

Species, Varieties, Cultivars, Hybrids
T. grandiflorum (grand-ih-*flor*-um). Great white trillium, white wake robin. Eastern North America. Grows 18 inches tall and as wide. Each upright stalk bears three pointed, wavy-edged, oval plain green leaves 3 to 6 inches long. Short-stalked, 2- to 3-inch white, maturing to soft pink, flowers in spring. The easiest to grow and showiest of the trilliums. 'Flore-pleno' has double flowers. Zones 4 to 9.

Trillium grandiflorum.

TROLLIUS
(*troh*-lee-us)
Globe flower
Ranunculaceae—buttercup family

Found growing naturally in moist to wet meadows in the cooler parts of the temperate areas of the Northern Hemisphere, globe flowers require similar conditions in the garden. Given these conditions, they reward the gardener with repeated blooming of golden yellow flowers. The many cultivars available offer various shades of yellow, with all lasting well as cut flowers. The genus name comes from the old German word *trollblume*, round flower.

Growing Guide
Full sun in cool-summer climates; partial shade in hotter areas. Humus-rich, moist soil. Deadhead for repeat bloom. Cut back fading foliage in late summer. May take several years to become established. Staking may be necessary.

Trollius.

Propagation
Division.

Uses
Wet meadows, partially shaded wild gardens, bog gardens. Cut flowers.

Species, Varieties, Cultivars, Hybrids
T. x cultorum (kul-*tor*-um). Hybrid globe flower. Hybrid origin. Grows 2 to 3 feet tall and 18 inches wide. Hybrids between *T. asiaticus*, *T. chinensis*, and *T. europaeus*. Basal clumps of deeply divided or lobed, dark green leaves. Slender stems with a few leaves each bear several globe-shaped, 2- to 3-inch, yellow flowers with many stamens in late spring. Many cultivars, with flower color varying from dark orange to creamy white. Zones 3 to 7.

T. europaeus '**Superbus**' (yew-*roh*-pay-us suh-*per*-bus). Common globe flower. Europe. Grows 1 to 2 feet tall and 18 inches wide. Similar to the hybrid globe flower, but more prolifically flowering with 1- to 2-inch, lemon-yellow flowers in early spring. More tolerant of well-drained soil. Zones 4 to 7.

T. chinensis (chi-*nen*-sis). Usually offered as *T. ledebourii*. Siberian globe flower. Siberia. Grows 2 to 3 feet tall and 18 inches wide. Vigorous plants with deeply divided, lobed, and toothed leaves. Globular, 2-inch, deep orange flowers in spring. 'Golden Queen' grows to 4 feet with 3- to 4-inch golden-orange flowers. Zones 3 to 6.

U

UVULARIA
(yew-vew-*lah*-ree-ah)
Merrybells
Liliaceae—lily family

As befitting the name merrybells, these are delightful perennials that grace shaded borders and woodland gardens with their pale yellow, nodding flowers in spring. Widely adaptable, they are easily grown, with the rhizomatous roots slowly spreading to form luminous patches.

Growing Guide
Partial to half shade. Humus-rich, moist but well-drained soil.

Propagation
Division, seed.

Uses
Beds and borders, woodland gardens.

Species, Varieties, Cultivars, Hybrids
U. grandiflora (gran-dih-*flor*-ah). Merrybells. Eastern and central North America. Grows 18 to 24 inches tall and 12 inches wide. Clump-forming plants with upright stems. Oblong, pale green leaves to 4 inches long, sometimes drooping and with edges rolled under. Spring blooming, with bell-shaped, 1½-inch-long, pale yellow flowers with six twisted petals hanging down singly or in pairs from the tops of the stems. Zones 4 to 9.

Uvularia grandiflora.

V

VALERIANA
(vah-leh-ree-*ahn*-ah)
Common valerian
Valerianaceae—valerian family

Grown and used since ancient times as a medicinal herb, valerian has a beneficial effect on gardens as well. Long, graceful stems bear clusters of delicate white or pink flowers in summer. These are fragrant and good for cutting. Cats find it attractive, too. The genus name is from the Latin, *valere*, to be healthy. Widely adaptable, it has naturalized in many parts of the United States.

Growing Guide
Full sun to partial shade. Average to humus-rich, moist but well-drained to wet soil. Tolerates drier, alkaline soil.

Propagation
Division, seed. May self-sow.

Uses
Beds and borders, meadow gardens, near streams or pools, bog gardens. Cut flowers.

Species, Varieties, Cultivars, Hybrids
V. officinalis (oh-fis-ih-*nal*-is). Common valerian, vervain, cat's valerian, all heal. Europe, Asia. Grows 3 to 4 feet tall and 3 feet wide. Basal clumps of egg-shaped, deeply lobed leaves, with stem leaves divided into seven to ten pairs of lance-shaped, toothed leaflets to 3 inches long. Long stems bear rounded heads of tiny fragrant white or pink flowers in summer. Zones 4 to 9.

Valeriana officinalis.

VERBASCUM
(ver-*bas*-kum)
Mullein
Scrophulariaceae—
figwort family

Verbascum.

Many people may be familiar with the felty-leaved common mullein, *V. thapsis,* found in fields and along roadsides, but there are also a number of biennial and short-lived perennial verbascums more suited to the garden. These provide a strong vertical element with their tall flower spikes in summer. Verbascums readily hybridize among the species, with the resulting named hybrids offering choice, longer-lived selections. The genus name is thought to be derived from the Latin *barbascum,* beard, in reference to the hairy leaves.

Growing Guide
Full sun. Average, well-drained soil. Deadhead for repeat bloom. Staking may be necessary. May take several years to establish.

Propagation
Division of cultivars, hybrids and species; seed of species.

Uses
Beds and borders; best when planted in groups of at least three.

Species, Varieties, Cultivars, Hybrids
V. x hybridum (hih-*bri*-dum). Hybrid mullein. Hybrid origin. Grows to 5 feet tall and 2 feet wide. Basal rosettes of pointed oval leaves to 10 inches long. Leaves are usually thick, white-hairy, but some are wrinkled and dark green. Flower colors include shades of yellow, pink, apricot and white, often with a contrasting eye. Zones 6 to 9.

Among the species, the best for the perennial garden include *V. chaixii,* growing 2 to 3 feet tall, with yellow or white flowers (Zones 5 to 8); *V. olympicum,* growing 4 to 6 feet tall, with branching spires of yellow flowers (Zones 6 to 8); and *V. phoeniceum,* growing 2 to 4 feet tall with spikes of purple, pink, red or white flowers (Zones 6 to 8).

VERBENA
(Ver-*bee*-nah)
Brazilian verbena
*Verbenaceae—*verbena family

Mainly native to subtropical and tropical North and South America, verbenas are usually thought of as colorful annuals. Several species are hardier, with one being particularly useful for the airy effect it brings to perennial gardens. The species *bonariensis* is named for Buenos Aires, where it was first found.

Growing Guide
Full sun. Average, well-drained soil. Winter mulch is beneficial in the northernmost areas of its hardiness range. With pruning, plants become more shrub-like.

Propagation
Root cuttings, stem cuttings, seed. Self-sows.

Uses
Beds and borders, hedges. Use one to three plants as filler or plant in masses.

Species, Varieties, Cultivars, Hybrids
V. bonariensis (boh-nah-ree-*en*-sis). South American verbena. South America. Grows 3 to 4 feet tall and 2 feet wide. Basal clumps of toothed, lance-shaped leaves to 4 inches long. Wiry, somewhat branching stems, with few leaves, bear 2-inch clusters of ¼-inch, purplish red flowers from early summer though fall. Zones 6 to 9.

Verbena bonariensis.

VERNONIA
(ver-*non*-ee-ah)
Ironweed
Compositae—daisy family

Only the most callous and cynical person could see a meadow filled with ironweed on an early fall morning, with the mist rising, and not fall in love with it. Among the 1000 or so species of vernonia, mostly native to subtropical regions of the world, only a few are native to temperate North America. If the New York ironweed were rare, gardeners would be clamoring for it. Be daring, try at least a few among other fall-blooming perennials. The common name is from the color of the faded flowers.

Growing Guide
Full sun. Humus-rich, moist soil is ideal, with drier soils tolerated.

Propagation
Division, seed.

Uses
Beds and borders, meadow gardens.

Species, Varieties, Cultivars, Hybrids
V. vernonia (ver-*non*-ee-ah). New York ironweed. Eastern North America. Grows 3 to 5 feet tall and 2 to 3 feet wide. Clump-forming plants with stiff, upright stems. Pointed, toothed, oval to lance-shaped, rough-textured leaves to 8 inches long. Loose, open, somewhat flat clusters of ½-inch, fluffy, purplish red flowers in late summer and fall, aging to a rust color. Zones 4 to 9.

Veronica prostrata *'Rosea'*.

VERONICA
(veh-*ron*-ih-kah)
Speedwell
Scrophulariaceae—figwort family

Veronicas are widely used in gardens because of their blue, purple, pink, red or white flowers for many weeks in summer, relatively low growth but vertical form, easy care, long life, wide adaptability and the large number of species and cultivars available. As a bonus, the flowers are good for cutting. The genus name is said to have come from the similarity of markings on the flowers with those of the handkerchief of St. Veronica.

Growing Guide
Full sun to partial shade. Humus-rich, moist but well-drained soil. Deadhead to prolong blooming. Soil must not dry out, so use summer mulch.

Propagation
Division or stem cuttings of species and cultivars; seed of species.

Uses
Beds and borders.

Species, Varieties, Cultivars, Hybrids
V. alpina **'Goodness Grows'** (al-*pine*-ah). Goodness Grows alpine speedwell. Hybrid origin. Grows 10 to 12 inches tall and 12 inches wide. Creeping, mat-forming plants with pointed, oval, shiny leaves to 1½ inches long. Foliage is evergreen in milder climates. Narrow, dense spikes to 6 inches long of dark blue, ¼-inch flowers in late spring and early summer, then again in fall. Also a white-flowered form of the species. Zones 3 to 8.

Veronica *'Sunny Border Blue'*.

Veronica teucrium *'Crater Lake Blue'*.

V. gentianoides (gen-tee-ah-*noi*-deez). Gentian speedwell. Caucasus. Grows 18 inches tall and as wide. Spreading, mat-forming plants with basal rosettes of narrow, pointed, glossy, dark green leaves to 3 inches long. Leafy stems with 4- to 10-inch spikes of ½-inch, pale blue, darker-veined flowers in early summer. 'Variegata' has white-margined leaves. Zones 4 to 8.

V. incana (in-*kan*-nah). Also listed as *V. spicata incana*. Woolly speedwell. Russia. Grows 12 to 18 inches tall and as wide. Spreading, mat-forming plants with oval to lance-shaped, toothed, silver-gray, felty leaves to 3 inches long. Narrow, dense, 3- to 6-inch spikes of long-lasting, ¼-inch, blue flowers. Good edging plant. Does not do well with hot or rainy weather. Several varieties and cultivars. Zones 3 to 7.

V. longifolia (lon-gi-*fol*-ee-ah). Long-leaf veronica. Grows 2 to 4 feet tall and 1 to 2 feet wide. Clump-forming plants with oval, pointed, toothed leaves to 3 inches long. Stiff, narrow, dense, 12-inch spikes of ¼-inch, lilac-blue flowers for many weeks from early to midsummer. Several varieties and cultivars, not widely available, varying in height or flower color. May need staking. Zones 4 to 8.

V. prostrata (pros-*trah*-tah). Also listed as *V. rupestris* and *V. teucrium* var. *prostrata*. Prostrate speedwell, harebell speedwell. Europe, Asia. Grows 8 to 12 inches tall and 12 to 18 inches wide. Spreading, mat-forming plants with oval, toothed, gray-green, hairy leaves to 1 inch long. Narrow, dense, 4- to 10-inch spikes of ⅓-inch, deep blue flowers for several weeks in summer. Several cultivars available. Zones 5 to 8.

V. spicata (spee-*kah*-tah). Spiked speedwell. Europe, Asia. Grows 1 to 2 feet tall and 18 to 24 inches wide. Spreading, clump-forming plants with toothed, oval to lance-shaped, glossy leaves to 2 inches long. Narrow, dense, 3-inch spikes of ¼-inch blue flowers for many weeks in summer. Most popular veronica; many varieties and cultivars, varying in height and flower color, with shades including dark purple, dark blue, rose-pink, rose-red and white. Zones 3 to 8.

V. 'Sunny Border Blue'. Grows 18 inches tall and 12 inches wide. Sunny Border Blue veronica. Hybrid origin. Clump-forming plants with oval, pointed, wrinkled, shiny, dark green leaves. Narrow, dense, 3- to 6-inch spikes of ¼-inch, violet-blue flowers for many weeks in summer and early fall. Zones 4 to 8.

V. teucrium (*tewk*-ree-um). Also listed as *V. austriaca teucrium* and *V. latifolia*. Hungarian speedwell. Grows 18 inches tall and as wide. Highly variable species, but generally spreading, mat-forming plants with oval to lance-shaped, pointed, toothed or deeply cut leaves to 1½ inches long. Dense, 4- to 10-inch spikes of bright blue flowers for a month in early summer. Best known cultivar is 'Crater Lake Blue', growing to 12 inches tall. Zones 4 to 8.

Veronica gentianoides *'Blue Gentian'*.

VERONICASTRUM
(veh-ron-ih-*kas*-trum)
Culver's root, bowman's root, blackroot
Scrophulariaceae—figwort family

Closely related to the veronicas, where taxonomists sometimes place it, culver's root provides stately size as well as late-blooming flowers for the garden. Culver's root was used both as a medicinal and ritual herb by Native Americans. The genus name is a combination of veronica and aster.

Growing Guide
Full sun to partial shade. Moist but well-drained soil. May be slow to establish.

Propagation
Division, seed, stem cuttings.

Uses
Beds and borders, meadow gardens, at the edges of woodlands.

Species, Varieties, Cultivars, Hybrids
V. virginicum (vir-*jin*-ih-kum). Culver's root, bowman's root. Eastern United States. Grows 4 to 6 feet tall and 2 to 3 feet wide. Clump-forming, upright plants. Toothed, lance-shaped, shiny leaves to 4 inches long arranged in whorls of three or six on strong stems. Plants branch at the top into narrow spikes of small, flaring, tubular flowers of white, pale pink or purplish in late summer and fall. Zones 3 to 8.

Veronicastrum virginicum.

VINCA
(*ving*-kah)
Vinca, myrtle, periwinkle
Apocynaceae—dogbane family

Among the toughest, most dependable, and widely adaptable of the perennials used as groundcovers, vinca can also be appreciated for its beautiful blue flowers in spring, sprinkled over the ground like so many fallen stars. A number of varieties and cultivars offer these blooms in different colors or plants with variegated foliage. The genus name is from the Latin *vincio*, to bind, in reference to its creeping stems.

Growing Guide
Partial to full shade. Average to humus-rich, moist but well-drained soil.

Propagation
Division, stem cuttings.

Uses
Groundcover. Slow-growing forms in beds and borders.

Species, Varieties, Cultivars, Hybrids
V. major (*may*-jor). Large periwinkle. Europe. Grows 18 to 24 inches tall and 24 inches wide. Wiry stems with rounded, pointed, evergreen leaves, 2 to 3 inches long. Nonflowering stems creep on the ground, rooting at the tips where they touch the ground. Upright flowering stems bear flowers in spring that are 1 to 2 inches wide, blue, and funnel-shaped with 5 flaring lobes. Occasional repeat blooming. 'Reticulata' has leaves with netted yellow lines; 'Variegata', also offered as 'Elegantissima', has white-blotched leaves and is often used in container plantings. Zones 7 to 9.

V. minor (*mine*-or). Common periwinkle. Europe. Grows 6 to 12 inches tall. Wiry, spreading stems, rooting at all nodes. Oval, pointed, glossy, evergreen leaves, 1½ inches long. Blooms in spring with flowers that are ¾ to 1 inch wide, blue, and funnel-shaped with 5 flaring lobes. Occasional repeat blooming. Numerous cultivars, with most having more restrained growth and single or double flowers in shades of dark purple, plum, blue or white; some have leaves that are variegated or edged. Zones 4 to 9.

Viola cornuta.

VIOLA
(*vye*-oh-lah)
Violet
Violaceae—violet family

A genus with thousands of years of history, having been grown by the ancient Greeks and Romans, violas are a prodigious, promiscuous lot, what with some 500 species and untold numbers of readily produced natural hybrids. Some are irritating weeds, while others are rare plants for the collector's garden. The large-faced, annual pansies, *V.* x *wittrockiana*, are staples of cool-season gardens. Native-plant enthusiasts will seek out those from North American shores. For the perennial garden, there is a handful of species with those familiar rosettes of heart-shaped leaves and uniquely shaped, spurred, five-petaled flowers, even some with that haunting, elusive fragrance. An unusual feature of many violets is the production of two types of flowers: the showy, infertile ones and the inconspicuous, fertile ones, borne close to the soil and often with no petals. The name viola is the Latin form of the Greek word, *ione*, from the myth of Zeus providing violas as the food for the white cow he turned his lover into to hide her from his wife.

Growing Guide
Partial shade. Humus-rich, moist but well-drained soil. Deadhead for repeat bloom.

Propagation
Division, seed.

Uses
Beds and borders, edging, wildflower gardens.

Species, Varieties, Cultivars, Hybrids
V. cornuta (kor-*new*-tah). Horned violet, tufted violet. Pyrenees. Grows 4 to 12 inches tall and 12 inches wide. Tufted plants with oval, toothed, pointed, evergreen leaves 1 to 2 inches long. Leaf-like appendages at the leaf nodes. Purple, 1-inch, somewhat star-like, long-spurred, slightly fragrant flowers on 2- to 4-inch stems in spring, with some repeat. Several varieties and cultivars, with flowers in shades of light blue, apricot, yellow, red and white. Zones 6 to 9.

V. labradorica (lab-rah-*doh*-rih-kah). Labrador violet. North America, Greenland. Grows 2 to 4 inches tall and 8 to 12 inches wide. Clump-forming plants with rounded, pointed, finely toothed, shiny leaves to 1 inch wide. Bluish lavender, ¾-inch flowers in spring, and occasionally in summer. Self-sows. Combines well with hellebores, pulmonarias and primulas. The variety 'Purpurea', with purplish green leaves, is seen more than the species. Zones 3 to 8.

Viola obliqua *'Freckles'*.

V. obliqua (ob-*lih*-kwa). Also listed as *V. cucullata*. Marsh blue violet. Eastern North America. Grows 3 to 6 inches tall and 12 inches wide. Clump-forming plants with leaves and flower stems arising directly from the roots. Oval to heart-shaped, wavy-edged, toothed, evergreen leaves to 4 inches wide. Violet, ½-inch flowers with purple veins on the lower petal and dense hairs on the lateral petals. Grows best in moist, shady places. Good groundcover. Self-sows. Several well-known cultivars, including purple-spotted 'Freckles', rose-red 'Red Giant', deep blue 'Royal Robe', and 'White Czar'. Zones 4 to 9.

V. odorata (oh-doh-*rah*-tah). Sweet violet. Europe, North Africa, Asia. Grows 6 to 8 inches tall and 12 inches wide. Spreading, tufted plants with oval to heart-shaped, toothed, dark green leaves to 2

Viola odorata *'Royal Robe'*.

inches long arising directly from the roots. Violet, fragrant, ¾-inch flowers from fall to spring in mild climates and in spring in colder ones. Prostrate runner root at the tips. Best known for the large, double-flowered, very fragrant,

long-stemmed Parma violets, of which there are several named cultivars. Other cultivars include deep-violet 'Czar', dark blue 'Queen Charlotte', rose-pink 'Rosina' and 'White Queen'. Zones 6 to 9.

W

WALDSTEINIA
(wald-*stein*-ee-ah)
Barren strawberry
Rosaceae—rose family

If you have suffered the agonies of weeding out the pernicious mock

Waldsteinia fragarioides.

strawberry, *Duchnesia indica*, do not fear with the barren strawberry. It is much more civilized, spreading as a dainty, sun-loving evergreen groundcover, but not invasively.

Growing Guide
Full sun to partial shade.
Average, well-drained soil.

Propagation
Division.

Uses
Groundcover.

Species, Varieties, Cultivars, Hybrids
W. fragarioides (frah-gah-ree-*oi*-deez). Barren strawberry.

Eastern North America. Grows 4 to 6 inches tall and 12 to 18 inches wide. Creeping, mat-forming plants with lightly hairy to smooth, evergreen leaves divided into three wedge-shaped, toothed parts. Flat, ¾-inch, five-petaled, bright yellow flowers in spring on horizontal stems. Zones 4 to 7.

W. ternata (ter-*nat*-ah). Siberian barren strawberry. Europe, Siberia, Japan. Grows 4 to 6 inches tall and 12 to 18 inches wide. Rosettes of leathery, glossy, hairy three-parted, toothed leaves to 1 inch long. Flat, ½-inch, five-petaled, bright yellow flowers in spring on vertical stems. More compact than *W. fragarioides* and best suited to cool-summer climates. Zones 4 to 7.

Y

YUCCA
(*yuk*-ah)
Yucca, Adam's needle
Liliaceae—lily family

Large clumps of sword-like leaves are striking enough, but add tall spikes massed with fragrant 2-inch flowers, and the result is a plant that definitely makes a statement. Used as an architectural feature in a garden or planted in masses, these widely adaptable perennials are easily grown.

Growing Guide
Full sun. Sandy to average, well-drained soil. Drought tolerant.

Propagation
Separate young plants from the mother plants.

Uses
Beds and borders. Specimen plant. Meadow gardens. Drought-tolerant gardens.

Species, Varieties, Cultivars, Hybrids
Y. filamentosa (fill-ah-men-*toh*-sah). Adam's needle. Southeastern United States. Grows 4 to 6 feet tall and 3 feet wide. Clump-forming plants with bluish to gray-green, leathery, sharply pointed, sword-shaped, evergreen leaves to 15 inches long and 1 inch wide, with curly threads along the edges. Branching, woody-stemmed sprays arising from the center of the plant with nodding, bell-shaped, creamy white, fragrant, 2-inch flowers in summer. Several cultivars, mainly with cream or yellow leaf margins or leaves striped in cream. Zones 5 to 10.

Y. glauca (*glaw*-kah). Adam's needle. Central and southwestern United States. Grows 3 feet tall and 2 to 3 feet wide. Clump-forming plants with gray-green, white-margined, sharply pointed, sword-shaped leaves to 30 inches long and ½ inch wide, with a few white threads along the edges. Straight or slightly branching woody-stemmed sprays arising from the center of the plant with nodding, bell-shaped, greenish white with a red-brown tinge, fragrant, 2½-inch flowers in summer. Zones 6 to 10.

Y. gloriosa (glow-ree-*oh*-sah). Adam's needle. Southeastern United States. Grows 6 to 8 feet tall and 4 feet wide. Very stiff, sharply pointed, sword-shaped, evergreen leaves to 2 feet long and 2½ inches wide, borne on a single stiff stem. Branching, woody-stemmed sprays arising from the center of the plant with nodding, bell-shaped, creamy white, sometimes tinged with red or purple, fragrant, 2-inch flowers in summer. Zone 7.

Yucca filamentosa.

FERNS

Gardeners interested in perennials should start a fern awareness campaign. As a group, ferns are among the most underutilized of perennials. Often relegated to the more inhospitable spots in a yard, they deserve better as they offer gardeners a wide range of easily grown, long-lived plants with a great variety of sizes, shapes, textures and even colors, albeit, predominantly shades of green. The fronds are superb for use in flower arrangements.

Growing ferns only in the deepest shade does them a disservice, as they do best with partial to medium shade, with some even tolerating full sun. With exceptions, a wide range of soils and climates is tolerated, too, with most ferns thriving in moist, humus-rich soil, much as in their native habitats. Emerging ferns are coiled and called fiddleheads. The leaves are called fronds, with each consisting of two parts, the stipe, or leaf stalk, and the blade, which may be undivided, or simple, or finely cut, with each type of division having a specific term. Most ferns spread by means of rhizomatous roots, which makes division easy. Ferns do not produce seeds, but rather single-celled spores, which are held in small clusters or spore cases called sori (singular, sorus) on the backs of fronds. Growing ferns from spores is a rather challenging process.

There are over a thousand different species of ferns from

Adiantum pedatum.

temperate climates around the world. Many of these are well suited to gardens but have limited availability. The ones listed below are all easily grown and are available from either local or mail-order nurseries.

Growing Guide

Partial to heavy shade. Humus-rich, slightly acid, moist but well-drained soil. Summer mulching helps to keep the soil moist. Ferns tolerating dry soil include *Dennstaedtia, Cheilanthes, Dryopteris affinis* and *Dryopteris filix-mas*. Ferns tolerating the most sun include *Matteuccia, Thelypteris palustris, Osmunda, Dryopteris affinis, Dryopteris filix-mas, Athyrium filix-femina*, and *Dennstaedtia punctiloba*.

Propagation

Division.

Uses

Beds and borders, groundcover, near pools and streams, woodland gardens, as accents or massed.

Species, Varieties, Cultivars, Hybrids

Adiantum capillus-veneris (ah-dee-*ahn*-tum ka-*pill*-us veh-*ner*-is).

Southern maidenhair. North America. Fronds 10 to 22 inches long, arching, deciduous. Zones 7 to 10.

A. pedatum (ped-*ah*-tum). Maidenhair fern. Eastern North America. Fronds 12 to 30 inches long, erect-arching, deciduous. Several subspecies. Zones 2 to 8.

A. venustum (veh-*nus*-tum). Himalayan maidenhair. Himalayas. Fronds 8 to 12 inches long, arching, semi-evergreen. Zones 5 to 8.

Asplenium platyneuron (ah-*splay*-nee-um plah-tee-*new*-ron). Ebony spleenwort. Eastern North America. Fronds 8 to 18 inches long, sterile prostrate, fertile erect, evergreen. Several varieties. Zones 4 to 8.

A. trichomanes (tri-*kom*-ah-neez). Maidenhair spleenwort. North America, Europe, Asia. Fronds 4 to 7 inches long, arching, evergreen. Zones 2 to 9.

Asplenosorus ebenoides (ass-plen-oh-*sor*-us eb-eh-*noi*-deez). Scott's spleenwort. Hybrid origin. Fronds 6 to 12 inches long, erect, evergreen. Zones 5 to 8.

Athyrium filix-femina (ah-*thi*-ree-um fih-lix-*fay*-mih-nah). European lady fern. Europe, Asia. Fronds 1 to 2 feet long, erect, deciduous. Many different varieties and cultivars, with crested, dwarf or finely dissected fronds. Zones 4 to 8.

Athyrium filix-femina.

Athyrium niponicum var. pictum.

A. niponicum var. pictum (nip-on-ik-um *pik*-tum). Also listed as *A. goeringianum* 'Pictum' and *A. iseanum* 'Pictum'. Eastern Asia. Japanese painted fern. Fronds 8 to 20 inches long, arching, deciduous, tricolored. Zones 4 to 9.

A. thelypteroides (thuh-lip-ter-*oi*-deez). Also listed as *Diplazium acrostichoides* and *Deparia acrostichoides*. Silvery spleenwort, silvery glade fern. Eastern North America, Eastern Asia. Fronds 1½ to 4 feet long, erect-arching, deciduous. Zones 4 to 9.

Blechnum penna-marina (*blek*-num *pen*-nah mah-*rin*-ah). Little hard fern. Australia, New Zealand, Chile. Fronds 4 to 8 inches long, erect-arching, evergreen. Zones 5 to 8.

B. spicant (*spee*-kant). Deer fern, hard fern. Northwestern North America, Europe. Fronds, sterile, 8 to 20 inches long, prostrate; fertile, 16 to 30 inches long, erect; evergreen. Many cultivars. Zones 5 to 8.

Cheilanthes lanosa (kye-*lan*-theez lah-*no*-sah). Hairy lip fern. United States. Fronds 6 to 16 inches long, erect, deciduous. Zones 5 to 8.

Cyrtomium caryotideum (sir-*tom*-ee-um kare-eh-oh-*tid*-ee-um). Holly fern. Asia. Fronds 1 to 2½ feet long, arching, evergreen. Zones 6 to 10.

C. falcatum (fal-*kah*-tum). Japanese holly fern. Asia. Fronds 1 to 1½ feet long, arching, semi-evergreen. Several cultivars. Zones 6 to 10.

C. fortunei (for-*tune*-ee-eye). Holly fern. Asia. Fronds 1½ to 2½ feet long, erect, semi-evergreen. Zones 5 to 10.

Cystopteris bulbifera (kis-*top*-tah-ris bul-*bif*-er-ah). Bulblet bladder fern, berry fern. North America. Fronds 1½ to 3 feet long, arching, deciduous. Zones 3 to 8.

C. fragilis (frah-*jil*-is). Fragile fern, brittle bladder fern. North America, Europe. Fronds 5 to 16 inches long, erect-arching, deciduous. Zones 2 to 9.

Dennstaedtia punctilobula (den-*stet*-ee-ah punk-tee-*lob*-yew-lah). Hay-scented fern, boulder fern. North America. Fronds 15 to 30 inches long, erect-branching, deciduous. Zones 3 to 8.

Dennstaedtia punctilobula.

Diplazium pycnocarpon (dye-*play*-zee-um). Also listed as *Athyrium pycnocarpon*. Narrow-leaved spleenwort, glade fern. Eastern North America. Fronds 1½ to 3½ feet long, sterile erect-arching, fertile erect, deciduous. Zones 4 to 9.

Dryopteris affinis (*dree*-op-teh-ris af-*feen*-is). Also listed as *D. borreri* and *D. pseudomas*. Golden-scaled male fern, scaly male fern. Europe, Asia. Fronds 2 to 3 feet long, erect, semi-evergreen. Many cultivars. Zones 4 to 8.

D. x bootii (*boot*-ee-eye). Boott's wood fern. Hybrid origin. Fronds 1½ to 3 feet long, erect, deciduous. Zones 3 to 7.

D. carthusiana (kar-*thooz*-ee-an-ah). Also listed as *D. spinulosa*. Spinulose wood fern, toothed wood fern. North America, Europe, Asia. Fronds 1 to 3 feet long, erect-arching, deciduous. Zones 2 to 7.

D. cristata (kris-*tah*-tah). Narrow swamp fern, crested wood fern. North America. Fronds 1 to 3 feet long, erect, evergreen. Needs constantly moist soil. Zones 3 to 7.

D. cycadina (sye-kah-*deen*-ah). Also listed as *D. atrata* and *D. hirtipes*. Black wood fern, shaggy wood fern. Asia. Fronds 1½ to 3 feet long, erect, semi-evergreen. Zones 5 to 8.

D. dilatata (dil-lah-*tah*-tah). Also listed as *D. austriaca*. Broad wood fern. Europe, Asia. Fronds 2 to 3½ feet long, erect-arching, deciduous. Several cultivars. Zones 4 to 8.

D. erythrosora (ehr-ah-*throw*-soh-rah). Autumn fern. Asia. Fronds 1½ to 2 feet long, arching, evergreen. Zones 5 to 8.

D. filix-mas (*fil*-iks-mas). Male fern. North America, Europe, Asia. Fronds 2 to 4 feet long, erect, deciduous. Many cultivars. Zones 4 to 8.

Dryopteris filix-mas.

D. goldiana (gohl-dee-*an*-ah). Goldie's wood fern, giant wood fern. Northeastern North America. Fronds 3 to 4 feet long, arching, deciduous. Zones 3 to 8.

D. intermedia (in-ter-*mee*-dee-ah). Also listed as *D. spinulosa* var. *intermedia*. Evergreen wood fern, glandular wood fern, fancy fern. Northeastern North America. Fronds 1½ to 3 feet long, erect-arching, evergreen. Zones 3 to 8.

D. marginalis (mar-jih-*nal*-is). Marginal wood fern, leather wood fern. Northeastern North America. Fronds 1½ to 2½ feet long, erect-arching, evergreen. Zones 2 to 8.

D. purpurella (pur-pur-*el*-lah). Also listed as *D. erythrosora* var. *purpurescens*. Japan. Fronds 3 to 3½ feet long, arching, evergreen. Exceptional. Zones 5 to 9.

Matteuccia struthiopteris.

Gymnocarpium dryopteris (jim-noh-*kar*-pee-um dree-*op*-ter-is). Also listed as *Dryopteris disjuncta*. North America, Europe, Asia. Fronds 9 to 12 inches long, erect-arching, deciduous. Zones 2 to 7.

Matteuccia struthiopteris (mah-*too*-kee-ah stroo-thee-*op*-ter-is). Also listed as *M. pensylvanica*, *Pteretis nodulosa* and *Struthiopteris filicastrum*. Ostrich fern, shuttlecock fern. North America, Europe, Asia. Fronds 2 to 6 feet long, erect, deciduous. Fiddleheads edible. Spreads rapidly. Zones 2 to 6.

Onoclea sensibilis (oh-*nok*-lee-ah sen-*sih*-bil-is). Sensitive fern, bead fern. Eastern North America. Fronds 1 to 3 feet long, erect, deciduous. Fertile fronds are pod-like and used in flower arrangements. Spreads rapidly. Zones 2 to 10.

Onoclea sensibilis.

Osmunda cinnamomea (os-*mun*-dah kin-ah-*moh*-mee-ah). Cinnamon fern. North America. Fronds 2½ to 5 feet long, erect, deciduous. Cinnamon-colored fertile fronds. Tolerates sun. Zones 2 to 8.

O. claytoniana (klay-ton-ee-*ah*-nah). Interrupted fern. Eastern North America, Eastern Asia. Fronds 2 to 4 feet long, erect, deciduous. Spores borne in middle of frond. Zones 2 to 8.

O. regalis (ray-*gah*-lis). Royal fern. Eastern North America, Europe. Fronds 2 to 5 feet long, erect, deciduous. Several cultivars. Zones 2 to 10.

Osmunda regalis.

Phyllitis scolopendrium (*fill*-ih-tus sko-lo-*pen*-dree-um). Also listed as *Asplenium scolopendrium* and *Scolopendrium vulgare*. Europe. Fronds 8 to 16 inches long, erect-arching, evergreen. Need neutral to alkaline, very well drained soil and a summer mulch. Many cultivars, with crested, crisped or dissected margins on fronds. Zones 5 to 9.

Polypodium vulgare (pol-lee-*pod*-ee-um vul-*gah*-reh). Common polypody. Europe, Asia. Fronds 3 to 10 inches long, erect, evergreen. Many cultivars, with crested or dissected fronds. Zones 5 to 8.

Osmunda claytoniana.

Polystichum acrostichoides (pol-*lih*-stih-kum ah-kro-sti-*koi*-deez). Christmas fern.

Polystichum acrostichoides.

Polypodium vulgare.

P. makinoi (*mak*-ih-noi). Makino's holly fern. China, Japan. Fronds 20 to 30 inches long, arching, evergreen. Zones 5 to 9.

P. munitum (muh-*nih*-tum). Western sword fern. Western North America. Fronds 1½ to 5 feet long, arching, evergreen. Zones 6 to 9.

P. polyblepharum (pol-ee-bleh-*far*-um). Also listed as *P. setosum*. Japan, Korea. Fronds 1 to 2 feet long, arching, evergreen. Zones 5 to 8.

Polystichum setiferum.

P. setiferum (say-*tih*-feh-rum). Also listed *P. angulare* and *Aspidium angulare*. Southern Europe. Fronds 1½ to 4 feet long, erect-arching, semi-evergreen. Many cultivars, with crested and finely divided fronds or dwarf growth. Zones 5 to 8.

Rumohra adiantiformis (rue-*moh*-rah ah-dih-an-tih-*for*-mis). Leather fern. South Africa, South America, New Zealand, Australia. Fronds 1½ to 3 feet long, erect-arching, evergreen. Zones 8 to 10.

Thelypteris decursive-pinnata (thuh-*lip*-teh-ris deh-*kur*-sehv pin-*nah*-tah). Also listed as *Phegopteris decursive-pinnata*. Japanese beech fern. Asia. Fronds 1 to 2 feet tall, erect, deciduous. Zones 4 to 10.

T. hexagonoptera (hex-ah-go-*nop*-teh-rah). Also listed as *Dryopteris hexagonoptera* and *Phegopteris hexagonoptera*. Broad beech fern, southern beech fern. Eastern North America. Fronds 15 to 24 inches long, arching, deciduous. Zones 5 to 9.

T. noveboracensis (no-vah-ohr-ah-*sen*-sis). Also listed as *Parathelypteris noveboracensis*. New York fern, tapering fern. Eastern North America. Fronds 1 to 2 feet long, erect, deciduous. Rapidly spreading. Zones 4 to 8.

T. palustris (pah-*lews*-tris). Also listed as *Thelypteris thelypteroides*, *Dryopteris thelypteris* and *Lastrea thelypteris*. Marsh fern. Eastern North America. Fronds 1½ to 2½ feet long, erect, deciduous. Needs wet soil. Zones 2 to 10.

T. phegopteris (feh-*gop*-ter-is). Also listed as *Dryopteris phegopteris* and *Phegopteris commectilis*. Narrow beech fern, Northern beech fern. North America, Europe, Asia. Fronds 8 to 18 inches long, arching, deciduous. Zones 2 to 5.

Woodsia ilvensis (*wood*-see-ah il-*ven*-sis). Rusty woodsia. North America, Europe, Asia. Fronds 3 to 8 inches long, erect-arching, deciduous. Good for rock gardens. Zones 2 to 6.

W. obtusa (ob-*tew*-sah). Blunt-lobed woodsia. Eastern North America. Fronds 5 to 16 inches long, erect, deciduous. Zones 3 to 10.

Thelypteris noveboracensis.

Woodwardia areolata.

Woodwardia areolata (wood-*ward*-ee-ah ah-ree-oh-*lay*-tah). Also listed as *Lorinseria areolata*. Netted chain fern. Eastern North America. Fronds 1 to 2 feet long, erect, deciduous. Zones 3 to 9.

W. fimbriata (fim-bree-*ah*-tah). Also listed as *W. chamissoi*. Giant chain fern. Western North America. Fronds 3 to 5 feet long, arching, evergreen. Zones 8 to 10.

Woodsia obtusa.

ORNAMENTAL GRASSES

Andropogon gerardii.

In the not so distant past, grass in the flower beds meant that weeding needed was overdue. Now if you don't have grasses there, at least those designated ornamental, you're hopelessly out of date. What gardeners have discovered is that ornamental grasses are easily grown, widely adapted plants that bring much-needed, graceful, fine texture to the garden. They offer year-round interest with the long-lasting seed heads and foliage that persists during the winter. Both foliage and "flowers" are also quite useful for cutting, either fresh or dried. The possibilities include a wide range of sizes, shapes and colors, with most growing in full sun.

Growing Guide

Full sun. Humus-rich, moist but well-drained soil. Average to poor soil and dry conditions are usually tolerated. Trim plants back to ground level before growth begins in the spring. May take several years for plants to become established. Staking may be necessary for taller types.

Propagation

Division.

Uses

Beds and borders, as specimens or massed, groundcover, meadow gardens. Cut flowers.

Species, Varieties, Cultivars, Hybrids

Andropogon gerardii (an-dro-*po*-gon jer-*rar*-dee-eye). Big bluestem. North America. Grows 5 to 6 feet wide and 2 to 3 feet tall. Clump-forming plant with blue-green stems and gray-green leaves ½ inch wide; turns bronze-purple in fall. Purplish flowers. Drought tolerant. Zones 3 to 9.

Arrhenatherum elatius spp. *bulbosum* 'Variegatum' (a-ren-*a*-ther-um ay-*lah*-tee-us bul-*boe*-sum var-ee-ah-*gat*-um). Striped oat grass. Grows 12 inches tall and 8 inches wide. Europe. Mounding plant with blue-green leaves striped white. Goes dormant in summer with hot temperatures. Zones 4 to 8.

Arrhenatherum elatius *spp.* bulbosum 'Variegatum'.

Arundo donax.

Arundo donax (a-*run*-doe *do*-naks). Giant reed. Southern Europe. Grows 14 to 18 feet tall and 6 feet wide. Semi-evergreen, blue- to gray-green, 1- to 2-feet-long, drooping leaves along upright stems. Plumed bronze-to-silver flowers in fall. Variegated form. Zones 7 to 9.

Briza media (*bree*-za *mee*-dee-a). Quaking grass. Europe. Grows 2½ feet tall and 1 foot wide. Tufted clumps with 4-inch, green leaves turning yellow by midsummer. Airy flower clusters in early summer. Cut to 1 foot in summer. Tolerant of dry, poor soil. Zones 4 to 8.

Calamagrostis x *acutiflora* 'Stricta' (kal-ah-mah-*gros*-tis ah-*kew*-tih-flor-ah strik-*ta*). Feather reed grass. Europe. Grows 6 feet tall and 2 feet wide. Very upright clumps of leaves to 3 feet long and ½ inch wide. Feathery, bronze-purple flowers fading to yellow. 'Karl Foerster' is similar. Zones 5 to 9.

Calamagrostis x acutiflora 'Stricta'.

Chasmanthium latifolium.

Chasmanthium latifolium (kas-man-*thee*-um lat-ee-fol-*ee*-um). Wild oats. Eastern North America. Grows 3 to 4 feet tall and 18 inches wide. Leaves 9 inches long and 1 inch wide; turns bronze in fall and yellow in winter. Drooping green flower clusters turn bronze in fall. Tolerates partial shade. Zones 5 to 8.

Cortaderia selloana (kor-ta-*de*-ree-a sel-o-*ah*-nah). Pampas grass. South America. Grows 8 to 12 feet tall and 6 feet wide. Clump-forming plants with gray-green, arching leaves. Showy flower plumes mature to silver-white. Many cultivars. Zones 8 to 10.

Cortaderia selloana.

Deschampsia caespitosa.

Deschampsia caespitosa (de-schamp-*see*-ah kie-spi-*toe*-sa). Tufted hair grass. Europe, Asia, North America. Grows 2 to 3 feet tall and 2 feet wide. Tufted, mounding plant with evergreen, arching leaves to 2 feet long. Airy, branching flower head to 8 inches wide, maturing to pale yellow in summer. Does best with cool summers. Several cultivars. *D. flexuosa*, crinkled hair grass, grows to 20 inches tall and tolerates shade. Zones 4 to 9.

Eragrostis curvula (e-ra-*gros*-tis kur-*vuh*-lah). Weeping love grass. North America. Grows 3 feet tall and 2 feet wide. Tufted, upright plant with arching leaves; yellow in winter. Arching flowers turn pale yellow by fall. Very drought tolerant. Zones 5 to 9.

E. trichoides (trik-*oye*-deez). Sand love grass. North America. Grows 4 feet tall and 2 feet wide. Clump-forming, upright plant with dark green leaves. Upright to arching flower, bronze maturing to pale yellow. Zones 4 to 9.

Erianthus ravannae (eh-rih-*an*-this ra-*van*-eye). Plume grass. Europe. Grows 12 feet tall and 4 feet wide. Clump-forming plant with gray-green, hairy leaves to 30 inches long. Plumes of silver-bronze flowers in fall. Zones 6 to 9.

Festuca cinerea (fes-*tu*-kah sin-er-*ay*-ah). Europe. Grows 14 inches tall and 8 inches wide. Tufted plant with blue leaves. Does best with cool summers. Many cultivars, which supersede *F. ovina* var. *glauca*. Zones 4 to 9.

Hakonechloa macra *'Aureola'*.

Hakonechloa macra 'Aureola' (ho-kon-ee-*klo*-a *mak*-rah ah-ree-*oh*-lah). Hakone grass. Japan. Grows 12 to 18 inches tall and 2 feet wide. Arching growth with variegated leaves, pink-tinged in fall. Does well in shade. Zones 6 to 9.

Erianthus ravannae.

Helictotrichon sempervirens.

Miscanthus sinensis.

Molinia caerulea.

Helictotrichon sempervirens (he-lik-to-*tri*-kon sem-per-*vi*-rens). Blue oat grass. Central Europe. Grows 3 to 4 feet tall and 1 foot wide. Tufted hummocks with stiff, blue- to gray-green leaves 16 inches long and ½ inch wide. Arching beige flowers in early summer. Evergreen in mild climates; may go dormant with hot summers. Zones 4 to 8.

Imperata cylindrica 'Red Baron' (im-per-*ah*-tah sih-*lin*-drih-kah). Japanese blood grass. Japan. Grows 18 inches tall and 12 inches wide. Upright growth with leaves green at the base, but the rest red, intensifying in fall. Zones 5 to 9.

Miscanthus sinensis (mis-*kanth*-us sih-*nen*-sis). Eulalia grass, Japanese silver grass. Eastern Asia. Grows 6 to 8 feet tall and 3 to 4 feet wide. Clump-forming, upright plants with arching leaves. Stiff stems bear clusters of feathery flowers, copper-bronze in summer turning silvery in autumn. Foliage turns pale yellow in fall. May need staking. Most widely grown of ornamental grasses. Many cultivars, varying in size, growth habit, flower color, leaf variegation and hardiness. Generally hardy in Zones 5 or 6 to 9.

Molinia caerulea (mo-leen-*ee*-ah kie-*ru*-lee-a). Moor grass. Europe, Asia. Tufted, mounding plant with blue-green leaves turning yellow in fall. Clusters of delicate, purple flowers in summer. Needs acid soil. Tolerates partial shade. Several varieties and cultivars, including a variegated form. Zones 4 to 8.

Panicum virgatum (*pah*-ni-kum vir-*gah*-tum). Switch grass. North to Central America. Grows 4 to 8 feet tall and 2 feet wide. Upright, clump-forming plant. Feathery clusters of green to pink flowers in late summer. Foliage and flowers become yellow in fall. Several cultivars, mainly turning red or burgundy in fall. 'Heavy Metal' has blue-green leaves turning yellow in fall. Zones 5 to 9.

Imperata cylindrica *'Red Baron'*.

Miscanthus sinensis *'Silver Feather'*.

Panicum virgatum *'Heavy Metal'*.

Melica altissima (meh-lik-*ah* al-tis-*ih*-mah). Melic grass. Europe. Grows 2 feet tall and 1 foot wide. Evergreen tufts of broad leaves. Arching clusters of beige flowers in summer. 'Atropurpurea' has purple-red flowers. May go dormant by late summer. *Melica ciliata* is similar but with blue-green leaves and white flowers. Zones 5 to 8.

Miscanthus sinensis *'Variegatus'*.

Pennisetum alopecuroides.

Pennisetum alopecuroides (pen-i-_say_-tum a-lo-pek-ew-_roi_-deez). Fountain grass. Eastern Asia. Grows 2 to 4 feet tall and 18 to 24 inches wide. Mounding plant with shiny, arching leaves. Bristly flowers in summer or fall. Flowers and foliage turn tan in fall. Exceptional garden plant. Many cultivars. Zones 5 to 9.

Phalaris arundinacea var. _picta_ (fah-_lah_-ris a-run-di-_nah_-kee-ah _pik_-tah). Variegated ribbon grass. North America, Europe, Asia. Grows 3 to 4 feet tall and 3 feet wide. Rapidly spreading plant with white-striped leaves. In hot-summer areas, cut to ground in midsummer to stimulate new growth. 'Feesey' is more tolerant of heat. Good groundcover. Zones 4 to 9.

Phalaris arundinacea _var._ picta.

Sesleria autumnalis (sess-_ler_-ee-ah aw-tum-_nah_-lis). Autumn moor grass. Europe, Asia. Grows 2 feet tall and 1 foot wide. Spiky, 16-inch hummocks with light green leaves. Upright flower stems with feathery clusters of silver-white flowers in summer. Evergreen in mild climates. Does well in hot climates. Zones 5 to 8.

S. heufleriana (hew-_fler_-ee-an-ah). Europe. Grows 20 inches tall and as wide. Hummocks with blue-green leaves. Feathery clusters of dark purple-brown flowers in spring. Drought tolerant. Zones 4 to 8.

Sorghastrum nutans (sor-_gas_-trum _new_-tanz). Indian grass. North America. Grows 6 feet tall and 2 feet wide. Upright plant with gray-green leaves ¼ inch wide forms clumps 3 feet tall. Flower stems to 6 feet with reddish pink plumes in fall. Foliage turns orange and flowers gold in fall. 'Sioux Blue' has blue foliage and is very upright. Zones 3 to 9.

Sorghastrum nutans _'Ramsey'._

Spartina pectinata (spar-_teen_-a pek-ti-_nah_-ta). Prairie cord grass. North America. Grows 6 feet tall and 2 to 3 feet wide. Upright plants with arching, leathery leaves with rough edges. Insignificant flowers. 'Aureomarginata' has glossy leaves with gold edges and golden yellow fall color. Native to moist, boggy soils but tolerates dry soil. Spreads rapidly. Zones 5 to 9.

Spodiopogon sibiricus (spoh-_dee_-oh-pog-on si-_beer_-ih-kus). Europe. Grows 4 to 5 feet tall and 18 inches wide. Stiff, clump-forming plants with short, pointed leaves held at right angles to stems. Feathery clusters of silvery flowers in midsummer. Foliage turns burgundy-red in fall, then brown with frost. Grows in partial to light shade. Zones 4 to 8.

Stipa gigantea (_stee_-pa gi-_gan_-tee-a). Giant feather grass. Southern Europe. Grows 5 feet tall and 3 feet wide. Mound-forming plant with gray-green, rolled leaves forming 2-foot hummocks. Flowering stems bear airy clusters of silver-yellow flowers in summer. Does best in mild climates with cool summers. Zones 7 to 8.

Stipa gigantea.

Spartina pectinata.

APPENDIX
ZONE, FROST AND RAINFALL MAPS

Plant Hardiness Zones

Throughout this book, the regional adaptability of many plants is summarized by naming the "Zones" in which they grow during the various seasons. The zones on this hardiness zone map, based on average winter temperatures, are the standard numbered zones used here and in almost all gardening books, magazines and seed catalogs. Sometimes the zone number is followed by a letter, as in Zone 6a or 6b. An "a" means that the area falls within the colder sections within the zone, and the "b" suggests warmer growing conditions than those that prevail elsewhere in the zone.

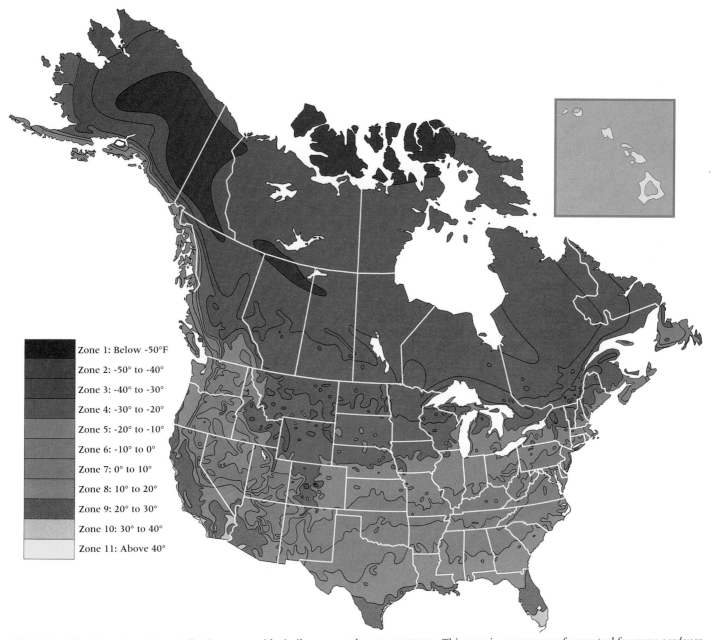

Zone 1: Below -50°F
Zone 2: -50° to -40°
Zone 3: -40° to -30°
Zone 4: -30° to -20°
Zone 5: -20° to -10°
Zone 6: -10° to 0°
Zone 7: 0° to 10°
Zone 8: 10° to 20°
Zone 9: 20° to 30°
Zone 10: 30° to 40°
Zone 11: Above 40°

USDA Plant Hardiness Zone Map, indicating areas with similar average low temperatures. This map is a necessary reference tool for every gardener.

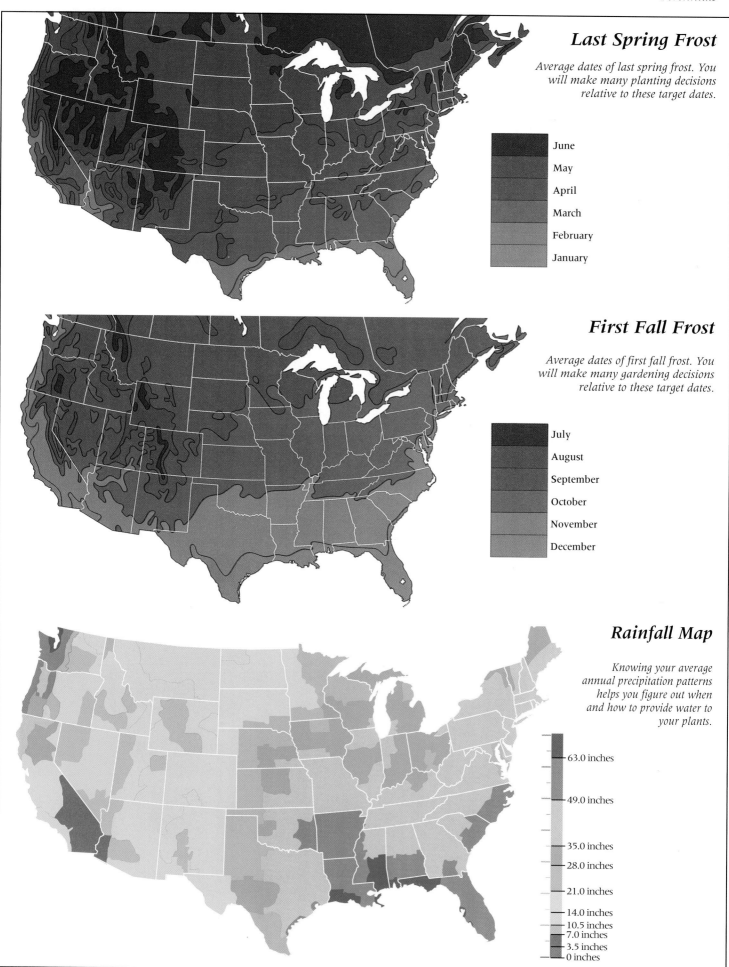

Last Spring Frost

Average dates of last spring frost. You will make many planting decisions relative to these target dates.

June
May
April
March
February
January

First Fall Frost

Average dates of first fall frost. You will make many gardening decisions relative to these target dates.

July
August
September
October
November
December

Rainfall Map

Knowing your average annual precipitation patterns helps you figure out when and how to provide water to your plants.

63.0 inches
49.0 inches
35.0 inches
28.0 inches
21.0 inches
14.0 inches
10.5 inches
7.0 inches
3.5 inches
0 inches

INDEX